DEPORTING OUR SOULS

In the past three decades, images of undocumented immigrants pouring across the southern border have driven the immigration debate, and policies have been implemented in response to those images. The Oklahoma City bombings and the tragic events of September 11, both of questionable relevance to immigration policy, have provided further impetus to implement strategies that are anti-immigration in design and effect. This book discusses the major immigration policy areas – undocumented workers, the immigration selection system, deportation of aggravated felons, national security and immigration policy, and the integration of new Americans – and the author suggests his own proposals on how to address the policy challenges from a perspective that encourages us to consider the moral consequences of our decisions. The author also reviews some of the policies that have been put forth and ignored and suggests new policies that would be good for the country economically and socially.

Bill Ong Hing is Professor of Law and Asian American Studies and the director of law clinical programs at the University of California, Davis. He has litigated before the U.S. Supreme Court and was co-counsel in the precedent-setting case *INS v. Cardoza-Fonseca* (1986), which established a more generous standard for asylum seekers. He is the author of many books on immigration including *Defining America through Immigration Policy* and *To Be an American – Cultural Pluralism and the Rhetoric of Assimilation*.

Deporting Our Souls

. . . . VALUES, MORALITY, AND IMMIGRATION POLICY

Bill Ong Hing

University of California, Davis

CAMBRIDGE UNIVERSITY PRESS

CAMBRIDGE UNIVERSITY PRESS
Cambridge, New York, Melbourne, Madrid, Cape Town, Singapore, São Paulo

Cambridge University Press
32 Avenue of the Americas, New York, NY 10013-2473, USA

www.cambridge.org
Information on this title: www.cambridge.org/9780521864923

First published 2006

Printed in the United States of America

A catalog record for this publication is available from the British Library.

Library of Congress Cataloging in Publication Data

Hing, Bill Ong.
Deporting our souls : values, morality, and immigration policy / Bill Ong Hing.
    p.   cm.
Includes bibliographical references and index.
ISBN-13: 978-0-521-86492-3 (hardback)
ISBN-10: 0-521-86492-5 (hardback)
1. Immigrants – Government policy – United States.   2. Illegal aliens – Government
policy – United States.   3. United States – Emigration and immigration.   I. Title.
JV6483.H564   2007
325.73 – dc22   2006011102

ISBN-13   978-0-521-86492-3 hardback
ISBN-10   0-521-86492-5 hardback

For

Kim Ho Ma, Yuthea Chhoueth, the Cuevas family, Manuel Garcia, Louen Lun, José Luis Magaña, Chanphirun Meanowuth Min, Jonathan Peinado, Mao So, Sor Vann, José Velasquez, and the countless others who have been deported since 1996 without receiving a second chance

And my friends

Many Uch and Andrew Thi, who are facing deportation and deserve a second chance

Contents

Foreword

Senator Edward M. Kennedy

Immigration is the story of American history. From the earliest days of our nation, generation upon generation of immigrants has come to be part of a land that offers freedom and opportunity to those willing to do their part. Immigrants built our great cities. They cultivated our rich farmlands. They built the railroads and highways that bind America from sea to shining sea. It is said that under every railroad tie, an Irishman is buried.

Immigrants erected houses of worship to practice their faiths. They fought under America's colors in our wars. In fact, seventy thousand immigrants are serving in the U.S. armed forces in the world today. Immigrants worked hard so that their children could enjoy the ever-widening possibilities in our land. Over the centuries, immigrants came to America from every part of the globe and reached the American Dream. They created a nation that is the envy of the world.

That is our history. But it is also our present and our future. As recent years have made clear, however, our current system is broken and fails to meet our nation's modern needs. Our borders are out of control at a time of heightened concern about terrorism. Vast numbers cross our borders and remain illegally, creating an underground society that is vulnerable to exploitation and abuse. I heartily agree with Professor Hing's philosophy. There are certain fundamental values that we should not compromise away for political expedience – values that are fundamental to our nation and our humanitarian tradition and fundamental to our heritage and history as a nation of immigrants. We cannot turn our back on the eloquent words of Emma Lazarus engraved in stone on the base of the Statue of Liberty in New York Harbor:

> Give me your tired, your poor,
> Your huddled masses yearning to breathe free,
> The wretched refuse of your teeming shore,
> Send these, the homeless, tempest-tossed to me,
> I lift my lap beside the golden door!

I also agree with Professor Hing's call for reaching out to newcomers for greater civic and economic participation. When immigrants do well, we all do well. To do so is to set a path, a way forward for the nation as a whole to a new prosperity and greater opportunity for all. It's a vision of the country we can become – an America that embraces the values and aspirations of our people now and for coming generations.

As we face the forces of globalization, we must affirm anew what it means to be an American. A new American majority is ready to respond to our call for a revitalized American Dream, grounded firmly in the Constitution and in the endless adventure of lifting this nation to new heights of discovery, prosperity, progress, and opportunity. A fundamental part of that revitalized American Dream is the inclusion of immigrants.

Acknowledgments

I am indebted to all of my good friends and relatives who have contributed to the ideas on progressive immigration policy that are presented in this text. They deserve credit for anything in these pages that makes sense. Everyone mentioned here has inspired me to think widely and broadly, while challenging me to put my time and effort into seeking fair and just change in our nation's approach to immigration.

I had the benefit of excellent research assistance from a group of dedicated students including Jennifer Chu, Candice Lee, Yoonjin Park, Diana Geng, Lindsay Bennett, Evelien Verpeet, Wynter O-Blanquet, Vicky Choy, Daniel Rizk, Rene Juarez, Carla Romero, Kristy Kunisaki, and Chanlee Sheih. The entire library staff at UC Davis School of Law has always been phenomenal in responding to my requests, and two reference librarians – Susan Llano and Peg Durkin – have been particularly helpful. Linda Cooper and Jennifer Thompson Fuentes of the law school's support staff assisted me with the preparation of the manuscript.

At UC Davis, I am lucky to be a part of two amazing programs. My law faculty colleagues have been supportive of my work in every important way. Cruz Reynoso, Jennifer Chacón, Madhavi Sunder, Anupam Chander, and Tom Joo have played important roles in the development of my most recent scholarship. And I cannot imagine a better pair of "bosses" than Dean Rex Perschbacher and Associate Dean Kevin Johnson, who are most responsible for creating an environment in which I have been able to thrive. My talented Asian American Studies colleagues push me to maintain a strong commitment to scholarship, our students, and our communities: Billie Gabriel, Darrell Hamamoto, Richard Kim, Sunaina

Maira, Susette Min, My Diem Nguyen, Rhacel Parreñas, Caroline Kieu Linh Valverde, Nolan Zane, and especially Wendy Ho and Stan Sue, who have been amazing leaders.

The inspiration for many of my efforts has been shaped by my good friends and prolific academic colleagues Kevin Johnson and Jerry López. My attorney friends who are in the front lines of day-to-day immigration work regularly teach me about the injustices of our immigration system: Jay Stansell of the Federal Public Defender's office in Seattle, Stan Mark and Margaret Fung of Asian American Legal Defense and Education Fund in New York, Sin Yen Ling and Joren Lyons of the Asian Law Caucus in San Francisco, Lucas Guttentag of the ACLU Immigrant Rights Project in Oakland, Bill Tamayo of the Equal Employment Opportunities Commission in San Francisco, and of course my clinical faculty colleagues at UC Davis: Amagda Pérez, Jim Smith, Holly Cooper, Millard Murphy, Cappy White, and Sarah Orr.

My information, knowledge, and any expertise in the field I may have is derived primarily from my more than twenty-five-year association with the entire staff of the Immigrant Legal Resource Center (ILRC), a legal services support center in San Francisco. Over the years, this talented group of support staff, administrators, bookkeepers, development experts, and lawyers has included Kathy Brady, Eric Cohen, Judy Golub, Jonathan Huang, Angie Junck, Sally Kinoshita, Shari Kurita, Susan Lydon, Irene Nyein, Rene Pérez, Nora Privitera, Elizabeth Romero, Tim Sheehan, Mark Silverman, Adam Sopko, and Shellie Stortz. Like any nonprofit organization, the ILRC has needed a board of directors to guide the organization through financially good times and bad times. Fortunately, a number of dedicated individuals has stepped up to the plate to serve on the ILRC board to ensure its viability in different periods: Sallie Kim, Lisa Spiegel, Dick Odgers, Don Ungar, Roger Wu, Lee Zeigler, Lupe Ortiz, Richard Boswell, John Burton, Angeli Cheng, Maribel Delgado, Howard Golub, Jerry López, Drucilla Ramey, Matt Schulz, Lynn Starr, Clark Trevor, Ruben Abrica, and Jackson Wong.

I also have enjoyed the benefit of serving on the National Advisory Council of the Asian American Justice Center in Washington, D.C., led by Karen Narasaki, with whom I regularly work on formulating policy positions. Karen and her staff members – Traci Hong and Katherine Newell Bierman – are extraordinary. I also must acknowledge the hard work and dedication of a number of my other D.C. friends who try to push Congress to do the right thing on immigration policy. I do not always agree with their specific strategies or positions, but they are accessible and respect all immigrant communities. They deserve our respect: Kevin Appleby, Jeanne Butterfield, Marshall Fitz, Doris Meissner, Cecilia Muñoz, Demetri Papademetriou, Rick Schwartz, and Frank Sharry.

The values that I express in this text have been shaped by my work with the colleagues and friends mentioned here. However, this all started as I was growing up in the small, copper mining town of Superior, Arizona, where most of my friends were of Mexican ancestry. That experience as well as getting to know my own Chinese immigrant relatives in Superior and Phoenix formed my early views about immigration. To say the least, those early views were all positive and have remained that way ever since. Those views were supported and validated by my parents, Ong Chung Hing and Helen Annie Soo Hoo, and by every one of my older siblings: Lilly, Minnie, Ally, Holy, Bob, Mary, Grace, Joyce, and Johnny. Their example of friendship, love, and respect for our Mexican American friends in particular has never been forgotten.

None of what I do would be possible without the love and support of my wife, Lenora Fung. Her incredible commitment to health care, volunteer work, and family is matched only by her own staunch support for immigrant rights. Most important to me, I can always count on Lenora for a smile and the start of a good day with her there. We have been blessed with three wonderful children who have blossomed as young adults. In their own way and on their own time, Eric, Sharon, and Julianne have developed deep commitments to social and economic justice for subordinated groups and individuals. I learn from them constantly. What they do with the rest of their lives is, of course, up to them and dependent upon circumstances that none of us can foresee. But I'm confident that they will lead their lives with open minds, dedicated to fairness and respectful of others, irrespective of race, gender, or background. I cannot be more proud nor can I ask for much more.

Bill Ong Hing
Davis, California
Summer 2006

DEPORTING OUR SOULS

INTRODUCTION

. . . . Hysteria and Shame

We are a nation of immigrants, but we also are a nation that loves to debate immigration policy. Except for western Europeans, virtually every new immigrant group that arrived experienced derision from nativists. But each newcomer group had its supporters as well. Thus, depending on the era and which side had the most influence, legislative and enforcement policies might be friendly or hostile toward newcomers. For example, these battles led to Asian exclusion laws from 1882 to 1917 and national origin quota systems in the 1920s that disfavored Asians and southern and eastern Europeans, but the debate resulted in more fair immigration categories in 1965 and a limited amnesty program for undocumented aliens in 1986 as well.

Sometimes, the hysteria over immigration policy can lead to cruelties that we later regret, usually implemented when anti-immigrant forces are particularly strong. These include instances of mean-spiritedness that extend beyond a decision simply to admit fewer immigrants per se or to deny admission to prospective immigrants who are criminals or suffering from infectious disease. The Asian exclusion laws and the quota provisions targeting southern and eastern Europeans are prime examples of such disgraceful enactments. Another shameful example is Operation Wetback in 1954, when more than a million undocumented Mexican workers were deported after being recruited and used by American growers for years. The turning away of destitute European Jewish refugees on the SS *St. Louis* in 1939 by the U.S. Coast Guard was another act of tragic callousness; they were murdered by the Nazis after being forced back to Europe.

Unfortunately, the heartless side of U.S. immigration policy is on full display today; anti-immigrant fervor has been quite effective of late. The cold, antiseptic version of U.S. immigration policy requires the deportation of a young Cambodian refugee who has lived here since the age of six; growing up in a crime-ridden inner-city ghetto where we resettled his family, he turned to gang violence as a means of self-protection. These policies lead to the criminal prosecution of a humanitarian worker for driving a dying illegal border-crosser to an emergency room. Reminiscent of the *SS St. Louis,* they require the coast guard to intercept and turn back Haitian refugees before they have reached our shores, even though many of them may have valid claims for asylum. They uphold the deportation into chaos of a Somali national to a country with no formal government that can protect him from random violence once he steps off the airplane. And the anti-immigrant contempt that supports these policies would deny a public school education or medical care to a U.S. citizen child, simply because her parents are undocumented.

The anti-immigrant movement in the United States is as strong as ever. Immigrant bashing is popular among politicians, talk radio hosts, private militiamen, and xenophobic grassroots organizations. The complaints are wide-ranging, from the vitriolic – "we must protect our borders from the wave of non–English speaking, nonwhite masses who threaten our way of life" – to those who are less apprehensive about change, but who believe that more modest numbers of immigrants should be admitted to better facilitate the Americanization of those who are admitted. They include those who claim that immigrants "take away jobs from native workers" and those who recognize the need for some workers – especially the low-wage workers – but only want to extend temporary as opposed to permanent status to those workers.

Today's nativists take full advantage of the high-tech era in which we live. At one moment we can tune in to CNN host Lou Dobbs warning of the "illegal alien invasion." Then we might be directed to the Web site of the pseudo think tank Center on Immigration Studies citing "studies" on the effects of immigrants with little empirical basis, all reaching the same conclusion: that immigrants hurt our economy. Then there are press releases and more Web-based "reports" from the Federation for American Immigration Reform (FAIR) warning of the "country's immigration emergency." Certainly, politicians who are reminiscent of the race-baiters during the Chinese exclusion era also can be located today. Consider

Representative Tom Tancredo, a Colorado Republican, who heads the Immigration Reform Caucus. C-Span brings him into living rooms where he chastises business for being "addicted to cheap [immigrant] labor" and spreads fear of a "radical multiculturalism" if immigration is not restricted.

By definition, the common thread that one finds in today's xenophobic rhetoric is fear as a means of persuasion. Somehow, if we do not take radical steps, the idea goes, the United States is doomed to be turned into a Spanish-speaking nation or a land that is unrecognizable without a trace of the American institutions we value. Whether intended or not, the fear evolves into hate or disdain for newcomers and eventually into draconian laws and enforcement policies. Thus, in 1994, California voters overwhelmingly supported Proposition 187, excluding citizen and undocumented children from public schools if their parents were undocumented. In 1996, Congress moved to cut off food stamps and welfare benefits to lawful immigrants and refugees irrespective of how truly needy they might be. The same year, Congress wanted to impose a thirty-day filing deadline on anyone entering who might be seeking asylum, even though refugees are hard pressed to enter with the neat bundle of evidence needed to establish a claim so quickly and most need time to adjust mentally because of post-traumatic stress disorder.

The fear-based strategies can become deadly. Beginning in 1994, the Clinton administration implemented Operation Gatekeeper, a strategy of "control through deterrence" that involved constructing fences and militarizing the parts of the southern border that were the most easily traversed. Instead of deterring migrants, their entry choices were shifted to treacherous terrain – the deserts and mountains. The number of entries and apprehensions were not at all decreased, and the number of deaths because of dehydration and sunstroke in the summer or freezing in the winter dramatically surged. In 1994, fewer than 30 migrants died along the border; by 1998, the number was 147; in 2001, 387 deaths were counted; and by 2005, 451 died. The pattern continued in 2006. Given the risks, why do migrants continue the harrowing trek? The attraction of the United States is obvious. The strong economy pays Mexican workers, for example, eight to nine times more than what they can earn in Mexico. For many, it's a matter of economic desperation, and some observers think that migrants would continue to come even if we mined the border. In a sense, they do not have a choice. Besides, jobs are plentiful here, because a variety of industries rely on low-wage migrant workers. They may know the risks but figure that the risks are outweighed by the benefits of crossing. Motivations for continued migration call into question the likely effectiveness of the expansion of Operation Gatekeeper if the goal is to discourage border-crossers. Beyond the economic situation in Mexico, a socioeconomic phenomenon is at play. The phenomenon is the long, historical travel patterns between Mexico and the United States, coupled with the interdependency of the two regions. Migration from Mexico is the manifestation of these economic problems and social phenomena. The militarization of the border does nothing to address these phenomena. Instead, it is killing individuals who are caught up in the phenomena. And yet we condone this enforcement strategy knowing that needless deaths will continue.

Our deportation policies also provide little flexibility because of our fears. Consider the case of Kim Ho Ma. At first blush, his deportation may not be surprising. He was the member of a tough gang from the streets of Seattle. In 1995, at age seventeen, Kim Ho and two friends ambushed a member of a rival gang. He was convicted of first degree manslaughter and sentenced to thirty-eight months' imprisonment. After serving more than two years, Kim Ho was released into the custody of immigration officials and eventually was deported because of this conviction.

Did Kim Ho Ma deserve a second chance? Consider more of his story. Kim Ho was born in Cambodia in 1977, in the midst of the Khmer Rouge regime's sinister oppression and genocide. His mother, eight months' pregnant, was sentenced to dig holes in one of Pol Pot's work camps. The idea was to teach her humility, and when she collapsed from exhaustion, she expected to be killed. Instead, the guards walked away. She was among the lucky ones who were not victims of Pol Pot's "killing fields" genocide from 1975 to 1978. U.S. involvement in Cambodia delayed the influence of the Khmer Rouge until 1975. U.S. forces bombed Cambodia in the early 1970s, dropping more than a hundred thousand tons of bombs on the Cambodian countryside. Between 1971 and 1973, the U.S. bombings targeted populated areas, displacing many Cambodian citizens. Led by Pol Pot, the Khmer Rouge ousted the U.S.-installed Lon Nol in 1975, and the Communist Party of Kampuchea (CPK) ruled Cambodia until 1979. The Khmer Rouge's main goal was to eradicate all things Western in Cambodia. During its reign in Cambodia, the Khmer Rouge regime committed unspeakable acts of horror, namely genocide, against the people of Cambodia – all in the name of socialism. An estimated two million people, 30 percent of the population, perished.

Kim Ho's matriculation into a Seattle street gang essentially represents the natural progression of his unique American life story as structured by the U.S. refugee resettlement program. After his infancy, Kim Ho's story is not even remotely connected with growing up in Cambodia. When Kim Ho was two, his mother carried him through minefields, fleeing the oppression of the Khmer Rouge, taking him first to refugee camps in Thailand and the Philippines and eventually to the United States when he was seven. Kim Ho's first home in America was a housing project in Seattle, where he and other Cambodian refugees had the misfortune of being resettled in the middle of a new war – one between black and Latino gangs. Both sides taunted Kim Ho and his friends, beating them up for fun. Still affected by the trauma she experienced in Cambodia and preoccupied with two minimum-wage jobs, his mother did not understand what was happening to her son. Determined that they would not be pushed around, Kim Ho and his friends formed their own gang.

When Kim Ho was turned over to immigration authorities, the United States did not have a repatriation agreement with Cambodia, so after a series of court appeals he was released from custody. Unfortunately, things changed in March 2002, when the United States reached an agreement with Cambodia, and Kim Ho was among the first to be deported to Cambodia in fall 2002. His shooting conviction was classified as an "aggravated felony," and under 1996 legislation, an aggravated felon was deportable without any opportunity to introduce evidence of remorse, rehabilitation, family hardship, or other sympathetic factors before an immigration court. Shortly after Kim Ho's deportation, his federal public defender Jay Stansell wrote:

> Kimho Ma was deported to Cambodia with 9 others, landing in Phnom Penh on October 2, 2002.
> I cannot write this in "reporter" mode, so I must take a breath and speak from my heart. The situation requires that I comment on the courage and example of this young man, who bore the weight of "The Ma Decision" and the hopes of "lifers" across the country through his three years of release; who sat there in the Supreme Court hearing his precious freedom dismissed as expendable in the face of the government's "plenary power"; and who, ironically, held throughout the utmost confidence that a cause as just as the lifers' would surely turn out in their favor. It did turn out that way, and it was a momentous victory for all of us who worked for the rights of

all human beings, regardless of which side of which border they are born on.

And still, throughout this, Kim knew that he would someday be deported, and now he has been.

Over the course of his three years of freedom, Kimho spent a lot of time with me and my family. Beginning in the Spring of this year when rumors were swirling that a repatriation agreement had been signed, Kim and his family became even more of a fixture at our house. We would come home to find him dropped in for a visit, or bags of odd fruit from the Cambodian market at our doorstep with no note. Instead of languishing in detention, as the INS so aggressively sought, Kimho was "allowed back into the community" where, ("oh my!!"), he spent three years celebrating the beauty and wisdom of his parents; where he became closer to all of his siblings and extended family; where he worked, laughed, wrote, and breathed the Seattle air free from iron bars. He became a son and a brother to me and my wife. A big brother to our now 10 and 6 year old boys. A fan at Adam's baseball games, a wrestling partner for Toby. A gentle friend and kind soul. And he knew that he most certainly was on the top of the Ashcroft wish-list for travel documents.

Turns out that he was. On September 19, 2002, I received a call that the INS was sending Kim a "bag and baggage letter." I am thinking of getting that ugly document framed. Many of us have seen dozens if not hundreds of these form letters but it is the first time after all these years caring about the lives of non-citizens that I felt what family members for decades must have felt when receiving that letter. A loved [one] is banished from the United States and will no longer be here in my home. I will frame it as a monument to 130 years of cruelty to immigrants in the United States, and as a reminder of the courage of Kimho and all immigrants who step forward in the struggle for justice.

. . .

Ultimately, Kimho and his family, my wife and I, and colleagues at the [federal public defender's office] took Kim to the same [Immigration and Naturalization Service] building from which we had won his release. Mr. Danger-to-the-Community and Mr. Flight-Risk walked right into that building with me. October 2, he was detained, and then deported.[1]

Kim Ho deserved a second chance. The United States had a hand in creating the political nightmare in Cambodia from which his mother had

---

[1] E-mail from Jay Stansell, Assistant Federal Public Defender, Seattle, Washington, Oct. 18, 2002, 4:02 p.m. (on file with author).

to flee. The U.S. resettlement program failed to provide his family a safe environment or resources to integrate into this society. Kim Ho's life essentially began on the streets of Seattle, and like it or not, he is a product of our society. You may not agree that Kim Ho automatically deserved a second chance, but I hope you agree that our deportation process should have afforded Kim Ho and his mother a chance for a fair hearing to present evidence on whether he deserved a second chance.

The age of hysteria over immigration in which we live leads to tragic policies that challenge us as a moral society. Policies that are unnecessarily harsh – that show a dehumanizing side of our character – are senseless. They bring shame to us as a civil society. When I meet and speak with immigrants – documented and undocumented – I find decent, hardworking folks who have traveled to join relatives or to work, or, in the case of refugees, fled here seeking freedom. I find individuals who want to be Americans and who definitely want their children to be Americans. If we were in their shoes (in fact, many of our parents or grandparents *were* in their shoes), then I am confident that we would want to be treated with simple, human respect.

In the chapters that follow, I set forth some of the major immigration issues that are up for debate and that likely will be debated for years to come. These are the issues related to undocumented immigration, the deportation of long-time residents, kinship versus employment-based immigration, national security, and how and why we should be integrating new immigrants. In the process, my hope is that the venom toward immigrants be put aside while the issues are considered. The debate over these issues provides our nation an opportunity to shed the cold side of our character and demonstrate the human values of which we are proud. I believe that the vast majority of Americans not only understand the value that immigrants bring to our shores but also believe that our energy is better spent following reasonable approaches that will not shame and embarrass us later. We will be better for doing so, and, with the right approach, we can invite newcomers to step forward and take on their American responsibilities as well.

1 . . . . . Illegal Immigration: Give Them a Parade

The furor over illegal immigration is palpable. Things are out of control. We are being overrun. They have broken the law. They take jobs away from native workers. They use our resources. They don't share our values. They don't speak English. Simply put, this is a crisis!

My solution is simple. Calm down. Welcome undocumented workers. We have recruited and relied upon them for generations. They have contributed to the economic greatness of our country. Welcome their families. Their children have become part of the social fabric of the nation. Like newcomers of the past, they are here to seek a better life through hard work and dedication to their families. To welcome them is to do the right thing. In fact, let's give them a parade.[1]

As we have seen recently, segments of the U.S. media, policy leaders, and populace continue to be obsessed with the issue of undocumented immigration to the United States. Turn on CNN and you may find Lou Dobbs chastising President Bush for failing "to enforce immigration laws that would slow the invasion of illegal aliens."[2] Open up the *Los Angeles Times,* and you can read about California Governor Arnold Schwarzenegger singing praises for the Minutemen Project, the volunteer group of

---

[1] The parade idea comes from former executive editor and op-ed columnist of the *N.Y. Times,* A. M. Rosenthal, who urged us to give a parade for Chinese who paid smugglers to bring them to the United States illegally, and welcome them as heroes after fleeing China for a better life aboard the *Golden Venture.* A. M. Rosenthal, *Give Them a Parade,* NY TIMES, June 8, 1993, at A25.

[2] Lou Dobbs, *Broken Borders,* Apr. 14, 2005, at http://www.apfn.net/messageboard/04-14-05/discussion.cgi.10.html.

vigilantes formed to patrol the U.S.–Mexico border.[3] Check out the Web, and read about Colorado Republican Congressman Tom Tancredo, who has launched a political career animated by his obsession to stem the tide of immigration from Mexico and Central America. Open a paper in Las Cruces, New Mexico, and you can read about Mexican workers in Chihuahua, Mexico, waiting for the right time to cross the border illegally to find work as ranch hands in New Mexico or in construction in Chicago.[4] In Boise, Idaho, a letter to the editor complains about "illegal immigrants [and contractors] willing to pay cheap wages under the table . . . in lieu of hiring American citizens."[5] In a Washington, D.C., debate over immigration policy involving the Christian Right, the Family Research Council that sponsored the event polled its members and reported that nine out of ten believe undocumented immigrants should be "detected, arrested and returned to their country of origin."[6] In response, hundreds of thousands who support immigrants – documented and undocumented – have taken to the streets for peaceful rallies – more than a million on May 1, 2006, alone. Catholic and other religious leaders have denounced draconian enforcement proposals aimed at the undocumented, and pro-immigrant politicians have reminded us that we are a nation of immigrants.

With an estimated eleven to twelve million undocumented aliens in the United States, advocates for immigration reform have become louder and more visible. The issue hit the front burner for Congress in 2006 after being pushed aside for more than four years by the events of 9/11. If anti-immigrant legislators have their way, illegal immigration would be a crime punishable by death, being undocumented would be a felony, and raids of restaurants, hotels, and construction sites would be common daily occurrences.

What to do about millions of undocumented immigrants is not a new question for U.S. policymakers. When the Immigration Reform and Control Act of 1986 (IRCA) was passed, Congress chose a narrow legalization

---

[3] Anna Gorman, *Volunteers to Patrol Border near San Diego*, LA TIMES, May 5, 2005, at B1.

[4] Diana M. Alba, *Jobs Lure Migrants North*, LAS CRUCES SUN-NEWS, June 19, 2005, at A1.

[5] Letters to the Editor: Robert Vasquez, IDAHO STATESMAN, June 16, 2005, at 6.

[6] Carolyn Lockhead, *Immigration Debate Splits Christian Right*, SF CHRONICLE, Apr. 28, 2006, at A1.

(or amnesty) as the answer, coupled with employer sanctions in theory to dissuade future undocumented migration by making it unlawful for employers to hire the undocumented. At the time, members of Congress perceived only a handful of alternatives: first, to legalize many of the immigrants; second, to find and deport them; or third, to do nothing. The third option was not an option given mounting pressure to do something, and the second option (which is touted by many today) was considered unworkable, given the expense and effort that would be necessary to round up and deport millions of individuals, while possibly violating the civil rights of many during the process.[7] Today a fourth choice – a large-scale guestworker program – is being advocated by President Bush.

In the first post-9/11 volley on immigration reform, the House of Representatives passed H.R. 4437 in late 2005. Sponsored by Republican Congressman James Sensenbrenner, the law would increase enforcement against employers who hire undocumented workers, make it a felony to be undocumented, and promote immigration enforcement cooperation between federal and local officials. The legislation also includes the construction of a 700-mile fence along the U.S.–Mexico border. These ideas were incorporated in Senate legislation introduced by Republican Senate Majority Leader Bill Frist, another Republican, a few months later. One of Sensenbrenner's earlier brainchilds, the REAL ID Act,[8] actually was enacted by being attached to an emergency $82 billion appropriations bill to fund America's military involvement in Iraq and Afghanistan in May 2005. REAL ID bars states from providing driver's licenses to undocumented aliens; one provision that eventually was eliminated would have established centers to encourage bounty hunters to help round up alien absconders.

In an environment where the debate over undocumented migration is one of the hottest political issues, proposals to do the right thing receive limited political traction. To his credit, President Bush reignited a discussion beyond a let's-round-up-and-deport-them approach with a proposal for a large-scale guestworker plan. In many respects, his plan reflects

---

[7] Bill Ong Hing, DEFINING AMERICA THROUGH IMMIGRATION POLICY 161 (2004).

[8] REAL ID is discussed more fully in Chapter 4.

smart politics as well as a method to address the undocumented challenge. Under the president's plan, first presented on January 7, 2004, and reiterated shortly after his re-election, each year 300,000 undocumented immigrants and workers from abroad would be able to apply for a three-year work permit; the permit could be extended once for a total of six years. Workers would be allowed to switch jobs and to move from one type of work to another. Those coming from abroad would be able to bring family members.[9] The political shrewdness of the proposal begins with the idea that no automatic path toward citizenship is provided to the workers, addressing concerns of some anti-immigrant groups. But by providing an opportunity to work for up to six years, many undocumented workers would step forward and reveal themselves, while a large pool of low-wage workers would make the business community extremely happy. In fact, providing a perpetual pool of low-wage temporary workers would revolutionize the labor market.

Although the proponents of the round-them-up-and-deport approach to undocumented immigration are led by Tancredo and his House Immigration Reform Caucus, with almost a hundred members who are 98 percent Republican, the debate over the guestworker solution does not divide along neat partisan lines. Democratic U.S. Senator Dianne Feinstein, the AFL-CIO, and immigrant rights organizations who recall the abuses of the Bracero program oppose guestworker programs. Republican Congressmen Lamar Smith and Tancredo as well as the restrictionist Federation for American Immigration Reform are also quite vocal in their opposition. Yet President Bush, Senators John McCain and Ted Kennedy, Republican Congressmen Jeff Flake and Jim Kolbe, businesses, and even some farmworker organizations have come to embrace guestworker proposals. The proposals raise a number of questions including the basic question of whether a broad guestworker program should be established; whether such a program would reduce undocumented migration and, if so, whether the reduction of undocumented migration in this manner is in the national security interest of the United States; whether the program should include more than agricultural workers; and whether such a program should provide a path to legalization.

---

[9] Ricardo Alonso-Zaldivar, *Bush Would Open U.S. to Guest Workers*, LA TIMES, Jan. 8, 2004, at A1.

As the debate over undocumented immigration shifted to the Senate in 2006, moderate Republicans such as Senators McCain and Sam Brownback joined forces with Senator Kennedy and Democratic Minority Leader Harry Reid to push for more than an enforcement-only approach to reform. They reached a compromise (Hagel–Martinez) that would include a guestworker plan and a path toward legalization for undocumented aliens who had been in the country for at least two years. But key House negotiators have taken an enforcement-only approach, leaving little hope that either a guestworker plan or legalization program would be enacted before November 2006 mid-term elections. Enforcement-only could still rule the day.

In this chapter, I scrutinize the Bush guestworker proposal as a solution to the undocumented migration issue and conclude that with certain modifications, the plan should be supported. The major modification required is, in fact, the inclusion of a path toward legalization. I explain that with this modification, the proposal should be supported not only by labor, immigrant rights groups, and others who believe that the nation benefits from the availability of low-wage immigrant workers, but also by everyone because the integration of undocumented workers is critical to the social, economic, and national security interests of the nation. However, I also explain why no such plan should be supported if the tradeoff includes conditions that would make millions in the undocumented population ineligible while adding onerous enforcement provisions.

The Undocumented Population

The undocumented population in the United States grows by 300,000 to 500,000 per year. In 2006, researchers at the Pew Hispanic Center estimated that twelve million undocumented immigrants resided in the United States.[10] Of that figure, 57 percent were from Mexico, 24 percent from other parts of Latin America, 9 percent from Asia, 6 percent from Europe and Canada, and 4 percent from Africa and other areas.[11] Almost two-thirds (68 percent) of the unauthorized population lives in eight states: California (24 percent), Texas (14 percent),

---

[10] Jeffrey Passell, *Estimates of the Size and Characteristics of the Undocumented Population*, Mar. 21, 2005, at http://pewhispanic.org/reports/report.php?ReportID=44.
[11] Id. at 4.

Florida (9 percent), New York (7 percent), Arizona (5 percent), Illinois (4 percent), New Jersey (4 percent), and North Carolina (3 percent).[12] Almost a third of the undocumented population (32 percent) is spread throughout other parts of the country.[13] States such as Georgia, Colorado, Maryland, Massachusetts, Virginia, and Washington have more than 200,000 undocumented immigrants. Nevada, Oregon, Pennsylvania, Michigan, Ohio, Wisconsin, and Tennessee each have more than 100,000. Connecticut, Utah, Minnesota, Kansas, New Mexico, Indiana, Iowa, Oklahoma, and Missouri have more than 55,000 undocumented immigrants.[14]

Most undocumented immigrants are adults (8.8 million); 56 percent of these adults are men, and 44 percent are women.[15] About 1.5 million families have at least one parent who is undocumented along with children who are all U.S. citizens. Another 460,000 are mixed-status families in which some children are U.S. citizens and some are undocumented.[16]

Undocumented immigrants account for about 4.3 percent of the civilian labor force – about 6.3 million workers out of a labor force of 146 million. Although they can be found throughout the workforce, undocumented workers tend to be overrepresented in certain occupations and industries. They are much more likely to be in broad occupation groups that require little education or do not have licensing requirements. The share of undocumented immigrants who work in agricultural occupations and construction and extractive occupations is about three times the share of native workers in these types of jobs. In contrast, undocumented immigrants are conspicuously sparse in white collar occupations. Whereas management, business, professions, sales, and administrative support account for half of native workers (52 percent), fewer than one-fourth of the undocumented workers are in these areas (23 percent).[17]

This table shows the proportion of workers in "detailed occupation groups" who are unauthorized. Those shown are where the proportion of undocumented workers exceeds the proportion in the workforce (4.3 percent).[18] For example, more than one out of every four (27 percent) of drywall/ceiling tile installers in the United States is an undocumented worker.

[12] Id. at 11.
[14] Id. at 14.
[16] Id. at 19.
[18] Id. at 27.

[13] Id. at 11.
[15] Id. at 18.
[17] Id. at 26.

Drywall/ceiling tile installers	27%
Roofers	21%
Painters, construction, etc.	20%
Carpenters	12%
Grounds maintenance workers	26%
Hand packers and packagers	22%
Butchers/meat, poultry workers	25%
Cooks	18%
Food preparation workers	13%
Maids and housekeepers	22%
Cleaning/washing equipment operators	20%
Metal/plastic workers, other	13%
Cement masons and finishers	22%
Construction laborers	20%
Brick/block/stone masons	19%
Miscellaneous agricultural workers	23%
Graders and sorters, agricultural products	22%
Dishwashers	24%
Dining and cafeteria attendants	14%
Janitors and building cleaners	12%
Sewing machine operators	18%
Packaging/filling machine operators	17%

So the story of a "typical" undocumented worker in the United States certainly might be about a young male from Mexico who is a farmworker, construction worker, or dishwasher. However, given the diversity of the undocumented worker population, this New Bedford story in the *Boston Globe* is common:

Three times a week, the teenager sorts mounds of frigid clam meat in a damp, windowless warehouse on the waterfront.

The work drains the feeling from his fingers and the optimism from his days. Sometimes, though he risked much to leave there, he is nostalgic for Guatemala.

"I don't have anything over here," said Diego, 19, who asked that his last name be withheld, because he is an undocumented immigrant. "When you're back there, you have this dream of coming over here, the thought of having a little bit of money, maybe work a couple of years and go back home so you can study. Sometimes, that dream is turning into a nightmare."

Diego is one of at least 3,000 young Mayans from Guatemala mostly men who have flocked to New Bedford over the past decade. They have gathered loans, walked for days, packed into freight containers, and wedged themselves into boxes hung under trucks to journey from their mostly rural Guatemalan towns, through Mexico, over the Arizona border, and, eventually, to this once-booming fishing city.

They came to New Bedford with the same hopes as earlier generations of immigrants; hopes realized by Norwegian and Portuguese men who found an ocean teeming with fish, and whose wives found more work than they could handle in factories and fish houses, and whose children found lives in the middle class.

The wide path worn by those earlier immigrants has greatly narrowed in recent years. New Bedford's fishing industry, once seemingly boundless, has been constricted by growing monopolies and by stringent fishing limits that knot the shrinking fleet to the wharves. And the road out of the city's lowest-paid jobs is choked because Diego, like thousands of newcomers, arrived illegally.

The Mayan community dominates the unskilled workforce in New Bedford's seafood houses and is nearly invisible outside them. The Mayans walk or ride bikes to the squat warehouses that line the waterfront, working fitful stretches sorting, cleaning, and packing seafood. They share bedrooms in triple-deckers in the city's North and South End. They send as much as they can to Guatemala to help their families or to repay the coyotes, the smugglers who guided them here.

They find work in the seafood houses mostly through temporary-worker agencies, which send them to employers with assurances that they are allowed to work. Although most make minimum wage, the Mayans earn far better money than they could in Guatemala, where some had worked in coffee and sugar plantations since they were children, for as little as $1.50 a day.[19]

Another undocumented immigrant story concerns the Cuevas family from the Philippines. The assassination of opposition leader Benigno Aquino Jr. on August 21, 1983, as he returned from exile, coupled with the disillusionment following seventeen years of dictatorship under Ferdinand Marcos, left the country in a state of civil unrest. Numerous foreign corporations, fearing the political and economic instability to follow, began to retract their assets from the largely export-based country.

One firm to pull out was National Panasonic, a firm that employed Delfin Cuevas. As National Panasonic's wholesale manager, Delfin was earning P6,000 per month (about $545) – a salary that easily covered the rent and allowed his wife, Angelita, to stay home and raise their three young children. By the time National Panasonic pulled out of the Philippines, laying off hundreds of employees, the unemployment rate was bulging. With Delfin unemployed and the economy relentlessly continuing in a downward spiral, Angelita took an accounting job that paid a meager P9 per day (about $0.82).

---

[19] Yvonne Abraham, *Mayans' Invisible Struggle, New Bedford Arrivals Find Scant Opportunity*, BOSTON GLOBE, Mar. 15, 2005, at A1.

With their children's futures in mind, Delfin and Angelita made the difficult decision to leave the Philippines. An opportunity presented itself in 1984, when the Summer Olympic Games held in Los Angeles led to a relaxation of travel restrictions for entry into the United States. Delfin secured a six-month visitor's visa and arrived in San Francisco in December 1984 with only $200 in his pocket. About a year later, Angelita and their three children, Donna, six, Dale, four, and Dominique, one, followed with tourist visas as well. Delfin, working as both a gas station attendant and a janitor, was able to move the family into a converted garage that they called home for three years. Unlike the spacious three-bedroom home the family had in the Philippines, Delfin and Angelita now slept on a carpeted floor while the three children shared a sofa bed.

Delfin and Angelita spent the ensuing years striving to achieve the dream of an education for their children. Delfin performed maintenance jobs while Angelita held various positions at a gas station, a dry cleaner, a courier service, and a restaurant. Both accepted whatever work was available, with their children's future in mind. They sacrificed so that Donna, Dale, and Dominique could receive a Catholic school education. Despite living just two blocks from a public high school, the parents insisted on sending the kids to a Catholic school in an adjacent city. Even with the hefty price tag, it was well worth it to Delfin and Angelita.

For a while, the Cuevases lived the typical American life – eventually moving into a townhouse in 1994, driving a minivan, and commuting to work on public transit. Angelita, eventually working at a utilities company as an accountant, and Delfin, working at the state employment department, watched proudly as their three children blossomed into responsible young adults. As they fulfilled their parents' dreams, the children tried to realize their own expectations. In December 2003, Donna, at the age of twenty-four, completed her BA in psychology from California State University, Hayward, and was looking forward to applying to graduate school. Dale, twenty-three, was working his way toward an AA in Business at De Anza College and planning to transfer to San Jose State University where his sister Dominique, now nineteen, was a nursing student.

Friends, coworkers, and even the children never knew what Delfin and Angelita had kept secret for years – the family's tourist visas expired in 1986, and they were living in the United States in undocumented status. Since the time of their arrivals, Delfin and Angelita worked hard, paid taxes, had no problems with law enforcement, and put their children through school. They decided to do the right thing and come forward to legalize their status by applying for political asylum.Unfortunately, their plan failed. In 1996, the Cuevas family filed a petition for asylum, but after several hearings and appeals, the asylum claim was denied and they were ordered to leave the country in December 2004. Despite the support of San Francisco Mayor Gavin Newsom, eight members of the San Francisco Board of Supervisors, and a petition of support signed by more than twenty-five hundred private citizens, all avenues for remaining were closed. They were given an extension to leave, allowing the family to sell their house and cars and to tie up any loose ends. The extension allowed Delfin and Angelita to watch their first daughter cross the stage at graduation – a moment they envisioned since they left the Philippines all those years earlier. On June 30, 2004, amid media, friends, and plenty of tears, the five members of the Cuevas family boarded a flight back to the Philippines.

Should we craft a remedy for those undocumented immigrants from Mexico who work in agricultural fields, construction sites, and poultry farms? Should we do something for the Guatemalans who toil in New Bedford? Should relief be available for the Cuevas family who, like the others, are here for a better life, harming no one while pursuing the American dream? To me, the answer is clearly yes.

The Bush Solution

Addressing the challenge of undocumented migration was a front burner issue in the summer 2001. A day before 9/11, Mexico President Vicente Fox was making demands that the United States provide some type of relief for undocumented Mexican workers in the United States. President Bush was receptive. That all changed when the terrorist attacks relegated immigration reform to low-priority status. But with his announcement on January 7, 2004, President Bush got the debate rolling again.

While he was not the first to come up with the idea, President Bush proposed a guestworker program to address the undocumented immigration situation with great fanfare. In a move that surprised pro-immigration and anti-immigration forces alike, just days before his 2004 State of the Union address, Bush gathered an illustrious group of cabinet members, congressmen, Latino leaders, and others to reveal his plan in a speech that was remarkable for its praise of immigrants and their contributions to the nation. The entire text is noteworthy:

REMARKS BY THE PRESIDENT ON IMMIGRATION POLICY

Many of you here today are Americans by choice, and you have followed in the path of millions. And over the generations we have received energetic, ambitious, optimistic people from every part of the world. By tradition and conviction, our country is a welcoming society. America is a stronger and better nation because of the hard work and the faith and entrepreneurial spirit of immigrants.

Every generation of immigrants has reaffirmed the wisdom of remaining open to the talents and dreams of the world. And every generation of immigrants has reaffirmed our ability to assimilate newcomers – which is one of the defining strengths of our country.

During one great period of immigration – between 1891 and 1920 – our nation received some 18 million men, women and children from other nations. The hard work of these immigrants helped make our economy the largest in the world. The children of immigrants put on the uniform and helped to liberate the lands of their ancestors. One of the primary reasons America became a great power in the 20th century is because we welcomed the talent and the character and the patriotism of immigrant families.

The contributions of immigrants to America continue. About 14 percent of our nation's civilian workforce is foreign-born. Most begin their working lives in America by taking hard jobs and clocking long hours in important industries. Many immigrants also start businesses, taking the familiar path from hired labor to ownership.

As a Texan, I have known many immigrant families, mainly from Mexico, and I have seen what they add to our country. They bring to America the values of faith in God, love of family, hard work and self reliance – the values that made us a great nation to begin with. We've all seen those values in action, through the service and sacrifice of more than 35,000 foreign-born men and women currently on active duty in the United States military. One of them is Master Gunnery Sergeant Guadalupe Denogean, an immigrant from Mexico who has served in the Marine Corps for 25 years and counting. Last year, I was honored and proud to witness Sergeant Denogean take the oath of citizenship in a hospital where he was recovering from wounds he received in Iraq. I'm honored to be his Commander-in-Chief, I'm proud to call him a fellow American.

As a nation that values immigration, and depends on immigration, we should have immigration laws that work and make us proud. Yet today we do not. Instead, we see many employers turning to the illegal labor market. We see millions of hard-working men and women condemned to fear and insecurity in a massive, undocumented economy. Illegal entry across our borders makes more difficult the urgent task of securing the homeland.

The system is not working. Our nation needs an immigration system that serves the American economy, and reflects the American Dream.

Reform must begin by confronting a basic fact of life and economics: some of the jobs being generated in America's growing economy are jobs American citizens are not filling. Yet these jobs represent a tremendous opportunity for workers from abroad who want to work and fulfill their duties as a husband or a wife, a son or a daughter.

Their search for a better life is one of the most basic desires of human beings. Many undocumented workers have walked mile after mile, through the heat of the day and the cold of the night. Some have risked their lives in dangerous desert border crossings, or entrusted their lives to the brutal rings of heartless human smugglers. Workers who seek only to earn a living end up in the shadows of American life – fearful, often abused and exploited. When they are victimized by crime, they are afraid to call the police, or seek recourse in the legal system. They are cut off from their families far away, fearing if they leave our country to visit relatives back home, they might never be able to return to their jobs.

The situation I described is wrong. It is not the American way. Out of common sense and fairness, our laws should allow willing workers to enter our country and fill jobs that Americans are not filling. We must make our immigration laws more rational, and more humane. And I believe we can do so without jeopardizing the livelihoods of American citizens.

Our reforms should be guided by a few basic principles. First, America must control its borders. Following the attacks of September the 11th, 2001, this duty of the federal government has become even more urgent. And we're fulfilling that duty.

. . .

Second, new immigration laws should serve the economic needs of our country. If an American employer is offering a job that American citizens are not willing to take, we ought to welcome into our country a person who will fill that job.

Third, we should not give unfair rewards to illegal immigrants in the citizenship process or disadvantage those who came here lawfully, or hope to do so.

Fourth, new laws should provide incentives for temporary, foreign workers to return permanently to their home countries after their period of work in the United States has expired.

Today, I ask the Congress to join me in passing new immigration laws that reflect these principles, that meet America's economic needs, and live up to our highest ideals.

I propose a new temporary worker program that will match willing foreign workers with willing American employers, when no Americans can be found to fill the jobs. This program will offer legal status, as temporary workers, to the millions of undocumented men and women now employed in the United States, and to those in foreign countries who seek to participate in the program and have been offered employment here. This new system should be clear and efficient, so employers are able to find workers quickly and simply.

All who participate in the temporary worker program must have a job, or, if not living in the United States, a job offer. The legal status granted by this program will last three years and will be renewable – but it will have an end. Participants who do not remain employed, who do not follow the rules of the program, or who break the law will not be eligible for continued participation and will be required to return to their home.

Under my proposal, employers have key responsibilities. Employers who extend job offers must first make every reasonable effort to find an American worker for the job at hand. Our government will develop a quick and simple system for employers to search for American workers. Employers must not hire undocumented aliens or temporary workers whose legal status has expired. They must report to the government the temporary workers they hire, and who leave their employ, so that we can keep track of people in the program, and better enforce immigration laws. There must be strong workplace enforcement with tough penalties for anyone, for any employer violating these laws.

Undocumented workers now here will be required to pay a one-time fee to register for the temporary worker program. Those who seek to join the program from abroad, and have complied with our immigration laws, will not have to pay any fee. All participants will be issued a temporary worker card that will allow them to travel back and forth between their home and the United States without fear of being denied re-entry into our country. (Applause.)

This program expects temporary workers to return permanently to their home countries after their period of work in the United States has expired. And there should be financial incentives for them to do so. I will work with foreign governments on a plan to give temporary workers credit, when they enter their own nation's retirement system, for the time they have worked in America. I also support making it easier for temporary workers to contribute a portion of their earnings to tax-preferred savings accounts, money they can collect as they return to their native countries. After all, in many of those countries, a small nest egg is what is necessary to start their own business, or buy some land for their family.

Some temporary workers will make the decision to pursue American citizenship. Those who make this choice will be allowed to apply in the normal way. They will not be given unfair advantage over people who have followed legal procedures from the start. I oppose amnesty, placing undocumented workers on the automatic path to citizenship. Granting amnesty encourages the violation of our laws, and perpetuates illegal immigration.

America is a welcoming country, but citizenship must not be the automatic reward for violating the laws of America.

The citizenship line, however, is too long, and our current limits on legal immigration are too low. My administration will work with the Congress to increase the annual number of green cards that can lead to citizenship. Those willing to take the difficult path of citizenship – the path of work, and patience, and assimilation – should be welcome in America, like generations of immigrants before them.

In the process of immigration reform, we must also set high expectations for what new citizens should know. An understanding of what it means to be an American is not a formality in the naturalization process, it is essential to full participation in our democracy. My administration will examine the standard of knowledge in the current citizenship test. We must ensure that new citizens know not only the facts of our history, but the ideals that have shaped our history. Every citizen of America has an obligation to learn the values that make us one nation: liberty and civic responsibility, equality under God, and tolerance for others.

This new temporary worker program will bring more than economic benefits to America. Our homeland will be more secure when we can better account for those who enter our country, instead of the current situation in which millions of people are unknown, unknown to the law. Law enforcement will face fewer problems with undocumented workers, and will be better able to focus on the true threats to our nation from criminals and terrorists. And when temporary workers can travel legally and freely, there will be more efficient management of our borders and more effective enforcement against those who pose a danger to our country.

This new system will be more compassionate. Decent, hard-working people will now be protected by labor laws, with the right to change jobs, earn fair wages, and enjoy the same working conditions that the law requires for American workers. Temporary workers will be able to establish their identities by obtaining the legal documents we all take for granted. And they will be able to talk openly to authorities, to report crimes when they are harmed, without the fear of being deported.

The best way, in the long run, to reduce the pressures that create illegal immigration in the first place is to expand economic opportunity among the countries in our neighborhood. In a few days I will go to Mexico for the Special Summit of the Americas, where we will discuss ways to advance free trade, and to fight corruption, and encourage the reforms that lead to prosperity. Real growth and real hope in the nations of our hemisphere will lessen the flow of new immigrants to America when more citizens of other countries are able to achieve their dreams at their own home.

Yet our country has always benefited from the dreams that others have brought here. By working hard for a better life, immigrants contribute to the life of our nation. The temporary worker program I am proposing today represents the best tradition of our society, a society that honors the law, and welcomes the newcomer. This plan will help return order and fairness to our immigration system, and in so doing we will honor our values, by showing our respect for those who work hard and share in the ideals of America.[20]

The premises of President Bush's proposal define the debate over whether a guestworker program makes sense as a solution to the large number of undocumented workers in the country:

- American employers are turning to undocumented workers to fulfill labor shortages: "Our nation needs an immigration system that serves the American economy.... [W]e see many employers turning to the illegal labor market. We see millions of hard-working men and women condemned to fear and insecurity in a massive, undocumented economy.... [O]ur laws should allow willing workers to enter our country and fill jobs that Americans are not filling."
- We need to be "more compassionate. Decent, hard-working people [should] be protected by labor laws, with the right to change jobs, earn fair wages, and enjoy the same working conditions that the law requires for American workers."
- A "temporary worker program will bring more than economic benefits to America."
- As a matter of national security, "[o]ur homeland will be more secure when we can better account for those who enter our country, instead of the current situation in which millions of people are unknown to the law."
- However, amnesty should not be granted; guestworkers should "not be given unfair advantage over people who have followed legal procedures from the start."
- The "best way" to "reduce the pressures that create illegal immigration in the first place is to expand economic opportunity among the countries in our neighborhood."

Undocumented workers who participate in the president's plan would receive no special treatment if they want to reside in the United States permanently. Because no green card or lawful permanent residence legalization program for undocumented workers is part of the president's proposal, at the end of the three- or six-year period, the workers would have

---

[20] *President Bush Proposes New Temporary Worker Program*, Jan. 7, 2004, at http://www.whitehouse.gov/news/releases/2004/01/20040107-3.html.

to return to their native countries. Of course, if a worker is eligible to apply for immigration status under preexisting immigration laws, the person can pursue that avenue while working in the temporary worker status.

The political genius of the proposal is evidenced by the critique of the Bush proposal from both the right and the left. By simultaneously giving too much in the eyes of strict anti-immigrant forces and too little to pro-immigrant groups, the Bush proposal can be depicted as a moderate compromise. Juxtaposing critique from the right and the left places Bush in the center.

The Left

Many Latino groups were disappointed that the proposal did not provide a path to legalization. According to the policy director of the League of United Latin American Citizens, "[T]here has to be some innovative mechanism to allow for adjustment of status for those who are in the United States. . . . We have to protect the people who are already here."[21] Congressman Howard Berman charged that the Bush plan would put too much power in the hands of employers, who would be deciding whether to sponsor the immigrant.

The National Network for Immigrant and Refugee Rights issued this press release criticizing the president's proposal:

> BUSH ADMINISTRATION'S IMMIGRATION REFORM PITCHES FALSE HOPES
> NO CONCRETE PROPOSAL FOR COMPREHENSIVE LEGALIZATION
> OF UNDOCUMENTED IMMIGRANT FAMILIES
>
> **Oakland, CA** – The proposal for immigration reform outlined today by President George Bush promises little hope for fair wages or decent working conditions, much less opportunity for legal status, for the millions of undocumented immigrant workers in the U.S. Instead, the proposed "new" policy amounts to little more than another "guestworker" program, with even fewer protections and opportunities than programs currently under consideration in Congress. The Bush proposal might be good for employers wanting cheap and vulnerable labor, but does little to contribute to the human rights and well-being of immigrant workers.
>
> The *National Network for Immigrant and Refugee Rights* and other immigrant rights advocates hoped that the Administration would finally follow through on its pledge of over two years ago to consider a path to

---

[21] Alonso-Zaldivar, *supra* note 9.

permanent residency for the hundreds of thousands of undocumented immigrants who live and work in the U.S.

However, the main fix that the President proposes – a three-year, renewable temporary worker visa – provides no definitive path toward legalization, but rather, ensures a pool of cheap labor for "bad jobs" that American workers try to avoid. Nor did the proposal specify how immigrant families could be united or remain together in the U.S., only that participants could leave to visit home countries and gain re-entry.

The President also spoke of the tragic deaths of migrants at the U.S.-Mexico border, indicating that his proposals for temporary work visas would help migrants who have been victimized by smugglers. However, he also reaffirmed border security policies which themselves have contributed to discrimination, abuse and violence against immigrants in the border regions, sometimes at the hands of border patrol agents. After September 11, stepped-up "militarization" of the border has forced desperate men, women and children into more hazardous migration situations.

The President's proposal did not specify changes to the current legal immigration program, which is woefully backlogged and inadequate in addressing the demand for immigration access. Since participants in the new temporary worker program would have "fall in line" to apply for permanent residency status, they too would be thrust into the existing backlog that itself contributes to undocumented immigration.

The fact that the Department of Homeland Security, which is dedicated to national security, would be responsible for implementing the proposed program is also disturbing. DHS immigration enforcement programs, as described in NNIRR's recent report, Human Rights and Human Security at Risk, already jeopardize community safety and compromise access to immigration services. DHS oversight provides little incentive for undocumented immigrants to emerge from the shadows and identify themselves through a program that carries little hope for longterm legal residency. Comprehensive immigration reform must include opportunities for permanent residency and family reunification, labor protection, access to due process, safety and community security. Undocumented immigrant students, many of whom have lived in the U.S. most of their lives, have been waiting for President Bush to support pending legislation that would provide them with access to permanent residency and a future free from fear of deportation. Farmworker unions have negotiated with agribusiness to bring to Congress legislation that would protect their rights as workers and create a path for legal residency. President Bush's proposals made no mention of these efforts. Instead, his announcement, which comes less than a week before he is scheduled to meet with

Mexican President Vicente Fox, has the transparency of a pre-election appeal to Latino voters – not a serious attempt to chart a path towards a fair and just program of much-needed immigration reform.

The Farmworker Justice Fund issued this press release in opposition to the Bush proposal:

THE PRESIDENT'S TEMPORARY FOREIGN WORKER PROPOSAL IS ILL-CONCEIVED
THE AGJOBS COMPROMISE ON FARMWORKER IMMIGRATION SHOULD BE SUPPORTED AND PASSED IN 2004

The President's proposal in his immigration policy speech on Wednesday, January 7, 2004, was vague but is specific enough for us to know that he is essentially proposing a new era of indentured servants. This nation has experimented with indentured servitude and "guestworker" programs; they failed miserably and caused great misery. His proposal should be rejected as inconsistent with our nation's democratic traditions and our history as a nation of immigrants.

Under the President's proposal, Congress would create a new temporary foreign worker program. A person from another country, whether living here or abroad, could gain a temporary, nonimmigrant work visa if he or she finds an employer willing to participate in the guestworker program. If the employment ended, that person would not have a right to stay in the United States unless another employer was willing to participate in the guestworker program. The visa would end after three years, but a renewal of the visa may be possible if the employer agrees.

The temporary work visa will essentially be controlled by the employer. The worker's ability to remain in the U.S. will depend on keeping that employer satisfied. Consequently, the worker will know that he or she risks deportation by challenging unfair or illegal conduct. Employers will gain docile workers who often will work for lower wages and fewer benefits. With potentially several million guestworkers, the U.S. citizens and full-fledged immigrants will experience reduced bargaining power with their employers. Union organizing and bargaining will be impeded.

The President's proposal lacks the labor protections against exploitation that the notorious "Bracero" program had and that are present in the abusive H-2A and H-2B temporary foreign worker programs. There will be no protections against depression in wage rates through the use of exploitable guestworkers. The minimum wage is not enough. If a poultry processing plant is paying citizens and immigrants $12 per hour but has access to guestworkers, it might choose to offer $10 per hour. This bill does not protect wage levels or other working conditions from depression. This and other protections existed even under the old Bracero program despite its reputation for abuses. The President's proposal is a shocking departure from longstanding policy.

Generally, such programs are called "guestworker" programs because the participating employees have no right to become immigrants or citizens of the United States. In this case, the visas would be temporary but many of the jobs they would hold are permanent. Some of the undocumented workers who would want a legal status have been employed in the U.S. for a decade or more in year-round jobs. The disconnect is not explained. On the other hand, there is significant unemployment in some geographic areas and industries; the proposal seems to lack a meaningful labor market test as a prerequisite for bringing in new guestworkers from abroad.

These workers will not be able to earn their way to a "green card" with immigration status even after years of employment. Guestworkers would apparently only be permitted to apply for the multi-year, perhaps multi-decade, waiting list to become an immigrant. In this sense, such workers will not even be granted the right to earn their freedom that indentured servants had.

The fact that the President's proposal would grant a "legal status" to undocumented workers does not by itself mean anything: slavery was a "legal status" too. The President's proposal raises a fundamental question about the nature of citizenship and immigration status in this country and answers it in the wrong way.

This is a nation of immigrants, not a nation of guestworkers. It is also a nation of basic freedoms; guestworkers, however, are subjected to a status that deprives them of meaningful economic bargaining power and, as nonvoters, of political representation or influence. Undocumented workers who are contributing to this society and other foreign workers who are needed should be converted to legal immigrant status, not into indentured servants under a guestworker program.

The President's proposal should be rejected. As to farmworkers, the White House should support the AgJOBS compromise (S.1645, HR 3142). It would provide undocumented farmworkers with the opportunity to earn immigration status by continuing to work in agriculture and would revise the H-2A guestworker program. It's a reasonable compromise based on arduous negotiations after years of bitter battles in Congress. No more delay is warranted.

The Right

The Center for Immigration Studies issued a "report" attacking the underlying assumptions of the Bush guestworker program that (1) immigration is inevitable, (2) the poor are overpaid, (3) there are jobs Americans will not do, (4) free trade requires open immigration, (5) guestworkers will go

Although the Bush administration did not draft guestworker legislation prior to the November 2004 election, once Sensenbrenner's H.R. 4437 enforcement measure was passed in the House at the end of 2005 and the debate shifted to the Senate in 2006, the president reiterated his proposal. The president wanted to force a debate on his guestworker proposal in Congress, but again he was attacked by the right. Congressman Tancredo declared his resolve to block the legislation. Invoking his clout as head of the House Immigration Reform Caucus, which argues for stronger action to stop undocumented immigration and a reduction of legal migration, Tancredo charged:

> Why is this so important to the president? Is it just the corporate interests who benefit from cheap labor? Do they have such a strong grip on our president that he is actually willing to put our nation at risk, because open borders do put our nation at risk? Is it petulance, because we were able to stop it in the last Congress? Why is it so important to give amnesty to people who have broken the law? I'm willing to fight against this and I would say there are at least 180 members of our Republican caucus who are willing at least to stop amnesty for illegal immigrants.[25]

Assailed by the right and the left, the president was positioned squarely in the middle of the debate over illegation immigration.

Guestworker and Legalization Proposals

While the president's guestworker proposal was not introduced as independent legislation, his plan was incorporated into a bipartisan compromise in early April 2006 written largely by Senators Mel Martinez (R-Florida) and Chuck Hagel (R-Nebraska) (Hagel–Martinez bill). The compromise is best understood in the context of a number of other guestworker proposals that have been proposed in Congress. Some, like the Hagel–Martinez bill, have included a separate path toward legalization (permanent residence and eventual citizenship) for undocumented workers. Others are limited to agricultural workers. Their approaches to wages vary. The most noteworthy are summarized in the following sections.

AgJOBS

In 2003, the Agricultural Job Opportunity, Benefits and Security (AgJOBS) Act was introduced in the House (H.R. 3142) and the Senate

---

[25] Alan Elsner, *Republican to Lead Immigration Revolt against Bush*, REUTERS NEWS, Jan. 12, 2005.

(S. 1645) after several years of bipartisan efforts and earlier iterations. The sponsors of the House Bill were Representatives Chris Cannon (R-Utah) and Howard Berman (D-California). Senators Edward Kennedy (D-Massachusetts) and Larry Craig (R-Idaho) sponsored the Senate version. The bill would have granted lawful permanent residency to as many as 500,000 undocumented farmworkers and revised the current H-2A agricultural worker program. The bill represented a compromise between farmworker advocates and their employers and contained several concessions on both sides.

After six years, a worker would be eligible for legalization. Under the legislation, temporary resident status would be granted to undocumented farmworkers who could establish proof of 575 hours of agricultural work or 100 workdays during the eighteen-month period preceding the introduction of the legislation. After the grant of temporary resident status, the farmworker would be required to complete an additional 2,060 hours of agricultural work or 360 workdays during the next six years to be eligible for lawful permanent residency.

The proposed changes to the current H-2A guestworker program by AgJOBS are significant. The legislation would replace the labor certification process of the present H-2A program (requiring that recruitment efforts of available U.S. workers have been attempted and failed) with the labor attestation process found in the H-1B program (where the employer simply attests in a statement that U.S. workers are unavailable). This was a major concession by farmworker advocates who believe that the present labor certification process is more protective of farmworker wages than the proposed labor attestation process.

Changes to the wage structures were also contemplated in AgJOBS. The legislation would effectively freeze the Adverse Effect Wage Rate (AEWR) for three years. AEWR is used to determine the wages that farmworkers receive. Employers wanted to eliminate the AEWR altogether. Currently, employers must pay workers the highest of three rates: the state or federal minimum wage, the AEWR, or the local prevailing wage. The AEWR was created under the Bracero program as a necessary protection against the depression in prevailing wages that results from guestworker programs.

The proposal also would expand the H-2A program by allowing temporary workers to enter the United States for a period of up to three years. After three years, these guestworkers would be obligated to return to their countries of origin. This provision sounded very similar to the guestworker reform proposed by President Bush. However, AgJOBS' opportunity for legalization after six years was not part of the president's plan.

Hagel–Daschle

Soon after President Bush announced his temporary worker proposal in January 2004, Senators Chuck Hagel (R-Nebraska) and Tom Daschle (D-South Dakota) unveiled their bipartisan immigration reform package that contained a temporary worker provision. [Note: Senator Daschle was not reelected to the Senate in November 2004.]

A new H-2C category would be open to 250,000 nonimmigrant workers per year for five years and would not be limited to agricultural workers. Workers would be admitted for an initial period of two years, and employers would be allowed to petition for extensions for workers for an additional two years. Spouses and children of willing workers would be eligible for derivative status. Employers would be required to pay the prevailing wage, and H-2C employees would be allowed to maintain status and change employers after three months.

The legislation also contained a path to legalization ("earned adjustment of status") for undocumented immigrants who had resided in the United States for at least five years prior to the introduction of the legislation. They must also demonstrate aggregate employment in the United States for at least three of the five years immediately preceding introduction of the legislation and for at least one year following enactment. An alien who filed an application for earned adjustment of status would be required to pay a fine plus a $1,000 application fee.

An alien who was physically present in the United States on the date the legislation was introduced, but who did not satisfy the five-year physical presence or employment requirements, would be able to apply for "transitional worker status." Transitional workers would be eligible for adjustment of status to permanent residence if they were lawfully employed in the United States for an aggregate of more than two but fewer than three of the five years immediately preceding the introduction of the legislation and are employed for at least two years following enactment.

Goodlatte–Chambliss

In November 2003, Congressman Bob Goodlatte (R-Virginia) introduced legislation that would substantially alter the H-2A agricultural worker program. The program's application process would have be streamlined to

become a labor attestation program, rather than the current labor certification program. Employers would simply promise to comply with requirements (e.g., temporary nature of the work, benefits, wages, recruitment
of domestic workers). The Department of Labor would have seven days
to review and approve the employer's petition for workers. The employer
would still need to engage in "positive recruitment" (i.e., private market efforts) in areas of labor supply but would no longer be required to
recruit U.S. workers through government job service offices. The legislation would eliminate the AEWR. A special "prevailing wage" would apply
that could be determined by the employers' own prevailing wage survey.
Currently, H-2A employers must provide free housing to nonlocal U.S.
and foreign workers, but under this legislation, employers could choose
to provide a monetary housing allowance if the state's governor has certified that there is sufficient farmworker housing available in the area. With
philosophical undertones similar to that of the president, Congressman
Goodlatte felt that his legislation was a good way to address the problem
of undocumented workers in the United States, by providing a streamlined temporary visa program through which farmworkers could be hired.
Workers currently in the United States in undocumented status would be
given a one-time chance to return home and apply for the program legally.

Senator Saxby Chambliss (R-Georgia) introduced a Senate bill in March
2004 that was almost identical to the Goodlatte bill. The Chambliss bill
added a couple of noteworthy provisions. Currently, employers must reim-
burse workers for their transportation costs to and from their place of
recruitment. This bill would allow employers to pay for travel costs to and
from the place where the worker was approved to enter the United States,
which could be a U.S. consulate hundreds of miles from the worker's
home. The bill also sought to overrule the decision in *Arriaga v. Florida
Pacific Farms*,[26] regarding the Fair Labor Standards Act. It would essentially allow H-2A employers to reduce the workers' wages below the federal minimum wage by imposing on the workers the obligation to absorb
visa, transportation, and other costs related to entering the United States.
Although the current H-2A program is intended to fill agricultural jobs
that last fewer than eleven months, the Chambliss bill would distort the
definition of "seasonal" employment by allowing an employer to file an

---

[26] 305 F.3d 1228 (11th Cir. 2002).

unlimited number of applications for guestworkers during a twelve-month period.[27]

SOLVE Act

In May 2004, congressional Democrats introduced the Safe, Orderly, Legal Visas and Enforcement Act of 2004 (SOLVE Act), sponsored by such legislators as Senator Edward Kennedy (D-Massachusetts) and Representatives Bob Menedez (D-New Jersey) and Luis Gutierrez (D-Illinois). The comprehensive package, which proposed changes to facilitate family reunification in the immigrant visa categories and reductions in the waiting lists (backlog reduction) as well as adjustments to the income tests for sponsors and would have established a "future worker program." New programs would be established for workers in low-skilled positions. H-1D visas would be available to 250,000 workers for a period of two years, and the visas would be renewable for two additional terms (six years total). H-2B visas would be available to 100,000 workers for a period of nine months and renewable for up to forty months. After three months with one employer, the workers in each category could change employers (job portability). The Department of Labor would have to agree through a "strengthened" attestation process that U.S. workers are not available and that the employment of foreign workers will not adversely affect the wages and working conditions of U.S. workers. H-2B and H-1D workers would be paid the prevailing wage, as determined by the shop's collective bargaining agreement or, in its absence, under federal labor laws.

The programs would include a path to permanent residency for undocumented immigrants. Immigrants who have been in the United States for five or more years as of the date the legislation was introduced are eligible, if they can demonstrate twenty-four months in aggregate employment in the United States and payment of taxes. Applicants here fewer than five years are eligible for transitional status of five years, during which time they can work and travel abroad if necessary. After twenty-four months, they too would be eligible for permanent residence.

The Arizona Bill

Republican members of the Arizona congressional delegation came up with their own plan. H.R. 2899 was introduced by Congressmen Kolbe

---

[27] Farmworker Justice Fund, Inc. Policy Brief, September 2004.

and Flake in the House and Senator McCain (S. 1461) in the Senate in July 2003. The legislation would have created a new nonimmigrant worker visa category, H-4A. Employers would have to provide the same benefits, wages, and working conditions provided to other employees similarly employed; the visa would be portable – employers could not prevent nonimmigrants from accepting work for a different empoloyer. The employer would have to verify that the worker did not or would not displace a U.S. worker. The visa would be valid for an initial period of three years and could be extended once for another three years. The spouse and children of the worker would not be given a special visa to join the worker. A filing fee plus a $1,500 penalty would be required. Adjustment to legal permanent resident (LPR) status would be available to the H-4A nonimmigrant either by petition of employer or through self-petition, if the alien has maintained status for three years.

Critics of the McCain/Kolbe/Flake proposal included another Arizona Republican congressman, J. D. Hayworth. He claimed that the legislation was a "transparent path to amnesty" that would "only encourage a new wave of illegal aliens and make America's uncontrolled and unacceptable immigration debacle even worse than it is now." A local resident complained that the legislation was "not a solution because it does not address the true problem of uncontrolled borders with Mexico and Canada. It is a surrender because politicians from both parties are pandering to the Latino vote."[28]

McCain–Kennedy

With some fanfare and timed when the Migration Policy Institute announced the formation of an Immigration Task Force to analyze immigration policy, Senators McCain and Kennedy and Representatives Kolbe, Flake, and Gutierrez introduced sweeping immigration reform in May 2005 that included major guestworker components: H-5A and H-5B.

A new temporary worker visa (H-5A) would be created for nonagriculture or high-skilled jobs. To qualify, the person must have a job offer. H-5A workers would have the same rights as U.S. workers under applicable federal, state, and local labor and employment laws; they would not be treated as independent contractors. For the first year, at least 400,000 visas will be made available, with up to 80,000 more depending on demand.

[28] John P. Hoeppner, *Border Proposal Is a Surrender*, ARIZONA REPUBLIC, Aug. 5, 2003, at 8B.

Available visas in subsequent years will follow similar formulas. After four years of work, H-5A visa holders may apply for lawful permanent resident status through an employer or through self-petition.

The H-5B program is for aliens (including undocumented) who are in the United States before the date of introduction of the legislation (May 2005). The person's spouse and children may also apply. The applicant must pay an initial $1,000 fine. The initial period of authorized stay is for six (three plus three) years. After a period of time, the person is eligible for adjustment to LPR status if still working, must pay an additional $1,000 fine, must submit to security checks, and must demonstrate knowledge of English and U.S. civics.

While Senator McCain went through great pains to make sure that the legislation is not viewed as an amnesty by emphasizing the penalties that undocumented workers would have to pay to participate in the program, Representative Tancredo immediately expressed opposition: "There might be a little more lipstick on this pig than there was before," he said, "but it is most certainly the same old pig. Time and time again, history has shown us that amnesty actually increases illegal immigration."[29] Similarly, Rosemary Jenks, director of government affairs for Numbers USA, which advocates reducing the undocumented immigrant population, said her group also opposed the McCain–Kennedy proposal and only "would support an exit amnesty, like a tax amnesty, that would allow illegal immigrants to leave and not apply a ban on future reentry."[30]

Hagel–Martinez

For much of March 2006, the U.S. Senate wrangled over the issue of immigration. Although the McCain–Kennedy proposal sparked much of the debate that occurred first in the Judiciary Committee, Committee Chair Senator Arlen Specter (R-Pennsylvania) came up with his own legislation that attempted to balance McCain–Kennedy provisions with pressure from others to include strong enforcement provisions. For example, Republican Senate Majority Leader Bill Frist threatened to come up with his own Sensenbrenner-type bill if the Judiciary Committee failed to produce something. In fact, even though the committee did put forward a bill, Frist introduced his own bill (S. 2454) anyway, threatening to make

---

[29] Darryl Fears, *Immigration Measure Introduced*, WASHINGTON POST, May 13, 2005, at A8.
[30] Id.

his the central bill if an accord was not reached by the Easter break. The Senate debate raged on.

Two days prior to the congressional break, a major breakthrough was made when a bipartisan compromise was cobbled together by Senators Hagel and Martinez. The Hagel–Martinez bill (S. 2611) was embraced by two-thirds of the senators, including Senators Frist, McCain, Kennedy, and Reid. The deal came after days of negotiations designed to persuade Republicans who had supported the more lenient measure that emerged from the Senate Judiciary Committee to shift their backing to a a bill with more Republican ownership. The Democrats thought they still had enough votes to pass the Judiciary Committee version until two of the Judiciary Committee bill's primary sponsors, Senators McCain and Lindsey Graham (R-South Carolina), informed Kennedy that they were no longer with him and, instead, would back the Hagel–Martinez compromise. Able to secure a few changes in the compromise, Kennedy went to the Senate floor to urge Democrats to endorse the deal.

The Hagel–Martinez compromise in early April addressed the issue of undocumented immigrants in a number of manners. For those who could prove that they had been in the country for five years or more (perhaps eight million), a renewable work visa would be granted after paying a $2,000 penalty and back taxes, and undergoing a criminal background check. After five years, those individuals could apply for legalization provided they remained employed, learned English, and did not commit crimes. For those undocumented who were in the country for more than two years but less than five (perhaps three million), a temporary work visa was available if they left the country and applied for the visa outside. The bill also provided for a Bush-type guestworker program for 325,000 visas annually.

The compromise immediately received criticism from the right and the left. Senator Jon Kyle (R-Arizona) dismissed the deal as "artifical and meaningless," and former House speaker Newt Gingrich (R-Georgia) called it "a cave-in" to the Democrats. Congressman Tancredo chimed in, "The Senate amnesty deal is miserable public policy."[31] On the other hand, AFL-CIO President John Sweeney, desiring a broader legalization program, said the agreement "tears at the heart of true immigration

---

[31] Jonathan Weisman, *Senate Pact Offers Permits to Most Illegal Immigrants*, WASHINGTON POST, Apr. 7, 2006, at A1.

reform."[32] Immigrant rights advocates were opposed because of provisions such as those that would preclude the participation of anyone who had used a false Social Security number to obtain employment in the past, permit indefinite and possibly permanent detention of deportable immigrants, expand the use of expedited removal proceedings, give local and state police the authority to assist the federal government in enforcing federal immigration laws, and permit the deportation of someone who has never committed a crime if the attorney general has reason to believe that the person is a member of a gang.

On April 7, 2006, the day before Congress took its break, the agreement on Hagel–Martinez appeared to fall apart. Republicans blamed the Democrats and vice versa. The disagreement was over whether amendments could be introduced to the bill on the floor of the Senate and what rules would be used in a Senate–House conference that would ultimately reconcile the Senate bill with the enforcement-only Sensenbrenner House bill. The Democratic leadership also was concernd about the rules that would govern the conference between the two bodies of Congress. They feared that without a bipartisan agreement on rules limiting concessions to the House, Congressman Sensenbrenner, who certainly would be one of the House conferees, would have his way and the legislation would come out of the negotiations intensely anti-immigrant. With no agreement over process, the Senate took its Easter break.

However, discussions continued. President Bush met with a bipartisan group in late April that included Senators Martinez, McCain, Kennedy, Reid, Specter, and Frist, signaling to many that the president was willing to endorse the legalization provisions of Hagel–Martinez. When the Senate reconvened on April 24, 2006, these senators were committed to bringing the legislation to the Senate floor by Memorial Day. They worked tirelessly and considered countless amendments. On May 15, President Bush delivered a major primetime address to the nation on the immigrations issue, reiterating his earlier message but acknowledging that undocumented immigrants with "roots in the country" deserve a path to citizenship. By May 25, Hagel–Martinez passed the Senate by a 62–36 margin.

The May 25 legislation differed somewhat from the early April bill. Undocumented immigrants who have been in the country five years or more can continue working and eventually become lawful permanent residents and citizens after paying at least $3,250 in fines, fees, and back taxes

---

[32] Id.

and learning English. Those here from two to five years would have to depart the country and apply to reenter under a guestworker program. Anyone convicted of a felony or three misdemeanors is barred from these programs. Those undocumented here less than two years would have to leave the United States. AgJOBS was incorporated, which would put a million undocumented farmworkers on a path to legalization. A guestworker program would be created for up to 200,000 workers per year; visas would be good for three years with a possible three-year extension. An additional 370-mile, triple-layer fence along the U.S.–Mexico border would be constructed. The president is authorized to send six thousand National Guardsmen to help at the border. Employers are subject to increased fines and criminal penalties for hiring unauthorized workers. The names of overstayed nonimmigrants would be added to a national crime database.

As a Senate–House conference committee was formed to try to reconcile the enforcement-only Sensenbrenner House bill with the more comprehensive Hagel–Martinez Senate bill that contains a path to legalization for millions of undocumented, a compromise that would include legalization appeared doubtful. Certainly, Senator Frist's support remained important. Although he once supported the House version that would make illegal immigration a felony, he changed his position, remarking on how "a mature understanding" of the handling of undocumented immigration emerged in the Senate after weeks of debate. But Congressman Sensenbrenner, the chief negotiator for the House, stated that he would not accept any legislation that would put undocumented immigrants on a path to citizenship, and his intransigence could prevail.

Humanizing Guestworkers and Undocumented Immigrants

Short of doing nothing, the policy options available to lawmakers faced with the challenge of undocumented immigration today include massive deportations, a path to legalization, and a guestworker program. If anti-immigrant forces in Congress have their way, a round-up-and-deport strategy would be implemented along with making undocumented status a felony and building more death traps along the border. In this police-state environment, raids of restaurants, hotels, and construction sites would be common daily occurrences, and families would be torn apart. That scenario simply should not be acceptable to us as a civil society. Thus, the guestworker-legalization option must be seriously considered.

The idea of establishing a large-scale guestworker program as a way to reduce undocumented immigration is an option that has a great deal of support today. For immigrant rights advocates, a straight legalization program that is generous and broad is preferable.[33] However, the strength of congressional support for straight legalization is questionable. While legalization for some undocumented immigrants was part of the Hagel–Martinez Senate compromise, the trade-off included onerous and unjust enforcement provisions. One legalization bill (H.R. 2092) that was introduced in the House by Congresswoman Sheila Jackson Lee (D-Texas) got nowhere even though she is the ranking Democrat in the House subcommittee on immigration. In fact, the only immigration legislation that has emanated from the House in the past few years are Sensenbrenner's REAL ID Act and H.R. 4437, which represent a philosophy diametrically opposed to legalization. On the other hand, broad political support for the AgJOBS guestworker program was garnered in the past, and the degree of criticism aimed at guestworker proposals by the right are at least a bit less vitriolic than that spewed at straight legalization proposals. So pushing for a good and fair guestworker program is something that immigrant rights advocates seriously might consider given the political atmosphere. The potential benefit to undocumented immigrants is too real to facilely dismiss.

While political support for guestworker programs is significant, within that support, division over whether such a program must include a path toward legalization is evident. In the agricultural guestworker area, AgJOBS represents a compromise between the two camps that includes a legalization component. As a result, AgJOBS, at least during the 108th Congress, did enjoy substantial bipartisan support. Hagel–Martinez and McCain–Kennedy (and the SOLVE Act and Hagel–Daschele of past years) included rigorous provisions that could lead to legalization after the payment of penalties.

Those who favor guestworkers but oppose legalization are epitomized by Lorinda Ratkowski, a businesswoman who testified in favor of the

---

[33] I include myself among the advocates who would prefer a simple, straightforward legalization plan. For example, H.R. 2092, the Save America Comprehensive Immigration Act of 2005, introduced by Congresswoman Sheila Jackson Lee, offers legal status to undocumented immigrants who have resided in the United States for five years.

Goodlatte–Chambliss guestworker proposal. To her, legalization would not help preserve her cut-flower business and other seasonal agriculture in the United States, "because farms need a workforce that is willing to be transient and amnesty encourages workers to settle down in one location."[34] Couched in those terms, the question of whether a guestworker program should include a legalization component is, in the end, a question of whether we view guestworkers simply as commodities in the global economy,[35] or whether we view them as human beings with lives, feelings, hopes, aspirations, sensitivities, and families.

Opposition to the AEWR and the attitude of growers toward wages also is a reflection of the commodification of workers. William L. Brim, vice president of the Georgia Fruit and Vegetable Growers Association, who also favored the Goodlatte–Chambliss framework, testified that he began participating in the H-2A program in 1998 under threat of an INS crackdown on undocumented farmworkers during the next peak production season. The H-2A program "was the only alternative we had to employ a legal workforce." He added that if Congress does not reform the H-2A program, many Georgia growers will be forced to stop participating because of four problems: (1) the AEWR, which requires growers to pay $7.88 per hour and transportation to and from the country of the laborer's residence while employers who hire an undocumented workforce pay $5.50 per hour; (2) the requirement that growers protect the domestic workforce by offering domestic workers employment until 50 percent of the production contract is fulfilled; (3) the inflexible definition of "seasons," which does not take into account crop delays; and (4) the ongoing threat of legal action.[36]

The debate over whether guestworkers – especially as part of a solution to the challenge of undocumented migration – should be given a path toward legalization is a question of what value we place on these workers. That residents and politicians from the same region of the country of similar background may not view the issue monolithically tells us that the resolution may not be simple. Senator McCain and Congressmen Flake and Kolbe support such a path, but Senator Kyl and Congressman

---

[34] 81 INTERPRETER RELEASES 177, 179 (Feb. 9, 2004).

[35] See generally Rhacel Salazar Parreñas, SERVANTS OF GLOBALIZATION: WOMEN, MIGRATION AND DOMESTIC WORK (2001); Ruben Garcia, *Ghost Workers in an Interconnected World: Going beyond the Dichotomies of Domestic Immigration and Labor Laws*, 36 U. MICH. J.L. REFORM 737 (2003).

[36] 81 INTERPRETER RELEASES 177, 179 (Feb. 9, 2004).

Hayworth strongly oppose that approach.[37] All are Arizona Republicans. Why the difference? McCain, Flake, and Kolbe favor a path toward legalization because they are driven by personal experiences. They meet and talk regularly with service, construction, agriculture, and ranch workers in their state – individuals who would benefit from legalization. They have come to value the contributions of these individuals from a humanistic perspective, and their ethical subjectivism leads them to favor more than a simple guestworker framework.

Humanizing guestworkers rather than commodifying them helps us understand why providing them with a path to legalization is probably the right thing to do. For example, as a matter of distributive justice, Michael Walzer argues that what guestworkers provide us and our relationship with them demands that we provide them with membership in our society.

> [G]uest workers are not, in the usual sense of the word, guests; and they are certainly not tourists. They are workers, above all, and they come (and generally stay for as long as they are allowed) because they need to work, not because they expect to enjoy the visit. They are not on vacation; they do not spend their days as they please. . . . These guests experience the state as a pervasive and frightening power that shapes their lives and regulates their every move – to which they have no access. Departure is only a formal option, deportation a continuous practical threat. As a group, they constitute a disenfranchised class. They are typically an exploited or oppressed class as well – and they are exploited or oppressed at least in part because they are disenfranchised, incapable of organizing effectively for mutual aid and advancement. Their material condition is unlikely to be improved except by altering their political status. Meanwhile, tyranny is the right name for their subjection. And surely political community requires something else.[38]

The relevant principle here is not mutual aid but political justice. The guests don't need citizenship – not in the same sense in which they might be said to need their jobs. Nor are they injured, helpless, destitute; they are able-bodied and earning money. Nor are they standing, even figuratively, "by the side of the road"; they are living among the citizens. They do socially necessary work and they are deeply enmeshed in the legal system of the country to which they have come. Participants in economy and law, they ought to be able to regard themselves as potential or future participants in politics as well. And they must be possessed of those basic civil liberties the

---

[37] Recent legislation introduced by Senator Kyl with Senator John Cornyn of Texas provides for a guestworker program with no ability for participants to become lawful permanent residents.

[38] Michael Walzer, SPHERES OF JUSTICE: A DEFENSE OF PLURALISM AND EQUALITY 30 (1984).

exercise of which is so much preparation for voting and office-holding. They must be set on the road to citizenship. They may choose not to become citizens, to return to their homes, or to stay on as resident aliens. Many, perhaps most, will choose to return because of their emotional ties to their national family and their native land. . . . [U]nless they have that choice, their other choices cannot be taken as so many signs of the acquiescence to [our] economy and law. . . . A firmer recognition of the guests' civil liberties and some enhancement of their opportunities for collective bargaining would be difficult to avoid once they were seen as potential citizens.[39]

Leaving aside international arrangements of the sort just described, the principle of political justice is this: The processes of self-determination through which a territorial state shapes its internal life must be open, and equally open, to all those men and women who live in the territory, work in the local economy, and are subject to local law. Hence, second admissions (naturalization) depend on first admissions (immigration), and are subject only to certain constraints of time and qualification, never to the ultimate constraint of closure. When second admissions are closed, the political community collapses into something very different: a world of members and strangers, with no political boundaries between the two groups, where the strangers are the subjects of the members. Among themselves, perhaps, the members are equal, but it is not their equality but their tyranny that determines the character of the state. Political justice is a bar to permanent alienage – either for particular individuals or for a class of changing individuals.[40]

Thus as enfranchised, potential citizens (with human faces), guestworkers would less likely be subordinated and more likely be treated with respect. That makes recognition of their need for housing, health care, education (at least for their children), and fair treatment more likely. Addressing these needs is important for pro-immigrant critics of guestworker proposals who recall the exploitation of workers under the old bracero program of the 1950s. These critics may remain skeptical of a change in attitude toward guestworkers, but at least with a path toward legalization (and eventual citizenship), even the skeptic can see a chance for future political participation by the guestworker.

As prospective citizens, other possibilities for the workers also are evident. They can be made aware of options, such as schools, neighborhood organizations, churches, community groups, political entities, and the like, that they are less likely to engage in under a guestworker-only framework. As such, we have a better chance of getting those workers to be part of

[39] Id. at 30–31.   [40] Id. at 31–32.

our system and society, and more readily accept their responsibilities and duties of membership. A path toward legalization and eventual citizenship sends a signal of invitation and welcome.

Given the plight of undocumented workers – especially those from Mexico with which we share a long history – who simply are here seeking a better life, the morally right thing to do is to recognize their contributions and circumstances and provide them with a path toward legalization and membership. Guestworker legislation is designed to benefit our economy and our society, and its supporters likely believe that such a framework benefits the workers as well. But by imagining yourself in the shoes of a guestworker you begin to realize that we ought to provide a guest-worker legalization path to those from whose labor we have benefited. Establishing a guestworker program without a path to legalization auto-matically erects boundaries between the enfranchised and the disenfran-chised and institutionalizes a division within our society. That scenario not only smacks of second-class citizenship, but also has a familiarity to it that is reminiscent of the bracero days and even slavery.

Any policy related to "solving" the undocumented migration issue will be debated with value-laden rhetoric and overtones of what is the morally right thing to do. Policymakers may act on personal impulse and intuition or may look for objective guidance to help make a decision. For those looking for objective guidance, what will they find? The U.S. Chamber of Commerce cites these data:

> The Bureau of Labor Statistics (BLS) estimates that the number of people in the labor force ages 25 to 34 is projected to increase by only three million between 2002 and 2012, while those age 55 years and older will increase by 18 million. By 2012, those aged 45 and older will have the fastest growth rate and will be a little more than 50% of the labor force. According to estimates . . . by the United Nations, the fertility rate in the United States is projected to fall below "replacement" level by 2015 to 2020, declining to 1.91 children per woman (lower than the 2.1 children per woman rate needed to replace the population). By 2010, 77 million baby boomers will retire and, by 2030, one in every five Americans is projected to be a senior citizen.
>
> At the same time, we have, fortunately, projected job growth, including in lower-skilled occupations. Most jobs in our economy do not require a college degree. Close to 40% of all jobs require only short-term on-the-job training. In fact, of the top 10 largest job growth occupations between 2002 and 2012, all but two require less than a bachelor's degree. At the

same time, six of the top 10 occupations only require short-term on-the-job training. Some of these top 10 occupations that only require short-term on-the-job training include: retail salespersons, nursing aides, janitors and cleaners, waiters and waitresses, and combined food preparation and serving workers.

A panel on the future of the health care labor force in a graying society concluded that "[t]his will not be a temporary shortage. . . . Fundamental demographic changes are occurring in America, and the coming labor crisis will be with us for decades." Currently, the American Hospital Association reports high vacancy rates and more difficulty in recruiting workers for positions ranging from housekeeping and maintenance to nursing assistants and registered nurses. The impact of such workforce shortages, according to the Association, translates into severe emergency room overcrowding, emergency patients diverted to other hospitals, delayed discharge/increased length of stay, increased wait times for surgery, cancelled surgeries, discontinued programs, reduced service hours, and others.

However, shortages of essential workers are not limited to the largest growth occupations. In fact, the need for essential workers cut across industry sectors. In February 2004, Emily Stover DeRocco, Assistant Secretary of Labor for Employment Training, in a speech to the National Roofing Contractors Association, explained that BLS projected an increase in jobs between 2002 and 2012 for roofers of over 30,000, while at the same time there would be attrition in this occupation of about 40,000 – a net deficit of 70,000. The Construction Labor Research Council issued a labor supply outlook earlier this year where it found that the industry would need 185,000 new workers annually for the next 10 years.

The National Restaurant Association projects that the restaurant industry will add more than 1.8 million jobs between 2005 and 2015, an increase of 15%. However, the U.S. labor force is only projected to increase 12% during the next 10 years, which will make it more challenging than ever for restaurants to find the workers they need. The National Restaurant Association study notes that the 16 to 24 year old labor force – the demographic that makes up more than half of the restaurant industry workforce – is only projected to increase 9% during the next 10 years.

Our own surveys, not surprisingly, reflect the problems these employers have in finding the workers that they need. [The surveys included] chambers, businesses, and associations [representing] a wide range of industries . . . including arts, entertainment and recreation, professional scientific, technical services, social assistance, and nonprofit organizations. Difficulties in finding both entry-level and skilled workers, and developing solutions for this problem, ranked extremely high in importance to those surveyed.[41]

[41] Thomas J. Donohue, Statement of the U.S. Chamber of Commerce on "The Need for Comprehensive Immigration Reform: Serving Our National Economy," before the

The Cato Institute concurs:

> [W]hile the fastest-growing occupations in the next decade in percentage terms will require high degrees of skill and education, the largest growth in absolute numbers will be in those categories that require only "short-term on-the-job training" of one month or less. In fact, of the top 30 categories with the largest expected growth between 2000 and 2010, more than half fall into that least-skilled category. . . . Those categories include: combined food preparation and servicing workers, including fast food; waiters and waitresses; retail salespersons; cashiers; security guards; nursing aides, orderlies, and attendants; janitors and cleaners; home health aides; manual laborers and freight, stock, and materials movers; landscaping and groundskeeping workers; and manual packers and packagers. . . . Across the U.S. economy, the Labor Department estimates that the total number of jobs requiring only short-term training will increase from 53.2 million in 2000 to 60.9 million by 2010, a net increase of 7.7 million jobs.
>
> Meanwhile, the supply of American workers suitable for such work continues to fall because of an aging workforce and rising education levels. The median age of American workers continues to increase as the large cohort of Baby Boomers approaches retirement age. From 1990 to 2010, the median age of U.S. workers is expected to increase from 36.6 years old to 40.6. Younger and older workers alike are now more educated as the share of adult native-born men without a high school diploma has plunged, from 53.6 percent in 1960 to 9.0 in 1998. During that same period, the share with college degrees has gone up from 11.4 percent to 29.8 percent.
>
> With the number of low-skilled jobs expected to grow by more than 700,000 a year, and a shrinking pool of Americans willing to fill those jobs, Mexican migrants provide a ready and willing source of labor to fill the growing gap between demand and supply on the lower rungs of the labor ladder.[42]

Others might dissent. For example, David Bacon argues that "there is no great shortage of workers in the United States, immigrant or native-born. . . . There is a shortage of workers at the low wages industry would like to pay."[43] According to Bacon, if industries would pay fairer wages, then immigrant and native workers who are already available would come forward. I understand and respect this perspective, but to me a guest-worker/legalization proposal provides an attempt at balancing the needs

---

U.S. Senate Subcommittee on Immigration, Border Security and Citizenship of the Committee on the Judiciary, May 26, 2005, at 3–5.

[42] Daniel T. Griswold, *Willing Workers: Fixing the Problem of Illegal Mexican Migration to the United States,* Cato Institute Center for Trade Policy Studies, Oct. 15, 2002, at 9.

[43] David Bacon, *New Immigration Proposals: A Fast Track to the Past,* PACIFIC NEWS SERVICE, May 20, 2005.

of available U.S. workers with the interests of undocumented workers. Even Bacon acknowledges that undocumented workers "will not stop [entering] as long as huge differences persist between the world's rich and poor."[44] Until that time, balancing the interests of undocumented workers and those of U.S. workers must be worked out, premised on requirements that employers pay prevailing wages (or higher) and demonstrate shortages of available U.S. workers.

Nationality Security

After the tragic events of September 11, 2001, perpetrated by foreign nationals who entered as nonimmigrants, a call for more restrictive immigration policies might seem the natural response. Thus the restrictionist organization FAIR demanded more stringent visa issuance procedures, more agents for interior enforcement, and federal–local law enforcement cooperation.[45] But as part of its national security position, FAIR also criticized any proposals to grant legalization to undocumented aliens.[46] Linking the attacks of 9/11 and national security to the need to oppose legalization is puzzling.

As a matter of logic, granting legalization and encouraging the undocumented to surface would seem to be more conducive to national security. As a starting point, what do we know about the 9/11 perpetrators? None of the nineteen hijackers entered the country illegally across a land border. Most entered with tourists visas, and one with a student visa. Fifteen were Saudi nationals.[47] All but one obtained some form of U.S. identification document, some by fraud.[48] Given the disconnect between the terrorists and undocumented migration from Mexico, clamping down on undocumented migration as a response to 9/11 does not necessarily follow. In fact, a completely different, counterintuitive point of view might make more sense.

---

[44] Id.

[45] *Immigration Reforms to Combat Terrorism*, at http://www.fairus.org/site/ PageServer?pagename = iic_immigrationissuecenters6593.

[46] Id. Full title of FAIR report is *An Invitation to Terror: America Still at Risk: How Our Immigration System Still Leaves America at Risk*.

[47] *Staff Statement No. 1: Entry of the 9/11 Hijackers into the United States*, THE 9/11 INVESTIGATIONS 3–10 (Steven Strasser, ed., 2004).

[48] THE 9/11 COMMISSION REPORT: FINAL REPORT OF THE NATIONAL COMMISSION ON TERRORIST ATTACKS UPON THE UNITED STATES 390 (2004).

West Point Professor Margaret Stock has noted:

By bringing the people that are here out of the shadows, and creating an orderly mechanism for identifying and documenting the low-risk individuals who travel to this country to work, and by curbing policies such as separating families that entice otherwise low-risk individuals to cross the border illegally, a comprehensive immigration reform plan would help these initiatives better focus on those who have come here to do us harm. Quite simply, only an immigration reform program that deals with the current problem in its entirety would have such a positive effect. A program that fails to identify the reasons for illegal-crossings or one that inadequately deals with the undocumented population would not help [DHS] initiatives protect our citizens.

. . .

Because all nineteen of the September 11th terrorists were foreigners, some observers have been quick to blame our vulnerability to terrorist attacks on lax immigration laws. While such a response was predictable, it was misguided and has inevitably resulted in overreaction. Calls to impose a "moratorium" on immigration, halt the issuance of student visas, close the borders with Canada and Mexico, eliminate the Diversity Lottery visa program, draft harsher immigration laws, and similar types of proposals reflect a serious misunderstanding of the relationship between immigration policy and national security.

Although the attacks of September 11th revealed serious management and resource deficiencies in the bureaucracies that administer our borders, U.S. immigration laws in and of themselves did not increase our vulnerability to attack. In fact, U.S. immigration laws already are among the toughest in the world and have long provided the federal government with broad powers to prevent anti-American terrorists from entering or residing in the United States. A careful analysis of the September 11th attacks reveals that deficiencies in U.S. intelligence collection and information sharing, not immigration laws, prevented the terrorists' plans from being discovered.[49]

The Cato Institute also notes:

Long-time opponents of immigration have seized on September 11 to argue against legalization of Mexican migration and in favor of drastic cuts in existing levels of legal immigration.

The connection between the September 11 attacks and illegal immigration from Mexico is tenuous. None of the 19 hijackers entered the country

---

[49] Margaret D. Stock, *The Need for Comprehensive Immigration Reform: Strengthening Our National Security*, May 17, 2005, at 9 (unpublished paper on file with author).

illegally or as immigrants. They all arrived in the United States with valid temporary nonimmigrant tourist or student visas. None of them arrived via Mexico. None of them were Mexican. Sealing the Mexican border with a three-tiered, 2,000-mile replica of the Berlin Wall patrolled by thousands of U.S. troops would not have kept a single September 11 terrorist out of the United States.

. . .

[L]egalizing and regularizing the movement of workers across the U.S.-Mexican border could enhance our national security by bringing much of the underground labor market into the open, encouraging newly documented workers to cooperate fully with law enforcement officials, and freeing resources for border security and the war on terrorism.

Legalization of Mexican migration would drain a large part of the underground swamp that facilitates illegal immigration. It would reduce the demand for fraudulent documents, which in turn would reduce the supply available for terrorists trying to operate surreptitiously outside the United States. It would encourage millions of currently undocumented workers to make themselves known to authorities by registering with the government, reducing cover for terrorists who manage to enter the country and overstay their visas.

. . .

A system that allows Mexican workers to enter the United States legally would free up thousands of government personnel and save an estimated $3 billion a year – resources that would then be available to fight terrorism.[50]

And journalist Peter Laufer, arguing for a more open border policy with Mexico, sees things unfolding in the same way:

There is no question that the United States' southern border will be more secure if law-abiding Mexicans are allowed to pass freely. At present the bulk of the huge Border Patrol force and budget is used for chasing Mexicans. Once Mexicans no longer feel the need to sneak north, most of them undoubtedly will be happy to register with American authorities and carry whatever documents the United States requires for them to move between the two countries via official ports of entry. After that change occurs, the Border Patrol and other U.S. government agencies will be facing a trickle instead of tidal wave of illegal border crossers. With their advanced detection equipment and huge staff, the Border Patrol will then be well prepared to arrest and detain most of those who still try to cross into the United States illegally. . . . U.S. authorities will no longer be

---

[50] Griswold, *supra* note 42, at 18.

chasing Mexican workers needed and wanted in the north; they can pursue unwanted – and potentially dangerous – border violators.[51]

National security experts have recognized the connection between legalization and the nation's safety. In September 2003, former Secretary of Homeland Security Tom Ridge suggested that some sort of legalization program may be necessary to "come to grips with the presence of 8 to 12 million illegals." Speaking at a town hall meeting in Miami, Secretary Ridge responded to a question from the audience saying that it would be unworkable for undocumented people to leave the country and petition for reentry and that some sort of legal status, short of citizenship, should be considered. He emphasized that undocumented aliens should not be rewarded for breaking the law but that some form of legalization was necessary along with stricter border enforcement. Ridge's undersecretary of border and transportation security, Asa Hutchinson, appearing before a Senate committee in 2004, stated, "Illegal entry across our borders makes more difficult the urgent task of securing the homeland. Our homeland will be more secure when we can better account for those who enter our country, instead of the current situation in which millions of people are unknown."[52] Before a House subcommittee, Hutchinson testified that most undocumented aliens have overstayed their periods of authorized stay and that he saw a temporary worker program as being good law enforcement because it would mean fewer problems with undocumented workers.[53]

Reaching out to immigrants promotes national security. Following the July 7, 2005, London subway suicide bombings by British-born Muslim terrorists, Boris Johnson, a member of Parliament, noted that Americans did not grow their own suicide bombers, giving credit to Americans for acculturating its immigrants.[54] The National Commission on Terrorist Attacks Upon the United States (the 9/11 Commission) created by Congress to investigate the circumstances surrounding the 9/11 terrorist

[51] Peter Laufer, WETBACK NATION: THE CASE FOR OPENING THE MEXICAN-AMERICAN BORDER 244 (2004).

[52] *U.S. Guest Worker Program Would Allow Better Border Control*, February 13, 2004, at http://embajadausa.org.ve/wwwh2318.html.

[53] 81 INTERPRETER RELEASES 341, 343 (Mar. 15, 2004).

[54] *How They See Us: Britain's Response to Terror Beats America*, THE WEEK, July 29, 2005, at 13.

attacks recognized the national security benefits of an inclusive approach toward immigrants:

> Our borders and immigration system, including law enforcement, ought to send a message of welcome, tolerance, and justice to members of immigrant communities in the United States and in their countries of origin. We should reach out to immigrant communities. Good immigration services are one way of doing so that is valuable in every way – including intelligence.
>
> It is elemental to border security to know who is coming into the country. Today more than 9 million people are in the United States outside the legal immigration system. We must also be able to monitor and respond to entrances between our ports of entry, working with Canada and Mexico as much as possible.[55]

Thus, legalizing undocumented workers coupled with a large worker program is in the interest of our national security and constitutes a step that would aid our country in its efforts to combat terrorism. By offering a program that would encourage undocumented workers to come forward, we would be able to conduct background checks on a large group that currently lives underground, while freeing up investigative resources to concentrate on real threats of terror at the border and within our borders. These new community members would be more inclined to participate in civic society and aid law enforcement efforts directly. Legalization would promote family reunification and the psychological benefits derived from enjoying the comfort of family. With more definite status, wages and working conditions for the new Americans and consequently all Americans would improve.

Guestworker proposals like McCain–Kennedy and AgJOBS that provide a path toward legalization, without nasty provisions that would felonize undocumented status or preclude countless numbers who worked with false documents, can actually reduce future surreptitious migration. By providing an avenue for large numbers of low-wage workers to enter in the future, the need for illegal entry in the future is greatly reduced. As Congressman Flake, the Arizona Republican who cosponsored such legislation in the House notes, the worker program with a fair path to legalization is critical because it avoids the mistakes of IRCA in 1986. "[There we] just dealt with those who were here illegally, and we didn't

---

[55] The 9/11 Commission Report: Final Report of the National Commission on Terrorist Attacks Upon the United States 390 (2004).

recognize that there would be future needs for employment. And so the day that that act was signed into law in 1986, it was out of date, because we needed more workers."[56]

Conclusion

As a nation, the United States ought to do the right thing when it comes to undocumented immigrants. Given our long historical ties with Mexico, doing the right thing is especially in order in the case of Mexican migrants. We demonize the undocumented, rather than see them for what they are: human beings entering for a better life who have been manipulated by globalization, regional economies, and social structures that have operated for generations. We benefit from undocumented labor every day and in a vast range of occupations. The right thing to do is to develop a system to facilitate the flow of Mexican migrants to the United States who are seeking employment opportunities. Given the economic imbalance between the two nations, we know that the flow will continue – legally or otherwise. By legalizing the flow through a large guestworker program, we ease pressures at the border (thus freeing up personnel to concentrate on the serious challenge of looking for terrorists and drug smugglers), address the labor needs of employers, bring the undocumented out of the shadows, and end unnecessary border deaths that have resulted from current enforcement strategies.[57]

Doing the right thing requires us to humanize the guestworker upon whom we have come to rely. Thus, establishing a worker program must be done in a manner that provides the workers with hope for membership and respect from other Americans. A path toward legalization becomes a critical ingredient of any guestworker program. Only through that path can these individuals attain a sense of enfranchisement and freedom from political subjugation and servitude. Our moral, economic, social, and national security interests demand that we pursue such a program.

---

[56] Stephen Dinan, *McCain-Kennedy Bill Opens Citizenship Path*, WASHINGTON TIMES, May 13, 2005, at A4.

[57] I have argued elsewhere that the government's Operator Gatekeeper along the U.S.–Mexico border is immoral and results in countless unnecessary deaths among those attempting to enter without inspection. Bill Ong Hing, DEFINING AMERICA THROUGH IMMIGRATION POLICY 184–205 (2004).

2 . . . . . Deporting Our Souls

The headlines about Operation Community Shield could not be more appealing to law-and-order or anti-immigrant enthusiasts: *Hundreds from Violent Gangs May Be Thrown Out of U.S.*,[1] *Immigrant Gangs Targeted in Sweep – Federal Dragnet Snags Hundreds*,[2] *Immigration Sweep Hits Gangs – 34 Nabbed in Colorado*.[3] Apparently, the primary targets of the operation were Latin street gangs, many rooted in Central America. Department of Homeland Security (DHS) Secretary Michael Chertoff reported that over a six-month period, U.S. Immigration and Customs Enforcement (ICE) had made 1,057 arrests as part of its anti-gang initiative; 930 to 950 were "illegal immigrants."[4] That meant that more than a hundred were either lawful permanent residents or U.S. citizens.[5]

Immigrants who commit crimes are deported from the United States every day. They come from all over the world, including Mexico, Canada, Europe, Africa, and the Middle East. The U.S. Supreme Court even endorsed the removal of a Somalian refugee convicted of assault back

---

[1] Chronicle News Services, *Hundreds from Violent Gangs May Be Thrown Out of U.S.*, SF CHRONICLE, Aug. 2, 2005, at A3.

[2] Julia Malone, *Immigrant Gangs Targeted in Sweep – Federal Dragnet Snags Hundreds*, ATLANTA JOURNAL-CONSTITUTION, Aug. 2, 2004, at 4A.

[3] Alicia Caldwell, *Immigration Sweep Hits Gangs – 34 Nabbed in Colorado*, DENVER POST, Aug. 2, 2005, at B1.

[4] Chronicle News Services, *supra* note 1, at A3.

[5] In fact, the *San Francisco Chronicle* reported that locally at least three of the suspected gang members arrested were U.S. citizens. Henry K. Lee, *13 Bay Area Men Held in Gang Sweep*, SF CHRONICLE, Aug. 2, 2005, at A3.

to Somalia where no formal government exists.[6] In 2002, the United States began deporting Cambodian refugees convicted of crimes back to Communist-dominated Cambodia. So although ICE may indeed be rounding up and removing hundreds of so-called illegal immigrants who have committed crimes, the agency also is engaged in deporting convicted lawful permanent resident aliens (those with "green cards") or refugees legally admitted under U.S. refugee provisions. And these deportees have served their sentences in the criminal justice system before being deported.

As a legal services attorney in San Francisco in the 1970s, I represented a number of clients who were being deported because of crimes they had committed. One typical client was Fred Wong,[7] who immigrated with his parents from Hong Kong at the age of ten in 1966. They settled in Chinatown, where his parents found low-wage work. It did not take long for Fred to be running with other guys in a gang with nothing better to do. By the age of seventeen, Fred was arrested for robbery and extortion. A couple years later, he was busted for sale of heroin, convicted in federal court, and sent to Soledad State Prison. After his release, he was handed over to immigration authorities to face deportation charges back to Hong Kong. Fortunately, I was able to work with Fred, his new wife, drug counselors, employment counselors, job supervisors, probation officers, and a psychologist over a period of two years to prove that Fred was rehabilitated and would not recidivate. He was given a second chance by the immigration judge, and Fred has been law-abiding ever since. Another client was Linda Smith,[8] a native of Canada, who immigrated to the United States as a toddler. Somewhere along the line, she took to the streets and became a prostitute; a conviction for solicitation led to her deportability. Her mother, the "star" witness in her deportation hearing, was a straight-laced high school teacher. She pleaded with the immigration judge to give her daughter a second chance, admitting that she (the mother) had failed as a parent and wanted a second chance for herself as well as for her daughter. The judge agreed, granted the waiver, and today Linda is leading a law-abiding life.

---

[6] *Jama v. Immigration and Customs Enforcement,* 125 S. Ct. 694 (2005). Jama was convicted of third-degree assault, a moral turpitude crime, within three years of entering the United States. *Jama v. INS,* 329 F.3d 630, 631 (8th Cir. 2003).

[7] "Fred Wong" is not my client's actual name.

[8] "Linda Smith" is not my client's actual name.

Things have changed. Today, the law does not afford those in Fred's and Linda's shoes a second chance. In the process, many noncitizens of countless other nationalities are removed from the United States where they have spent many of their formative years. Most of the convicted lawful residents and refugees have one thing in common: Under U.S. immigration laws, they are regarded as aggravated felons. As aggravated felons, virtually no deportation relief is available from an immigration judge. Issues of rehabilitation, remorse, family support in the United States, and employment opportunities are irrelevant.

Deporting Immigrants Based on Criminal Convictions – "Aggravated Felony"

September 11, 2001, profoundly affected the immigrant community. The Department of Justice and the U.S. Congress passed at least two dozen statutes and federal regulations in response. For example, immigrants with criminal convictions are now a primary concern for the Department of Justice (DOJ) and DHS. Noncitizens, including lawful permanent residents, can be deported based on a criminal conviction. Lawful permanent residents are granted permission by the U.S. government to live and work in the United States for an indefinite period of time, establishing close relatives and ties. The Immigration and Nationality Act (INA) establishes three categories of crimes that place a lawful permanent resident at risk of deportation or prevent a noncitizen from ever becoming a lawful permanent resident: (1) aggravated felonies, (2) crimes involving moral turpitude, and (3) a variety of other crimes involving firearms, domestic violence, or controlled substances.[9]

Under the INA's aggravated felony provision, neither the adverse effect on the family of a lawful permanent resident nor the exile of someone to a country he or she never knew is considered. Despite the unfairness of these laws, courts continue to sanction them under the plenary power doctrine.[10] Deportation is clearly more detrimental to the life of a noncitizen than the imposition of a criminal sentence. Yet courts continue to treat

---

[9] Robin Bronen, *Immigration Consequences of Criminal Convictions*, Alaska Justice Forum (2003), at http://justice.uaa.alaska.edu/forum/20/1spring2003/c_immigcrim.html.

[10] David Cheng, *Emigres of the Killing Fields: The Deportation of Cambodian Refugees as a Violation of International Human Rights*, 25 B.C. THIRD WORLD L.J. 221, 223 (2005).

immigration proceedings as civil proceedings, failing to view deportation as a separate and additional punishment.[11]

A deported noncitizen faces the possibility of losing his or her family, friends, and livelihood forever. Many deported noncitizens are cast to countries with which they have virtually no ties. Surprisingly, courts continue to conclude that deportation is not an additional and unequal "punishment" for noncitizens. The aggravated felony provision subjects any noncitizen convicted of an aggravated felony to deportation from the United States.[12]

The courts no longer have authority to review an aggravated felony deportation, now termed "removal." According to the Ninth Circuit Court of Appeals, "few punishments are more drastic and final than expelling a person from his country when their family members are residents."[13] The legislation mandating deportation of long-time, lawful residents with strong family ties in the United States when these noncitizens are con-victed of an aggravated felony continues to be disguised as an exercise in good policy. Noncitizens convicted of serious crimes are then perceived as an intolerable threat to both U.S. citizens and resident noncitizens.[14]

People expect their government to protect them from dangerous for-eign nationals, particularly in the wake of 9/11. However, a closer look at the sweeping mandatory deportation scheme governing criminal grounds for deportation reveals that the aggravated felony category is so broad that it includes many crimes that bear little relation to an actual threat to public safety.[15] Thus, the distorted effect of current deportation laws results in automatic deportation for convictions as minor as petty theft, urinating in public, or forgery of a check for less than $20.

Deportation Provisions: Crimes Involving Moral Turpitude

Lawful permanent residents and refugees who have been convicted of certain crimes, or who have committed certain "bad acts" without being convicted, can be removed. Problems with drugs; crimes involving moral turpitude, prostitution, and firearms; sexual crimes; and a host of other

---

[11] Id. at 224.

[12] Valerie Neal, *Slings and Arrows of Outrageous Fortune: The Deportation of "Aggravated Felons,"* 36 VAND. J. TRANSNAT'L L. 1619 (2003).

[13] Id.   [14] Id.

[15] Id.

offenses can cause problems. Even very minor offenses can lead to catastrophe.

An immigrant can be deported based on one or two convictions involving moral turpitude. Only one conviction of a crime involving moral turpitude is needed to render a lawful permanent resident deportable, if the crime was committed within five years after admission and if the offense had a potential sentence of one year. A noncitizen is deportable if convicted of two separate crimes involving moral turpitude at any time, regardless of the sentence and the time since admission.

Moral turpitude crimes include theft and robbery, crimes involving bodily harm, sex offenses, and acts involving recklessness or malice. Passing bad checks, credit card scams, burglary, and even perjury can involve moral turpitude. Assault with a deadly weapon, murder, rape, and arson involve moral turpitude because those offenses require an intent to do great bodily harm. Simple assault, simple battery, and simple driving under the influence generally do not involve moral turpitude. However, a conviction for driving under the influence while the person's license was suspended is a crime involving moral turpitude.[16]

Under a separate deportation provision, aliens who are convicted of any law relating to use or possession of a firearm (e.g., a gun) or "destructive device" (e.g., a bomb) are deportable.

Aggravated Felonies

Many offenses, including murder, certain drug offenses, alien smuggling, and even theft (with a suspended sentence of one year), have been designated as aggravated felonies. These carry the most severe immigration consequences, with little hope of relief from deportation.

Under immigration laws, an alien convicted of an aggravated felony at any time after admission is deportable.[17] An aggravated felony is defined as murder, rape, sexual abuse of a minor, any illicit trafficking in any controlled substance (including drugs, firearms, or destructive devices), money laundering, or any crime of violence (except for purely political offenses) for which the term of imprisonment imposed is at least one year.

---

[16] *Matter of Lopez-Meza*, Int. Dec. 3423 (BIA 1999). This holding, concerning an Arizona statute, was overturned by the Ninth Circuit, but just because the Arizona statute also included sitting in a parked vehicle while drunk. *Hernandez-Martinez v. Ashcroft*, 329 F.3d 1117 (9th Cir. 2003).

[17] 8 U.S.C. §1227(a)(2)(A) (2004).

The definition also includes offenses of theft, if the term of imprisonment imposed is at least one year; treason; child pornography; operation of a prostitution business; fraud or deceit in which the loss to the victim or victims exceeds $10,000; tax evasion in which the loss to the U.S. government exceeds $10,000; crimes relating to the Racketeer Influenced and Corrupt Organizations (RICO) Act, if the term of imprisonment imposed is at least one year; alien smuggling, except in the case of a first offense involving the assisting, abetting, or aiding of the alien's spouse, child, or parent and no other individual; document trafficking, if the term of imprisonment imposed is at least one year; failure to appear to serve a sentence, if the underlying offense is punishable by imprisonment for a term of five years; and bribery, counterfeiting, or forgery for which the term of imprisonment is at least one year. An attempt or conspiracy to commit any of the crimes just mentioned is also included.[18]

So what we might think of as minor crimes – for example, selling $10 worth of marijuana or "smuggling" one's baby sister across the border illegally – also are aggravated felonies. And being convicted of a misdemeanor as opposed to a felony does not automatically preclude aggravated felon status. For example, several offenses are classified as aggravated felonies once a one-year sentence is imposed. These include theft, burglary, perjury, and obstruction of justice, even though the criminal court may classify the crime as a misdemeanor.[19] A misdemeanor statutory rape (consensual sex where one person is under the age of eighteeen) will also

---

[18] The breadth of aggravated felonies has constantly expanded since the term was introduced in the immigration laws in 1988. See Anti-Drug Abuse Act of 1988, Pub. L. No. 100-690, §7344(a), 102 Stat. 4181, 4470–4471 (1988). The crimes treated as aggravated felonies prior to the 1996 changes in the law can be found at Immigration and Naturalization Act, §101(a)(43), 8 U.S.C. §1101(a)(43) (2003). Prior to 1996, the aggravated felony ground for deportation was essentially similar to the other grounds for deportation. For example, drug convictions that constituted aggravated felonies were also independent grounds for deportation under a provision for deporting persons convicted of drug crimes. Similarly, any person who had two crimes involving moral turpitude was deportable, so it did not matter if the crimes were aggravated felonies. In some cases, however, the aggravated felony definition served to authorize deportation for a single crime, where the person would not otherwise have been deportable. For example, a person convicted of a murder committed more than five years after entering the country, who had no other criminal record, would have been deportable only as an aggravated felon. A noncitizen is only deportable by reason of an aggravated felony if the conviction occurred after 1988, which is the year in which the aggravated felony deportation ground was added.

[19] See, for example, *United States v. Campbell*, 167 F.3d 94, 98 (2nd Cir. 1999).

be treated as an aggravated felony. And a misdemeanor conviction can be an aggravated felony under the "rape" or "sexual abuse of a minor" categories.[20]

Conviction of an aggravated felony results in harsh immigration consequences. For example, an aggravated felon is ineligible for release on bond, is ineligible for asylum (although the person might be eligible for "restriction of removal" or the protections of the Convention Against Torture), is ineligible for discretionary cancellation of removal (see Section 212(c) Waiver section), can be deported without a hearing before an immigration judge (if the person is not a permanent resident), and is not eligible for a waiver for moral turpitude offenses upon admission.

One of the worst effects of aggravated felonies arises if the person returns to the United States illegally. A person who is convicted of an aggravated felony and removed and then returns illegally to the United States can be sentenced to up to twenty years in federal prison just for the illegal reentry.

Section 212(c) Waiver: Its Rise and Fall

Discretionary relief from deportation for long-time lawful permanent residents convicted of serious crimes, even those eventually classified as aggravated felonies, was available from 1976 to 1996. During that time, an immigration judge could consider issues of rehabilitation, remorse, family support in the United States, and employment opportunities for aggravated felons who had entered as refugees or as immigrants, if they had become lawful resident aliens and had resided in the country for at least seven years.

In 1976, the INA did not contain a provision that would have explicitly provided relief to someone like Fred or Linda. The language and application of INA §212(c), however, provided the impetus for an interpretation that benefited many aliens:

> Aliens lawfully admitted for permanent residence who temporarily proceeded abroad voluntarily and not under an order of deportation, and who are returning to a lawful unrelinquished domicile of seven consecutive years, may be admitted in the discretion of the Attorney General without

---

[20] *Matter of Small*, 23 I. & N. Dec. 448 (BIA 2002).

regard to the provisions of paragraphs (1) through (25) and paragraph (30) of subsection (a).[21]

Importantly, the "provisions of paragraphs (1) through (25) . . . of subsection (a)" included grounds of exclusion that barred the entry of aliens convicted of serious crimes involving moral turpitude and narcotics offenses.[22] Therefore, under INA §212(c), a lawful permanent resident who had resided in the United States for seven years could proceed abroad voluntarily and be readmitted at the discretion of the attorney general, even if he or she had been convicted of a serious crime that rendered him or her excludable. In essence, INA §212(c) provided a waiver of exclusion. In practice, the attorney general could grant the waiver in exclusion or deportation proceedings, as long as the person had proceeded abroad voluntarily at some point.[23]

That similar lawful permanent residents convicted of identical crimes would be treated differently only because one had never left the United States after immigrating and the other happened to leave and return after committing the deportable offense troubled the Second Circuit Court of Appeals in *Francis v. INS*.[24] The latter person would be eligible for the 212(c) waiver, while the former would not under the Board of Immigration Appeals' (Board) interpretation of the statute. The Second Circuit ruled that the Board's interpretation violated equal protection, and, therefore, held the waiver applicable to any lawful permanent resident who had resided in the country for at least seven years.[25] Soon thereafter, the Board adopted the *Francis* decision.[26] The result was that a lawful permanent resident who had resided in the United States for seven years could apply for and be granted a waiver under INA §212(c) in deportation proceedings, thereby allowing the person to remain in the United States as a

---

[21] 8 U.S.C. §1182 (c).   [22] Id. §1182 (a)(2)(A)(i) (1976).

[23] *In re L*, 1 I. & N. Dec. 1 (BIA 1940).

[24] *Francis v. INS*, 532 F.2d 268 (2d Cir. 1976).

[25] Id. at 273 (holding that "[r]eason and fairness would suggest that an alien whose ties with this country are so strong that he has never departed after his initial entry should receive at least as much consideration as an individual who may leave and return from time to time"). In fact, this ruling was consistent with the Board's own interpretation of a similar provision that was part of the statute decades earlier: In re A, 2 I. & N. Dec. 459 (BIA 1946), approved by the attorney general (1947) (holding that an alien had not reentered country following his conviction was not bar to exercise of discretionary relief in deportation proceeding).

[26] *In re Silva*, 16 I. & N. Dec. 26 (BIA 1976).

lawful permanent resident. To be granted the waiver, the person had to persuade an immigration judge to exercise favorable discretion.

In *In re Marin*,[27] the Board summarized the major factors for immigration judges to consider in Section 212(c) cases, although each case was to be judged "on its own merits."[28] In general, the immigration judge was required to balance the adverse factors evidencing an alien's undesirability as a permanent resident with the social and humane considerations presented on his or her behalf to determine whether granting of relief appeared "in the best interests of this country."[29] The alien had the burden of showing that the positive factors outweighed the negative ones. Favorable factors included such considerations as

> family ties within the United States, residence of long duration in this country (particularly when the inception of residence occurred while the respondent was of young age), evidence of hardship to the respondent and family if deportation occurs, service in this country's Armed Forces, a history of employment, the existence of property or business ties, evidence of value and service to the community, proof of a genuine rehabilitation if a criminal record exists, and other evidence attesting to a respondent's good character [for example, affidavits from family, friends, and responsible community representatives].[30]

Factors deemed adverse to an alien included

> the nature and underlying circumstances of the exclusion [or deportation] ground at issue, the presence of additional significant violations of this country's immigration laws, the existence of a criminal record and, if so, its nature, recency, and seriousness, and the presence of other evidence indicative of a respondent's bad character or undesirability as a permanent resident of this country.[31]

Section 212(c) relief was not automatic. For example, in *Ashby v. INS*, that the applicant was convicted of three crimes, committed over a six-year period, which involved the use of force and weapons, and was incarcerated for eight years were critical to the Board's denial, despite twenty-seven years of lawful permanent residence.[32] Also, in *Arango-Aradondo v. INS*, the Second Circuit upheld the denial of INA §212(c) relief when the

---

[27] *In re Marin*, 16 I. & N. Dec. 581 (BIA 1978).
[28] Id. at 584.   [29] Id.
[30] Id. at 584–585.   [31] Id. at 584.
[32] *Ashby v. INS*, 961 F.2d 555, 557 (5th Cir. 1992).

immigration judge carefully and thoroughly weighed the evidence in the alien's favor (including his drug and alcohol rehabilitation efforts, his long-time residency in the United States, his close family ties, and the hardship he would endure in Colombia given his HIV status and his lack of ties there) against the detrimental evidence (including his sporadic employment record, his failure to file taxes, and, most important, his "very lengthy and very severe" criminal record, together with his long involvement in the drug culture).[33]

As the number of negative factors grew in a Section 212(c) case, the respondent had to introduce offsetting favorable evidence, often labeled "unusual or outstanding equities." Courts required this heightened showing when an alien was convicted of a serious drug offense, particularly one relating to the trafficking or sale of drugs. For example, in *Varela-Blanco v. INS*,[34] a conviction of lascivious acts with a child (sexual abuse of an eight-year-old niece) was a serious crime requiring a demonstration of "unusual or outstanding equities" for Section 212(c) relief.[35] Although the applicant had resided in the United States for eighteen years, the first ten were in an unlawful status. Therefore, employment during his undocumented status was not considered.[36] Furthermore, the presence of family and considerable evidence of rehabilitation was insufficient.[37]

In *Paredes-Urrestarazu v. INS*,[38] the Ninth Circuit upheld a denial of Section 212(c) relief, even though the alien demonstrated unusual and outstanding equities. He entered the United States at age twelve, was married, and had a child and numerous relatives. However, very serious adverse factors, including gang-related armed robberies, general court-martial and dishonorable discharge from the military, false testimony concerning military service, past drug abuse, and an arrest for drug possession (despite completing a diversion program), outweighed the equities.[39]

In *Diaz-Resendez v. INS*,[40] however, the Fifth Circuit found that an applicant who had been convicted of possession of twenty-one pounds of

---

[33] *Arango-Aradono v. INS*, 13 F.3d 610, 613 (2d Cir. 1994).
[34] *Varela-Blanco v. INS*, 18 F.3d 584 (8th Cir. 1994).
[35] Id. at 586.   [36] Id. at 587.
[37] Id. at 587–588.
[38] *Paredes-Urrestarazu v. INS*, 36 F.3d 801 (9th Cir. 1994).
[39] Id. at 817–821.
[40] *Diaz-Resendez v. INS*, 960 F.2d 493 (5th Cir. 1992).

marijuana with intent to distribute met the rigorous standards for Section 212(c) relief. The applicant was fifty-four years old and had been a continuous lawful resident for thirty-seven years. He had been married to a U.S. citizen for twenty-nine years, had three children who were fully dependent on him, faced imminent breakup of his marriage if deported, and otherwise had a clean criminal record except for a drunk driving charge that ended his drinking.[41]

In contrast, in *In re Roberts*, the Board denied relief to an applicant convicted of a cocaine sale constituting drug trafficking, who was separated from his wife and four children, did not financially support any of them, had an irregular employment history, and had not paid income tax for some time.[42] Similarly, in *Nunez-Pena v. INS*, the Tenth Circuit found that the applicant's ten years of residence, family ties in the United States, progress toward rehabilitation, and record of steady employment did not meet the outstanding equities standard.[43] The applicant, who would be deported to Mexico, had been convicted of a serious heroin offense, had served two years in prison, and involved his brother and common-law wife in his drug activity. The court found it relevant that the applicant was fluent in Spanish and that a sibling and his father lived in Mexico. In *Vergara-Molina v. INS*, the Seventh Circuit approved the Board's finding of no unusual and outstanding equities in a case involving an applicant convicted of two controlled substance violations.[44] Evidence of his rehabilitation, steady employment, service to the community as a drug counselor, and good character were considered, but the court would not second-guess the Board.[45]

The necessity of demonstrating unusual or outstanding equities was not triggered exclusively by serious crimes involving controlled substances. A particularly grave offense also demanded such a showing.[46] Additionally, such a showing could be mandated because of a single serious crime, or because of a succession of criminal acts that, together, established a pattern of serious criminal misconduct. A respondent who demonstrated

---

[41] Id. at 497.

[42] *In re Roberts*, 20 I. & N. Dec. 294 (BIA 1991).

[43] *Nunez-Pena v. INS*, 956 F.2d 223 (10th Cir. 1992).

[44] *Vergara-Molina v. INS*, 956 F.2d 682 (7th Cir. 1992).

[45] Id. at 685.

[46] *Cordoba-Chavez v. INS*, 946 F.2d 1244, 1249 (9th Cir. 1991); *In re Buscemi*, 19 I. & N. Dec. 628, 633–634 (BIA 1988).

unusual or outstanding equities, as required, did not automatically obtain a favorable exercise of discretion, but absent such equities, relief would not be granted in the exercise of discretion.[47] There were cases in which the adverse considerations were so serious that a favorable exercise of discretion was not warranted even in the face of unusual or outstanding equities.[48] On the other hand, Section 212(c) relief could not be categorically denied to drug offenders who served fewer than five years of incarceration.[49]

Rehabilitation of the respondent was a critical issue in Section 212(c) cases. The Board noted that an applicant with a criminal record "ordinarily" would be required to make a showing of rehabilitation before relief would be granted as a matter of discretion. Cases "involving convicted aliens [had to] be evaluated on a case-by-case basis, with rehabilitation a factor to be considered in the exercise of discretion."[50] In practice, the immigration judge would pay close attention to the testimony or statements from family members, friends, employers, parole or probation officers, counselors in or outside prison, and psychiatrists. The judge would want to discern whether the applicant would engage in criminal activity again and look for evidence that the person's life had changed to the point that such activity was a thing of the past.[51]

Thus, Section 212(c) cases permitted immigration judges to examine the respondent's crime, prison experience, current living situation, demeanor, attitude, job skills, employment status, family support, friends, social network, and efforts at rehabilitation in deciding whether to exercise favorable discretion. Judges were even able to postpone the case to monitor the respondent's behavior before rendering a decision.[52]

In 1996, however, Congress enacted legislation that eliminated Section 212(c) relief as it had been applied for twenty years. In its place, a cancellation of removal provision was added that precluded even the possibility of relief for many who had been able to at least apply for

---

[47] *Akrap v. INS*, 966 F.2d 267, 272–273 (7th Cir. 1992); *In re Roberts*, 20 I. & N. Dec. 294, 302–303 (BIA 1991).

[48] *In re Buscemi*, 19 I. & N. Dec. 628, 635–636 (BIA 1988).

[49] *Yepes-Prado v. INS*, 10 F.3d 1363, 1371 (9th Cir. 1993).

[50] *In re Edwards*, 20 I. & N. Dec. 191, 191 (BIA 1990).

[51] Bill Ong Hing, HANDLING IMMIGRATION CASES 388 (1995).

[52] See note 244, *infra*, and accompanying text.

discretionary relief from an immigration judge under the prior provision.[53] The new provision, INA §240A(a), permits the attorney general to "cancel removal" for certain aliens who commit crimes if the alien (1) has been a lawful permanent resident for at least five years, (2) has resided in the United States continuously for seven years after having been admitted in any status, and (3) has not been convicted of any aggravated felony.[54] The no aggravated felony requirement thus eliminated relief for many lawful resident aliens who would have been eligible for Section 212(c) relief.

Revisiting Fred

I recently had the opportunity to go back and revisit my client Fred Wong who was granted 212(c) relief back in the 1980s when the relief was available. His story is not surprising. Fred Wong was born in Hong Kong on March 27, 1956, the fifth of six children. His parents, originally from mainland China, immigrated to Hong Kong after World War II when the Communist Party took over. As tailors, they owned a small business making suits. As such, they were able to acquire property and had the time and money to provide for their children. Fred's aunt, however, lived in the United States and soon convinced Fred's parents that the United States offered a better future full of opportunity for their children. Thus, they sold all their possessions and decided to leave Hong Kong. Through the sponsorship of Fred's aunt in the United States, Fred's family arrived in San Francisco in 1963, when Fred was only seven years old. They settled down in San Francisco's Chinatown, where Fred's aunt owned a restaurant. Fred's parents worked twelve- to sixteen-hour days in the restaurant, mostly washing dishes. They were grateful for the opportunity to work and earn money but found themselves too tired to spend much time with their children. Their search for other work was severely limited by their almost nonexistent English (they could not invest any time in learning the language with their scarce resources). Eventually, both of Fred's parents were able to use their tailoring skills to obtain employment at a sewing factory and move the family into a two-bedroom apartment. After some time, Fred's mother remained in the factory, but Fred's father returned to working in the restaurant.

---

[53] See Katherine Brady, *Recent Developments in the Immigration Consequences of Crimes*, OUR STATE OUR ISSUES: AN OVERVIEW OF IMMIGRATION LAW ISSUES 129 (Bill Ong Hing ed., 1996).

[54] 8 U.S.C. §1229(a) (2004).

Life was drastically different in the United States for the Wong family. Thanks to the severe language barrier and resulting job opportunities, the family's socioeconomic status fell from middle class to low class. This made it much more difficult for the parents to support the family here than in Hong Kong. The long working hours kept Fred's parents from providing much supervision as Fred and his siblings faced complicated cultural and economic adjustments. Soon even Fred's siblings started working part time to help, as they were in high school. Fred felt a little spoiled since he was the youngest boy in the family and had much unsupervised time to do whatever he wanted. In grade school, he found companionship and understanding with neighborhood children who shared a similar background. Their parents were also very busy working and did not have much time to spend with them. Like Fred, these immigrant children also faced cultural and identity conflicts. Fred thought it would be easy to become accustomed to his new surroundings, but it turned out to be much more difficult than he had imagined. He had trouble learning English and did not have much outside support for his academics. His parents did not know about tutoring and did not have the time to provide help in school. At school, the American-born Chinese (ABC) children would pick on the foreign-born kids. Fred tried to be tough as early as in kindergarten as a result of his treatment from other kids. This created further incentive for Fred to hang out with children most like him. He performed satisfactorily in school but would get into frequent fights with the ABCs. These fights were not very serious, but they affected the formation of future relationships and ended in the creation of two groups that did not get along. Fred did not see the rivalries as a racial thing but simply the way things were in the neighborhood in which he grew up.

With little supervision and a group of friends who were struggling to fit in, Fred gradually lost interest in school. On a typical day, he would go to school to meet his friends and cut classes. They started stealing from local stores for fun. Fred did not have a sense that what he was doing was wrong or illegal; he just saw that he could obtain free things simply by putting them in his pocket. Because his parents could hardly afford to give him any spending money, this became an easy and exciting way to get the small things he wanted. In time, stealing allowed him to maintain a lifestyle he could not afford otherwise. By selling what he stole, Fred made enough money to party, go out for dinner, and drink with his friends. Smoking, drinking, and fighting became a regular occurrence in the neighborhood and Fred was caught participating in these activities several times. He started hanging out with his friends more often and cut classes in high school to do so. When Fred first started getting in trouble, his parents would hit him. It soon became clear that they could not control him, however, and they decided to allow the authorities take Fred to a boys' home in Palm Springs after he was sent to juvenile hall. This home consisted of at least one hundred boys and was structured like a hotel. During his year there, Fred was driven to school and taken on field trips. Still, he missed his parents and thought he would do better from then on. Unfortunately, this effort was short-lived and Fred ended up in juvenile hall a total of seven times by the time he reached the age of eighteen, mostly for stealing.

He was also sent to juvenile hall for fighting incidents, where he and his friends got into quarrels with groups of older kids. One day, Fred witnessed his friends fighting older youth. Although he did not participate, the police chased him just the same. While everyone else successfully escaped, Fred was smaller than the others. A policeman chased him into an alley, where he tripped on his baggy pants. The policeman proceeded to beat him before taking him to juvenile hall. Fred served six months for this "offense." During this time, he felt angry that he had been beaten and could not do anything about it. His hatred grew because he felt he had been apprehended for no reason. Fred grew determined to be tougher once he got out.

The other kids in juvenile hall were of different races and bigger than Fred. Fred was forced to stand up for himself because he was constantly picked on by these larger kids. Juvenile hall was similar to a dormitory with many levels. Each level was assigned according to how good the detainee's behavior was. Fred spent time on every level. The counselors at the time used methods Fred did not expect: Whenever two kids wanted to fight, the counselors would give them boxing gloves so they could settle their differences. Although there was no smoking allowed within the facilities, sometimes the cops themselves would hand out cigarettes to those they thought merited something extra for good behavior. By the time he was released, Fred was effectively tougher, and things got worse. Fred's friends would frequently get into similar trouble. Though the neighborhood did contain gangs that would fight and shoot at each other, Fred did not belong to any of these. His friends did not consider themselves a gang (they had no gang name and did not function like a typical gang). In fact, some of his friends would join different gangs and would find each other on opposite sides of a fight. Fred, however, only cared about having fun and making money. These goals and his reckless behavior led him to join a couple of friends in robbing an acquaintance. Fred was convicted of armed robbery at age nineteen and spent three years at Soledad Prison.

According to Fred, "If you're not a criminal and you're sent to state prison, you become a criminal." Accustomed to living among others physically like himself, Fred found himself as part of a tiny 1 percent Asian minority in prison. In comparison, there was a much higher population of African Americans, whites, and Latinos. It was a different world that taught him to sell drugs and offered him a heroin addiction. In this maximum security prison, many of the inmates were serving sentences for murder. Fred was new and only nineteen, whereas the people around him had been there for years and enjoyed seducing younger inmates. Hardened by his experiences, though, Fred held his own as a "tough guy." No matter how tough he tried to be, Fred still knew he needed to ally himself with a group. With the Asians, he made friends who would watch his back even as he did the same for them. At the same time, these friends exposed Fred to drugs. Each group (racial, for example, blacks, Asians, whites, Mexicans) had a representative who would organize the group and negotiate to provide whatever the group needed. By way of this organization, many drugs and much money flowed through the prison. Though the Asians did not have as much of a problem with other groups, where there were drugs, there was violence. Fred was involved in several fights and spent most of his time in lockdowns and solitary confinement. After serving three years in state prison, he was released on parole for good behavior to San Jose.

Fred spent six months at a halfway house, which he considered a rehabilitation period, and was required to report back periodically. If he violated any regulation, he would be sent back to jail. Thus he was drug free and crime free at this time. He received training in electronics and landed a job at General Electric. Soon he was able to move out of the halfway house and rent an apartment in San Jose. The taste of freedom was sweet and he quickly wanted more. Because his family and friends were still in San Francisco, Fred started commuting frequently and visiting his girlfriend. Fred grew bored of working and tired of commuting from San Jose to San Francisco to see his girlfriend. He knew that moving back to his San Francisco neighborhood would expose him to strong temptation to return to his old habits, but he missed his family's home cooking and the support that he could only find close to those who knew and cared for him. For him, the pros outweighed the cons. After his parole ended, Fred quit his job with General Electric and returned to San Francisco. Back in his old neighborhood, he reverted to hanging out with old friends, using drugs, and getting into fights. Prison had exposed him to heavy drugs, so that was what he sought. He was so used to someone supervising his every action that it was almost like he did not know what to do with so much freedom. Aware that he was slipping and could not afford drugs with his salary, he quit his construction job and started distributing drugs for a drug dealer to earn money. Though he did not consider himself an addict, he needed money and would deliver bags to specified locations. As a middle man, he often did not even look to see what was in the bags. On one such occasion, he was to deliver a brown paper bag to a hotel and pick up a piece of luggage in exchange. Instead, he was caught and arrested.

In 1979, just two years after being released from prison, Fred was sentenced in the U.S. District Court, Northern District of California, San Francisco. He pled guilty to a violation of Title 21 $\S841(a)(1)$ – possession with intent to distribute heroin – and was sentenced to two years in custody, with a special parole term of five years. Fred spent the first twenty months in rehabilitation for his heroin addiction. He found out that federal prison was much different from state prison. Before, he was in the company of people who had committed murder or assault. Though state prison was under maximum security, Fred would witness people killing each other. He had joined a group so he would not be dominated by another group (not so much a racial occurrence but because of drugs and the power associated with them). In federal prison, on the other hand, many of the inmates were educated. These people had not committed violent crimes, but were instead serving time for big time smuggling, embezzlement, and the like (white collar crimes). The environment in the federal prison led Fred to think more clearly about what he was doing and where he was headed. He completed his GED while serving time and also attended a drug rehabilitation program. This program tested him for drugs regularly. An important byproduct of this program was that it acted as a minimum security area, where Fred was able to meet "a lot of good people." One of these people was a seventy-three-year-old man who became his friend and mentor. This man, an Asian minister, taught

Fred to value his life and the life of others. This great influence on how Fred viewed himself and the world helped him see the importance of self-discipline. Unfortunately, Fred learned of his mother's death while he was still in federal prison. This caused him to feel great remorse for what he had done and how he had missed being with those he loved. "It hurt me a lot. I [would always] return [from jail] badder and badder." Upon release in 1981, Fred, now age twenty-five, decided to do things right.

Fred's resolution to stay out of trouble was strengthened further by his new role as a husband (he had married his girlfriend right before going to prison). However, he was afraid that nobody would hire him because he was an ex-felon. He applied for any job that was available but was met with only rejection and disappointment. Finally, he applied for a job in city hall, where an old friend helped him secure a job as a clerk for minimum wage. Because the job was only temporary, Fred continued to apply for all the jobs he could. After a year of working as a clerk, he applied to and was accepted into a program as a mechanic assistant because of his electrical training. This program trained him for two years to work for the municipal service of San Francisco. Though Fred found it difficult to maintain a "clean" life, he persevered for himself and his family. He had come to see that he had a lot to lose, and he did not want to take that chance anymore.

Although Fred's life appeared to be on track, he still faced a final obstacle. Because of his past criminal activity, the INS had a deportation detainer lodged against him. Fred never thought he would have problems with immigration. He had been in the United States for so long, more than twenty-five years, and thought he had paid for his crimes through serving time in prison. He therefore did not think his immigration status would be affected: "I did my time; I don't deserve getting deported." Since his initial immigration to the United States at the age of seven, Fred had never returned to Hong Kong. He knew no relatives or friends there and would have an extremely difficult time adjusting. His life, his home, his work, and family was in the United States. In addition, Fred had become the sole provider and caretaker of his elderly father. Dozens of letters supporting Fred came from friends, family, supervisors, coworkers, his parole officer, and a court-appointed psychologist. In 1985, Fred Wong was granted Section 212(c) by establishing his rehabilitation and the hardship to himself and his family that would result from his deportation. He was given a second chance to establish a life in the United States.

Fred not only maintained his status as a lawful permanent resident of the United States, but also applied and became naturalized as soon as he was eligible. He continues to live in San Francisco and has worked with the local transit authority for twenty years now. He is married and has three daughters, currently ages twelve, fourteen, and sixteen. His children are his inspiration – he is clean from all drugs and works daily to keep his life on track. Both he and his wife decided she would stay at home to raise the children because Fred understood the importance of proper parental supervision. Fred is eternally grateful for everyone's help.

Facing Deportation without the Opportunity for a Second Chance

Obviously, Fred should be proud of his accomplishments and how he turned his life around. Fred got a second chance, and as a society, we should be proud that we gave him that second chance to turn his life around. But after we eliminated the second chance opportunities in 1996 for others like Fred, we can only wonder what those like Kim Ho Ma (whom I described in the Introduction) or others would be able to accomplish with a second chance.

Jonathan Peinado

Elia Peinado still has fond memories of life in Mexico. Her husband, a photographer and business owner, owned several properties in the province of Durango as well as the home in which the family lived. Along with Elia, they raised their five children with a great deal of care and attention. As a Christian household, they would entertain missionaries as guests, some of whom would tell the family about the United States. These and other friends would often suggest that the family immigrate to the land of which they spoke so highly. Elia's husband decided to visit and see for himself what life in the United States was like and indeed liked what he saw. After some time, the family started making plans to move, selling their properties and those things they didn't need. They obtained the necessary legal papers to immigrate and moved as a family to the United States. Jonathan, Elia's middle child, was only four years old.

Three years after living in their new home, the family went back to Mexico to visit. After that, Elia sometimes returned alone, while the children stayed at home with their father. Her son Jonathan never again visited the land of his birth after that one trip shortly following his arrival in the

United States. Jonathan was the product of a happy home. He always had a good character, cheerful and laughing together with his family. He also would join in reading the Bible and singing when Elia gave the children daily biblical lessons. Jonathan's father became a pastor, and Jonathan was influenced to attend Riverside Baptist College after his graduation from high school.

After two years in the university, Jonathan decided to return home and start working. He enjoyed construction work and became a skilled finish carpenter employed by the Living Center, an organization that specializes in building and remodeling homes and hospitals. At age twenty-one he married and quickly built up an excellent work record. Everything seemed to be going well, until Jonathan's life took a turn for the worse. After eight years of marriage, Jonathan discovered that his wife had been unfaithful. Although he wanted to continue in the marriage, his wife wanted to be free, and they soon divorced. He suffered from this separation and eventually started hanging out with the "wrong crowd."

During this difficult time in his life, Jonathan was convicted of second-degree burglary. This involves stealing or intending to steal or commit a felony inside a building, not an inhabited dwelling place. Elia describes this event as "the incident with the check." "He took a check to see if he could deposit it for a man. The check was bad and he was charged for being involved," she says with sadness. Another man, a friend of Jonathan's also charged with the crime, was concerned about supporting his six children if he went to prison. Jonathan felt sorry for his friend, so he took the blame for the entire ordeal, and the other man was set free. Jonathan received a two-year stayed sentence.

"He is such a good person, that sometimes he is dumb," says Elia, recalling the second conviction her son received. Jonathan became involved with drugs and the people who made them. He allowed some of his friends to use his apartment, not knowing what they needed it for. These friends ended up using the space as a lab for making drugs. Jonathan was caught having the drugs in his home and was advised to admit his guilt to receive a lighter sentence. He did so and was convicted of manufacturing methamphetamine, a drug trafficking conviction.

After his release from jail, Jonathan decided to pick himself back up. He strengthened his ties with the community and became president of the Baptist Men's Brotherhood. He occasionally led the service and Bible study at the Baptist Church where his father had been pastor for more than forty years. Elia sadly remembers, "When Jonathan's father died of cancer two years ago, Jonathan took care of everything." Not only did Jonathan see to the burial arrangements for his father, but he also served as the sole provider for Elia, who has suffered from diabetes for forty years. But, even though he returned to work and acted as such a vital figure in his family during difficult times, and his parole and correctional facility officers agreed he was a good man, Jonathan was placed in removal proceedings a year after he was released from jail. This came as a complete surprise, because no one had ever warned him about the possible repercussions his criminal convictions could have on his immigration status.

Unlike his entire immediate family, who had naturalized and become U.S. citizens, Jonathan never saw the need to do so. He knew only one home, and he thought that because he had been in the United States as a lawful permanent resident for more than forty years that afforded him the rights of any other American. He soon found out this was a tragically false assumption. With his two convictions, Jonathan was ordered removed to Mexico with no consideration of mitigating circumstances. He knew this would be devastating not only to himself, but also to his whole family. He had recently discovered that his oldest sister was diagnosed with lymphoma, and he began taking her on regular trips to the hospital to receive chemotherapy. He took tests to see if he could be a bone marrow donor for his sister. He was deported to Mexico before the test results were received.

Elia wistfully contemplates her family's situation. "I have a son who was in the air force and worked as an engineer. He graduated from UC Berkeley. My husband went to school here [in the United States], learned English, and became a pastor. He went to Golden Gate Seminary. My children went to school. None of them has asked for welfare or been a burden for this country. Jonathan just messed up at one point in his life, and this [deportation] happened." With the rest of her children either out of the country or with their own families to sustain, Elia no longer has the strong support Jonathan provided. In fact, she lost most of her savings trying to help her son adapt to life in a strange country. She traveled with Jonathan to Tijuana when he was deported to try and help him find a place to live. At first, Jonathan was very homesick as he faced culture shock. He had no idea how things worked in Mexico, and he barely spoke Spanish. He would call home every week and ask how the family was doing, worried his mother would get sick.

Jonathan has lived in Mexico for two years now. When he first arrived, he barely had enough money to eat. Through a connection with friends, he was able to obtain employment as an English teacher in Puerto Vallarta. Still, he makes only enough money to pay for a small place to live. He struggles daily to survive, worrying about his mom even as she worries about him. "He should've had another chance" is all Elia can say.

José Luis Magaña

Jesse Magaña still remembers life in Mexico. Overall, the family was happy, and everything was going well. Eventually, however, Jesse's dad could no longer find employment and had to find a way to support the family. He soon immigrated legally to the United States and started work in 1959. After years of living apart, Jesse's dad decided to reunite the family and have everyone move to the United States. Jesse was thirteen years old when he arrived in the United States; José Luis, Jesse's younger brother, was only two.

Jesse speaks perfect Spanish as well as English, but José Luis grew up speaking mostly English and thus does not have a strong grasp on the Spanish language. Still, he got along well with everyone he knew. "He was a good kid, he was always happy, and he studied well. He didn't have problems with anything," says Jesse of his brother. Jesse and José Luis went to the same schools through high school. During these times, José Luis enjoyed all kinds of sports, showed an interest in the theater, and did not practice any vices. He was an average, calm, and helpful kid.

Upon graduating from high school, José Luis wanted to start working. He did several odd jobs here and there until finally settling on something he really enjoyed – karate. Having learned karate growing up along with a third brother, José Luis was a perfect candidate for karate instructor. He spent several years in this profession, as things started to change.

When José Luis was eighteen years old, he heard the tragic news that his little nephew, who was not even two years old, had been accidentally run over and killed. After that, José Luis started losing sleep and feeling depressed. Eventually, he would have "episodes" where he would talk loudly and sometimes angrily with no apparent provocation. Although José Luis became verbally and sometimes physically aggressive during his episodes, he never injured anyone. Jesse recalls that José Luis would say he was Bruce Lee and start yelling. He would also try to defend himself if anyone tried to restrain him. However, he would never attack another person. José Luis was suffering from severe bipolar disorder with manic psychotic features. From then on, he was taken periodically to the hospital, all but once involuntarily. These hospitalizations usually followed an emotionally charged event, such as the breakup with a girlfriend or the death of a friend. They also usually resulted from a failure to take his prescribed medication. He would spend from one month to six weeks in the hospital, on heavy medication and looking very tired. His family would frequently visit him. Once back home, José Luis would resume acting normally and being the friendly, calm person everyone knew.

In 1999, José Luis was convicted of interference with a flight crew by assault or intimidation, in violation of 49 U.S.C. §46504, for which he received a two-year prison sentence. Various doctors studied and tested José Luis, submitting their reports to the federal court dealing with what was essentially a hijacking case. These reports showed that the incident occurred while José Luis was in the midst of an emotional crisis, and he was probably insane at the time of the offense. He was acutely psychotic and in an extreme state of mania in which his attitude, thinking, and behavior were all substantially abnormal. One doctor described José Luis as suffering from manic grandiosity and irrational thinking that deprived him of the capacity to appreciate the wrongfulness of his actions under the insanity test. Another doctor's professional opinion was that José Luis clearly would be considered legally insane under the American Law Institute criteria, which includes the inability to adhere to right, even if the individual knew his or her actions were wrong. Two psychiatrists indicated that José Luis's medication helped but did not necessarily prevent him from experiencing his delusions and other symptoms of his mental disorder. He had a great deal of difficulty remembering what happened on the day of the incident as well as what he was thinking and feeling at that time. Despite these reports, José Luis was sentenced to jail time. No one ever told him the conviction could have immigration consequences.

Over the years, José Luis's parents and four brothers all had naturalized to become U.S. citizens. José Luis also attempted to naturalize but missed his scheduled interview appointment. He never tried again. After all, he had been in the United States since he was two, he barely spoke any Spanish, and he had never been back to Mexico. He had never known a world outside of the United States, so he never expected having to live elsewhere. This sense of security came crashing down soon after his release from jail. His family eagerly awaited his return, though they were notified that José Luis would have to present himself to a rehabilitation home six months after being free. Instead, when the time came for José Luis to come home, the family was told that he had been transported to Arizona for removal proceedings. It turned out that his two-year sentence made his crime an aggravated felony, for which even his legal permanent resident status could not protect him from automatic deportation.

José Luis does not have a criminal background, but he suffers from an ongoing mental disability. Despite the fact that deportation and exclusion from his home, where he has lived ever since he was a two-year-old child, away from his family and friends and while suffering from a chronic mental disability would be devastating and probably life-threatening to him, José Luis was deported to Mexico. Today, he lives in an apartment by himself in the Mexican province of Michoacan, focusing all of his energies on surviving. His family sends him the money they can spare. Although he has access to medicine and seems to be doing well emotionally, they worry about the next time his depression triggers uncontrollable episodes. They can no longer be by his side. José Luis is now in his thirties.

José Velasquez

The case of José Velasquez is another compelling example of the harsh criminal alien deportation statutes. Velasquez was born in the Republic of Panama to a member of the Panamanian diplomatic service in 1947. His mother was a U.S. citizen and Velasquez frequently accompanied his father to the United States for extended visits. At the age of thirteen, Velasquez was admitted to the United States as a lawful permanent resident and completed his high school education in Philadelphia. For many years, Velasquez operated a delicatessen and owned a home with his wife in Pennsylvania. Both of his older siblings are U.S. citizens, as are his wife of thirty-six years and his three adult children.

In 1998, deportation proceedings were initiated against Velasquez when he returned to the United States after a trip to Panama. Nearly two decades earlier, Velasquez pled guilty to two charges, conspiracy to sell and the sale or delivery of a controlled substance. The grounds of his removal were INA §212(a)(2)(C), which renders excludable "an alien who has been, or has aided or conspired with, an illicit trafficker in a controlled substance," and INA §212(a)(2)(C)(A)(i)(II), which renders excludable "an alien who has been convicted of . . . a violation of, or a conspiracy to violate, a state or federal law relating to a controlled substance."

In 1980, Velasquez was approached by a friend at a party who asked him if he sold cocaine. Velasquez answered that he did not but pointed out another man at the party who did. No evidence suggested that Velasquez expected compensation for any subsequent transaction between his friend and the man who Velasquez pointed to as a possible source of the drug. Upon his guilty plea, Velasquez was fined $5,000 and sentenced to five years' probation. As a result, Velasquez is subject to removal because his old conviction amounted to an aggravated felony under current immigration law. Neither an immigration judge nor the Board of Immigration Appeals has discretionary power to allow him to stay because of the 1996 changes to the law. Had the Immigration and Naturalization Service (INS) addressed Velasquez's criminal convictions while the Section 212(c) waiver was still available, there is little doubt the immigration court would have found outstanding circumstances and equities for relief from deportation.

Manuel Garcia

The case of Manuel Garcia also illustrates the harsh effect of current deportation laws. Manuel Garcia is a forty-year-old citizen of Mexico who has lived in the United States since 1983. Mr. Garcia graduated from high school in Mexico and then went on to a three-year technical college in 1983 to study economics and biochemistry. At the age of nineteen, he qualified for the special agricultural worker legalization provision in the Immigration Reform and Control Act of 1986 and intended to learn English and return to Mexico someday to become a teacher. Garcia soon realized, however, that he could not afford to attend school. He did agricultural work for many years, as well as work in a slaughterhouse and a mill. During this time, Garcia married and had a son in 1986. With roots firmly planted in the United States, Garcia became a lawful permanent resident in 1990.

In an unfortunate turn of events, Garcia's father passed away in Mexico. Unable to gather enough money for travel to Mexico, Mr. Garcia became depressed and frustrated. A neighbor who sold drugs, aware of the Garcia's financial hardship, approached him with the prospect of selling drugs to earn money. Garcia accepted the offer. Unbeknownst to him, the police were watching Garcia's neighbor. Garcia completed three illegal drug transactions and each were tracked by the police. In 1996, Garcia delivered approximately eight grams of methamphetamine and was arrested. He pled guilty to delivery of a controlled substance for consideration and was sentenced to thirty days in jail, drug evaluation, community service, and three years' probation. Garcia served twenty-seven days and successfully completed the other sentencing requirements.

Garcia went on to graduate with an associate's degree in human services and substance abuse. He also worked as a bilingual/bicultural substance abuse counselor. In 2003, DHS authorities arrested Garcia at his house, detained him, and initiated removal proceedings. DHS charged Garcia as removable for commission of an aggravated felony. The immigration judge had to order Garcia removed to Mexico, in spite of all his friends, family, and a good job.

Juan López

Another case involves Juan López, who arrived in the United States with his parents at the age of thirteen. López is a lawful permanent resident of the United States, is married to a U.S. citizen, and has two U.S. citizen children. In addition, López is part owner of a six-chain Mexican restaurant in the Twin Cities metropolitan area of Minnesota, is a member of the Chamber of Commerce, and gives antidrug lectures to Latino children in his community. In 1997, López pled guilty and was convicted of sale of controlled substances. He served one year in workhouse (work release from jail) and completed probation early. Years later, while at the police station to help a family member, López ran into an immigration agent who checked his alien registration number. López was arrested and placed him in proceedings as an aggravated felon. As a result, he faced removal for his prior conviction under INA §237(a)(2)(A)(iii).

In 2003, López was granted an extraordinary pardon by the Minnesota Board of Pardons because of the substantial and convincing evidence of his rehabilitation, because the crime was an unusual act in an otherwise law-abiding life, and because of the strong support that he had in his community. In addition, López also had his original sentence modified by a sentencing judge classifying his offense as a misdemeanor. As a result of the pardon, the aggravated felony ground of removability does not apply. However, López is still subject to removal under the controlled substance ground of removability.

Cambodian Refugees

The deportation of Cambodian refugees convicted of aggravated felonies, as illustrated by Kim Ho Ma's case, began in the summer 2002, The backgrounds of the potential returnees vary. The parents of Touch Rin Svay were among those who fled the killing fields of the Pol Pot regime, ending up in a Thai refugee camp. Touch was born in that camp, and, like thousands of other Cambodians, his family was eventually admitted to the United States as refugees. Touch grew up in Portland, Maine, and joined the Marines. At the age of twenty-two, however, Touch's life took a disastrous turn. He crashed his car while driving drunk, and his own sister, a passenger, was killed. In an awful twist that is one of those "only-in-America" stories of justice, Touch was convicted of manslaughter. The tragedy does not end there. Once Touch completed a term of eighteen months in prison, he faced deportation to Cambodia, a land with which he is totally unfamiliar.[55]

Mao So was one year old when he left Cambodia in 1979. His grand-mother took him across the border to Thailand and from there to the United States. Growing up, he always believed that she was his mother. Only when he was about to be deported did she tell him that his real mother was living in Cambodia. When he was fourteen, he began to sell drugs to fellow students at Santa Ana High School. At fifteen, he could make $500 in a day. He joined a gang and dropped out of school. He worked his way up in the gang until he was handling drug deals through-out the United States. Mao had twenty armed men working for him and sold cocaine, ecstasy, and "anything you can think of." Eventually, he was caught after he paid cash for an Integra. He pleaded guilty to drug charges and served two and a half years of a five-year sentence. By the time of his arrest, a rival gangster had put a price of $225,000 on his head. Mao was eventually deported in December 2002.[56]

Not all the potential Cambodian refugee deportees are murderers, drug dealers, or gang members. One returnee, Sor Vann, was a thirty-four-year-old construction foreman in Houston who was charged with indecent exposure – for urinating in public.[57] He was placed on six years' probation.

---

[55] Seth Mydans, *Dead End for Cambodians Who Grew Up American*, NY TIMES, Aug. 9, 2002, at A3.

[56] See Richard C. Paddock, *Cambodia's Black Sheep Return to Fold*, LA TIMES, Mar. 28, 2003, at A27.

[57] Mydans, *supra* note 55; Genevieve Roja, *Strangers in a Strange Land*, HYPHEN MAG., Summer 2003, at 35.

He was caught urinating in public again just one month before his six-year probation was completed. Although the offense was only a misdemeanor, violating probation was a felony, and he served four years in prison.[58] He has a wife and two young children in Houston, Texas. Before he entered the United States as a refugee, the Khmer Rouge murdered his parents.[59]

Louen Lun, who escaped the killing fields as a baby, committed a crime as a teenager: He fired a gun in a shopping mall as he fled a group of black teens.[60] Charged with second-degree assault, he served eleven months in county jail. For the next six years, he lived as a model American, building a family and maintaining steady employment.[61] Louen decided to apply for citizenship, and after two years he thought that the INS would finally approve his application. When he showed up at the INS office, he was incarcerated and held for deportation because of his prior conviction.[62] Within two weeks of his arrest, Cambodia signed the repatriation agreement, and, in May 2003, the United States deported Louen to Cambodia – twenty-two years after he first arrived in America.[63] For Louen, leaving the United States forever means being separated not only from his mother, but also from his wife and two young daughters.[64]

Yuthea Chhoueth grew up in a rough Sacramento neighborhood. At eighteen, his attempt to rob a bank was foiled, but that was enough to get him a three-year stint in federal prison.[65] After his release, U.S. immigration authorities required him to check in on a regular basis and to stay out of trouble.[66] More than a dozen years later, Yuthea was caught driving without a license. Ironically, he was traveling to the INS for his routine visit.[67] The problem was that the traffic infraction made him a parole violator, and he had to go back to jail. To make matters worse, the violation made him deportable. When travel documents are obtained, authorities plan to remove Yuthea back to Cambodia – the land he fled as a toddler.[68]

---

[58] Paddock, *supra* note 56.   [59] Id.

[60] Deborah Sontag, *In a Homeland Far from Home*, NY TIMES, Nov. 16, 2003, §6, at 48.

[61] Id.   [62] Id.

[63] Id.   [64] Id.

[65] Shonda Swilley, *Deported to Cambodia: A Love Story; A Sac State Student Follows the Man She Loves as He Returns to a Homeland He Doesn't Know*, SACRAMENTO NEWS AND REVIEW, Dec. 12, 2002, at http://www.newsreview.com/sacramento/Content?oid=oid%3A13780.

[66] Id.   [67] Id.

[68] Id.

As with many Cambodians, the Khmer Rouge killed Chanphirun Meanowuth Min's entire family after Pol Pot's takeover of Cambodia in 1975.[69] He, too, faces removal from his adopted San Gabriel Valley residence. With two accomplices, Chanphirun Meanowuth was found guilty of defrauding the Medi-Cal program, by selling blood and medical identification cards.[70] His sixteen-month prison sentence and $25,000 restitution order was enough to render him deportable.[71]

Many Uch also awaits deportation. Many believes that prison saved his life. Sadly, he had a better chance to survive and learn in prison than growing up in his poor Seattle neighborhood. Yet even after overcoming his past and winning his freedom, Many is again being threatened with deportation. Under the aggravated felony provision, he now faces deportation to the country he left as a young boy.

At the age of seven, Many, his mother, and his two older brothers came to the United States under horrific conditions. After their home country of Cambodia was pulled into war when the United States began bombing along the Vietnam/Cambodia border, the brutal Khmer Rouge regime came to power. Many's family was captured by the Khmer Rouge army, separated from their father, and forced from their home into the jungle. There they spent almost an entire year roaming around and foraging for just enough food to survive. In 1980, Red Cross workers found the family among the sick and the dead and placed them in a refugee camp.

Over the next four years the family bounced around from camp to camp, uncertain of their fate or the fate of loved ones left behind. They assumed the worst. When Many's family made it to a refugee camp in the Philippines, he began to pick up English and realized he was "a pretty smart kid." Yet life in the camps was dreary and they were willing to sit through incomprehensible "Jesus movies" just to take their mind off tragedy.

On April 14, 1984, Many's family arrived to the United States as refugees. Their first destination was Richmond, Virginia, a place where Many realized nobody there was like them. Scared and alone, their first days in the country came without any acculturation assistance. In their strange new environment, they were placed in low-income housing, given a welfare check, and left to fend for themselves.

A year later Many's family decided to move to Seattle where other Cambodians they knew had been placed. There they sought solace among

---

[69] Teresa Watanabe, *Cambodians Fear Possible Deportation*, LA TIMES, Feb. 21, 2003, at B1.

[70] Id.   [71] Id.

others who understood their trauma. Though these bonds helped, they could do little to assist Many when it came to actually succeeding in America.

Refugees, Many says, face many more obstacles than immigrants who willingly come here to work. Being forced from their homes to escape death, they are often unprepared for adjusting and still troubled by the sufferings of war. For Many, this abrupt move was especially tough because he came from a country of very different traditions. Because his mother could not speak English and did not understand American customs, she could not advise him about school nor could she easily seek help from others. She had never been educated and most of the other elders had been farmers back home. None of them knew what dreams he could have here.

Life at school was not much better for Many either. After his experiences with learning in the refugee camps, Many found the "alternative school" he was placed in completely unfit to teach him. "I didn't learn anything there, it was just too damn easy. They didn't expect anything from us, just to not cause any trouble." He notes that half the girls there were pregnant and almost all the guys were involved in something illegal. "How do I fit in with that?" he questioned.

Meanwhile in his neighborhood, Many faced the frustrations of poverty and discrimination. He always wondered why he could not have the things that other kids had. Kids at school would pick on Many for being different and poor. Riding the bus home from school, they would make fun of him for getting off in the "projects." They also would tell him to "go back to his country." Many didn't know how to respond so sometimes he would get into fights over it.

In his elementary school ESL class Many befriended a group of guys from similar backgrounds who had comparable problems. Growing up together, they became very close. As other kids would pick on them, they would stand up for each other. "If our friend got jumped, we didn't think twice. We'd go get those guys." Soon Many fell into the "tough mentality." If he did not fight, the other guys might look at him as weak. Sometimes he would have to steal to prove himself. And if someone would get in trouble with the law, he would never snitch.

Many and his large group of friends went everywhere together, something he says is common among Cambodians. To him they were a much-needed support group, but to police they were a gang. In the late 1980s, when gang life in Los Angeles was being popularized, the hysteria attached to Many and his friends. "We were never a gang, that title was given to us," he explained.

As Many became older, life on the street grew continually faster paced and he found himself committing worse crimes to get by. Fighting and stealing were not optional for Many, but rather a way of life. "You don't really think you're wrong 'cause everyone in the neighborhood is doing the same things," he explained. As the life of crime escalated, Many found himself trapped. To get the increasing amounts of money he needed, Many began to get involved with drugs and guns. When Many was eighteen, he was caught for a robbery and sent to prison.

Over the next six years Many was in some form of detention. He spent three plus years in prison and more than two in immigration detention. Sad but true, it was here that he would have the opportunity to cultivate himself, which he had been unable to do in his own neighborhood. Many took advantage of the opportunity. In prison he read books, went to school, and learned the law. Later he used this knowledge to petition for his release. After a tough battle, Many eventually won his freedom.

In many ways, Many is a success story of the ambivalent criminal rehabilitation system. Ironically, though, the same system he has persevered and succeeded through is the one threatening to take away the legitimacy he has earned by it. Since 2002, when the United States forced Cambodia to sign a repatriation agreement, the government has deported many people like Many and is threatening to deport him. He finds the damage from breaking up such families unnecessary, especially after the offender's debt to society has been paid.

Many has not let this threat stop him from working to improve lives of kids from his neighborhood who might fall victim to the same troubles he did. He has started a little league baseball league for Cambodian youngsters and also tutors students at a local elementary school. "I want to show them the options nobody showed me. These kids relate to me 'cause I know what they're going through."

Many's life now is quite different than it was before. He is now engaged to be married and owns his own delivery business. Growing up, Many never realized how tough life was in his neighborhood because his only other benchmark was a life of war. Now when he goes back the ills are painfully blatant to him. Though he has prepared himself to be separated from his family once again, for others he says, "it would be a disaster." That's why he works tirelessly to help them. "I just wish someone would've given me these tools back then; I really think I could have made it."

Another Cambodian refugee awaiting deportation is Andrew Thi, who wrote this to me:

My name is Andrew Thi. I was born on February 10, 1975 in Battambang, Cambodia. It was bad there, all the genocide and war. If the Communists saw you, they would put you in jail or kill you on sight. My family did what we had to do to escape to a Thai refugee camp where we began the long process to immigrate to the U.S. It was a long wait, but worth it. In 1981, my parents, three sisters and I arrived in San Francisco and made our home in Oakland.

When I was 8 or 9 years old, I got into a car accident in Oakland. I went into a coma and couldn't remember much afterward. I used to read Cambodian fluently, but now I can barely speak it. I think things would have been different if the accident had never happened.

I am the only son, so there was a lot of pressure on me to help out my dad in his landscape business. When he got hurt, everyone depended on me to help out. My dad is like Superman. Once he broke his leg doing a concrete job and wouldn't go to the hospital until he finished. My parents were farmers in Cambodia, so they continued to do labor work here. When asked by the authorities why we wanted to come to America, my dad said, "To give our kids an education." And that's what we all did. Everyone graduated from high school and two of us from college. Looking back, everything my dad told me was to set me on the right path and make me into a man. He was just a hardworking man providing for his family. He was so busy, but I know he loves me to death – he bailed me out when no one else believed in me. He probably did it to bring me back into the family and give me a wake-up call. I can't say I never had a father figure, but I didn't listen. I listened to my friends instead. I loved my dad, but I also loved bringing trouble home.

My family got public assistance for several years until everyone grew up and began working. One of my sisters owns a business in San Diego, and one is a beautician. Everyone is doing well except for me right now, but I'm getting there.

I don't remember anything about elementary school. I went to middle school in Oakland for one year, then in Hayward where I stayed for high school and two years of college. In Oakland, I had been surrounded with Cambodian friends. It was good to be separated from them for a while because a lot of them never graduated from high school. At Hayward, I was the only Cambodian in my school, except another guy who I didn't know was Cambodian at the time. We did what every normal American did – hung out, rode bikes, went to the mall and movies, went to Great America [amusement park]. I had black and Mexican friends. I can get along with almost any crowd. I would never be picked on, but would be the one picking on others. Still, I am a man with a heart – once I saw a guy get jumped in a poor area. I thought, that ain't right, so I got my friends to jump in the fight with me to help that guy out. We took on a whole gang and broke up when the cops came.

I was always on the honor roll and got good grades. School was easy for me. My dad could never criticize or control me because I always did well in school. My grades were a cover up. The other side of me kept getting into trouble, shoplifting and stealing things. We started stealing in eighth grade. We saw all these white people or whoever wearing brand name clothes and we wanted them too. It started out small and progressed to larger items. I was surrounded by both good and bad, and I wanted to do both. I found out that doing both doesn't cut it – if the bad gets involved, all the good is flushed away. I got caught a couple times for stealing clothes and small things in eighth grade and my dad beat me. I deserved all the beatings. I was lucky we weren't in Cambodia where I probably would have been hanged.

High school is when it really began. We went from stealing clothes to stealing cars for money and to get around. I wasn't in an organized gang; we would sell the parts to people. I taught my Hayward friends how to steal cars, and when they were caught by the cops they blamed me. That was so weak; they snitched on me. I wanted to go up there and snatch them.

I was also in honor roll in high school, and the class treasurer. I did my homework during school. During wrestling season, all the bad in me would go away. I was on the wrestling team all four years, and I would get so busy and tired out from after-school practice that I couldn't run around at night. Before or after wrestling season, my bad nature would come out again. So, I couldn't say I was addicted or that anyone pressured me. I thank God that I had self-control. Everything was my choice, and I made some bad choices. If I could go back, I would do it differently.

I wasted my youth. I wanted fun and excitement, I wanted to be independent and in control, but it cost me five years in prison. I went to juvenile hall when I was 16. After I got out, I was caught stealing a lot of cars and was charged with 18 counts of auto theft. I'm not happy about it, but it was my choice. I wanted to take classes in juvenile hall so I could go to college, but the classes were too easy. While on a home pass, I hooked up with some friends and we stole a car again. We were chased and one of my friends was caught and he told on us. I returned to juvenile hall and the punishment became more severe. I was sent to a one-year placement in Los Angeles.

In Los Angeles, I attended a male-only school, and the courses were still too easy. I worked hard, got straight A's, and transferred to a regular co-ed high school where I could take college-prep courses part-time. But I still hadn't learned my lesson; I was stealing cars again. I was so lost. When I graduated from the program, I surprised them by getting A's and B's. Then I went back to high school in Hayward.

The summer before my senior year, I applied to the Stanford Youth Science Medical Program for minorities who excelled in medicine and math. Somehow I was accepted with 21 other students. I think they just wanted me to sail back up and be good. I was surrounded by straight nerds from Berkeley, Modesto, central and northern California. It was a five-week scholarship-funded program and one of the best experiences of my life – I really enjoyed learning all kinds of sciences and math. Later they had a reunion, and I was so embarrassed because I felt like I disappointed all those people.

In college at Hayward State in 1995, I had financial problems. I was going to school and living with my girlfriend in Oakland. One day, I ran into some people who said we could make big money, at least $5,000 or $10,000, by stealing computer parts. I got involved with these big ball players. In our heists, I played the lowest role: the man with the gun. Nobody ever got hurt. I also began gambling. I would lose $10,000 in an hour and a half – money was easy come, easy go. It was exciting living on the edge. Getting money to survive became an addiction. That was when I got caught. We stole from a lot of Chinese and Vietnamese shops with large insurance policies. We would take $1 million and they would report a $2 million loss. That was how the feds got involved.

I was busted twice and charged with second degree robbery with possession of firearms. At first we were only charged with possession since the police had no evidence on us, but my friend snitched on us and they linked us to the robberies. I was offered 12 years but pled out at 5 years. I knew I could never beat them at trial.

While I was in custody, Congress passed a law in 1996 that subjected legal immigrants, including Asians, to immediate deportation or removal status for committing an aggravated felony. I was mad because I was only in jail because people opened their mouths. When I finished my time in November 1999, I went straight into INS custody. At that time, I was being charged with other crimes. People talked and more indictments would come down. Two federal agents came to see me and said I was looking at 100 years. I couldn't eat for a month!

Within a few months, I was ordered deported. It was frustrating because there was no telling how long I would be held. In state prison, it's fine because you have a date to look forward to. In INS custody, hope ends. You're living your life on someone's opinion and whether he has a good or bad day. I did have some help with administrative paperwork. I collected recommendation letters from my parole officer, counselor, teachers, administrators, and friends. You need to build a positive image; it's all about the letters. That helped me get out.

My only ticket out of INS custody was to sign a deportation agreement, which I did on January 14, 2000. Then they had 90 days to remove me. I signed because I knew they couldn't deport me to a Communist country (Cambodia). That's why a lot of people are in removal status. The feds started coming to see me again due to a new indictment in December 2000 for armed robbery. In April 2001, I got out of INS custody and went straight into federal custody. I was facing up to 45 years. My lifestyle was changing; God was putting angels in my life. It was crazy – everyone pled out or went to trial and got 45 years or became government witnesses. We all looked the same; we were all Asian. I borrowed $5,000 from my sister for a private lawyer, which was a waste. Now I have a private lawyer working pro bono. The problem is Cambodia signed a repatriation agreement with the U.S. in March 2001, and now the U.S. is deporting Cambodians.

For the next couple years, my family tried to bail me out or get me to a halfway house. I tried to use the recommendation letters with the feds, but they see only black and white. They looked at me and said, "Whoa, you're a violent man. We can't let you on the street." I tried to show them that I rehabilitated the last four years, but they denied bail. Thank God for my dad; he wanted to play a part in my life. My family risked a lot to get me out – my parents signed bonds and my sister put up her house and business. I would have to earn enough trust in nine months at the halfway home so I could go home.

At one point, I had three cases pending – state parole, federal, and INS. I was discharged from state parole after three years because I stayed clean. Over time, I have to check in with the feds and INS less often. It's getting easier now. I was bitter the first two years because I thought I was going back in. My heart was empty and I wasn't being faithful to any woman, just grabbing what I could before I had to go back in. Then, an angel came into my life. My woman is such a blessing, along with my family. I was in a living hell, but prayer has worked. I see it in court – on February 4, 2004, I was sentenced to five years of probation and 400 hours of community service. It was a miracle – no time for weapon possession and all those priors? My trials and tribulations with God have built up my faith. I think every life has its own purpose. He took me on a journey through His life, without books. Whatever happens now, He always has my heart and keeps me in check. Every day, the old Andrew wants to come out again, but He will just shut it down.

I have two months left in the halfway house. I am just so thankful. I believe in Jesus so much. I know He watches every little thing I do. I'm scared of Him, in a good way. The halfway house is co-ed with 60 to 80 people. People are just trying to get back into society and the community and build trust. For community service, I'm tutoring, doing senior outreach, administrative work, whatever they need. It's a court order, but I don't think of it that way. This is a new way of life. I've learned a lot about INS from Porthira Chimm, a director at the Cambodian Community Development center. He has had a huge impact on my life.

I tell my tutoring students that they don't have to go with the flow. My advice is, don't try to grow up too fast; just enjoy your young days, day by day. Don't worry about the money so much because it will be there. Don't try and find a shortcut in life.

Since getting out of custody, I don't fool with the law anymore. I do landscaping with my dad four days a week. I pay taxes. I have no complaints. Because of God, I have another chance at life. It could be a lot worse. I still check in quarterly with INS. I can potentially be deported back to Cambodia whenever they call my name. Every time I check in, I wonder if they're going to take me in, especially now that they want to know about my ancestors, village, and relatives – I know nothing. It would be hard if I go back, since I have no family there. One thing is, I will survive. It tears me up that you don't know when you'll be removed. You get so deep into American life, have a wife, have kids, then suddenly you have to go back. You know, I don't think about it anymore. Just have faith and everything will be all right. That's all I can live on now.

The examples do not end there. Most potential deportees are men who are the primary wage-earners for their families, who have lived in the United States for more than twenty years.[72] Some Cambodian refugees facing removal, however, are women. For example, one woman faces deportation after serving three years in jail for disciplining her children with unlit incense sticks. She is a single mother whose parents have died; the father of her children abandoned the family. Her children, who were born in the United States, will be placed in foster care when she is deported.[73]

Criminality in the Cambodian Refugee Community

The environment that many young immigrants and refugees fall into on their arrival in the United States is a far cry from images of America that

---

[72] Josie Huang, *Cambodians Fear Worst for Deportees*, PORTLAND PRESS HERALD, May 25, 2002, at 1A. One of the early returnees was an eighty-year-old man. Chris Decherd, *Home Isn't Sweet for Cambodians Deported from U.S; Law Says Noncitizen Criminals Cannot Stay Here*, SEATTLE TIMES, Jan. 14, 2003, at A10.

[73] Stephanie Ho, *Cambodia, U.S. Agree on Deportation of Criminals*, Voice of America, Jan. 2, 2003, at http://cambodiatoday.bravepages.com/Returnees.htm.

their parents have in their minds prior to arriving. Consider the world experienced by many young Cambodian refugees. Criminality in the Cambodian and other Southeast Asian refugee communities presents a serious challenge. Even back in 1990, when Southeast Asians made up only 1.5 percent of California's population, of the roughly nine thousand wards of the California Youth Authority (the state's most incorrigible youth), 4.5 percent were Southeast Asians.[74] Reflecting California's gang wars, many were young Cambodians. By 2000, an analysis of juvenile arrests in San Francisco and Alameda (including the city of Oakland) counties in California disclosed that Cambodian and Vietnamese youth have "higher arrest and recidivism rates as compared to most other racial and ethnic groups."[75]

What explains the relatively high levels of criminality in the Cambodian refugee community? Criminologists, social scientists, parents, and the criminals themselves offer a variety of explanations. All of these explanations seem to flow from refugee status itself.

Refugee Camp Environment and Experience

The experience and environment for refugees at the camps prior to entering the United States were not positive. Food and simple shelter were provided by a staff that was overwhelmed.[76] Activities were scarce, and there was little opportunity to be productive.[77] Men, the traditional "rulers" of the home, had lost control, and as one said: "I watch my children grow up behind barbed wire. . . . We [have been] here two years. And what can I do? What do I do? Nothing."[78]

Furthermore, refugee camps were breeding grounds for violence and crime. Most refugees were men between eighteen and thirty, with little to do and no means to support families they left behind.[79] Guilt, frustration, and anger often resulted in violence and then separate confinement by camp officials.[80] In some camps that were "open" to refugees coming and going during the day, drugs and other criminal acts were

---

[74] Tony Waters, CRIME AND IMMIGRANT YOUTH ix (1999). Southeast Asians also made up 8.5 percent of the 1991 incoming freshman class at the University of California, Davis. Id.

[75] See Thao Le et al., NOT INVISIBLE: ASIAN PACIFIC ISLANDER JUVENILE ARRESTS IN ALAMEDA COUNTY 43, 45 (July 2001).

[76] Patrick Du Phuoc Long, THE DREAM SHATTERED, VIETNAMESE GANGS IN AMERICA 111 (1996).

[77] Id.   [78] Id.
[79] Id.   [80] Id.

accessible.[81] Many unaccompanied minors, with no family in the camps, were attracted to gangs or older troublemakers. The environment in many camps reached a point where some refugees had to guard their families and belongings around the clock.[82]

Although most may have been safer in Thai camps compared to living with the terror of Pol Pot, Cambodian refugees were victimized in other ways. In one infamous event, Thai solders pushed forty-five thousand refugees down an embankment into a Khmer Rouge minefield.[83] Soldiers also exploited and assaulted refugees.[84]

Post-traumatic Stress Disorder

The task of acculturation is enormous for many newcomers, but Cambodians, who are ethnic Khmer, arrived with other challenges.[85] Many parents who survived the trauma of Pol Pot's autogenocide were in shock and continue to suffer from post-traumatic stress disorder (PTSD).[86] Some refugees suffered long instances of starvation, which caused long-term mental deterioration.[87] Many children are left unsupervised because their parents experience depression.[88] Even when at home, a parent may remain isolated in a corner, still depressed over the loss of a loved one in Cambodia.[89]

The constant environment of fear and terror in Cambodia resulted in an extremely high rate of PTSD. Although all Southeast Asian refugee groups have high rates of mental health illness, Cambodians show the highest levels of problems.[90] In Minnesota, 45 percent of adult Cambodians suffer from PTSD, and more than eight in ten were symptomatic.[91] Surveys of Cambodians seeking mental health treatment reveal that up to 90 percent suffer from PTSD.[92] These high rates of PTSD are of little wonder, given

[81] Id.   [82] Id.
[83] Dori C. Cahn and Jay W. Stansell, *From Refugee to Deportee: How U.S. Immigration Law Failed the Cambodian Community* (2004) (unpublished paper on file with author).
[84] Id.   [85] Id. at 5.
[86] Id.   [87] Id.
[88] Susanna J. Ko, *Examining the Contribution of Ethnic Attitudes, Collective Self-Esteem, and Spirituality to Delinquent Behavioral Outcomes among Cambodian Adolescents: An Exploratory Study* (2001) (PhD dissertation, University of Massachusetts) (on file with author).
[89] One teen spoke with bitterness of his mother, who lost her husband in Cambodia and now spends much time sitting quietly alone. Seth Mydans, *As Cultures Meet, Gang War Paralyzes a City in California*, NY TIMES, May 6, 1991, at A1.
[90] Cahn and Stansell, *supra* note 83, at 6.   [91] Id. at 5–6.
[92] Id.

the loss of loved ones at the hands of the Khmer Rouge. As Dr. Haing Ngor explained, many refugees understandably were traumatized by their own persecution:

> It was clear there was a massive mental health problem among Cambodian refugees. I understood it because I had my share of mental problems too. We had all been traumatized by our experiences. We had all lost parents or brothers or children. Many of us had horrible dreams, night after night. We felt isolated and depressed and unable to trust anyone. What made it worse was that we were in a culture totally unlike our own.... [I]n 1975 the communists put an end to our way of life. We lost everything – our families, our monks, our villages, our land, all our possessions. Everything. When we came to the United States, we couldn't put our old lives back together. We didn't even have the pieces.[93]

We may better understand the mental health challenges of refugees today. When large numbers of Cambodian refugees entered in the 1980s, however, the extent of the problem was not understood and mental health services were not readily provided.[94] To complicate matters, many refugees were reluctant to acknowledge depression to professionals or to discuss the past with their own children.[95]

Disruption of the Family

Refugee status itself can disturb the conventional family relationships and structures. Individual members negotiate new surroundings without familiar cultural cues.[96] The rates at which different family members adapt may be poles apart, placing strain on relationships and producing discord.[97]

Differences in English-speaking ability between parents and children have exacerbated the problem. Cambodians in the United States speak Khmer at home, and nearly three-fourths have trouble speaking English.[98] As in many newcomer families, parents cannot communicate with teachers and others in the neighborhood, so their children often serve as interpreters. This can be a role reversal challenge to the parents who are accustomed to full respect in the Khmer culture.[99] At the same time, while children adapt to the social settings of the school and neighborhood, many find it difficult to discuss these new surroundings with their parents.

[93] Id.
[95] Id.
[97] Id.
[99] Id.

[94] Id.
[96] Ko, *supra* note 88, at 24.
[98] Cahn and Stansell, *supra* note 83, at 5.

This challenge, grounded in differences in English literacy, disrupts the Cambodian family structure, and parents find it hard to enforce family traditions.[100]

Cultural Challenges to Parental Control

The new environment into which Cambodian refugees to the United States are thrust could not be more different than from where they came. Their family-oriented, Southeast Asian farming civilization was based on a "highly stratified social order."[101] Gender roles, deference to elders, and respect for parents were understood, and children accepted, without question, that they were permanently indebted to their parents.[102]

The world of the refugee family essentially has been "turned upside down," and many adults no longer work.[103] Southeast Asian homes are patriarchal, where the father is not to be challenged, and both parents are to be "respected and obeyed and not questioned."[104] Once in the United States, the father's authority is threatened. Dependent on public assistance, the father can lose face and position. The mother's authority suffers as well. "They don't have the power of experience anymore. The wisdom that they learned from their experiences doesn't fit into this culture."[105] The children are more adept at English, and the parents come to rely on them for everyday tasks, from grocery shopping to bill paying.[106] As the acculturation of the children progresses, the generation and culture gaps between children and parents grow. The urbanized child becomes "Americanized," in contrast to the "uneducated" refugee parents figuratively living in the rural past.[107] Thrown into this new environment, both children and parents are developing their own sense of culture within the context of U.S. culture.[108]

Cambodian refugee parents face huge challenges to raising their children in the United States. The trauma of fleeing persecution for all

[100] Id. at 5.   [101] Ko, *supra* note 88, at 26.

[102] Id.

[103] Alex Tizon, *A New World of Crime and Gangs – The Lure of the Streets Is Stealing away the Children of Southeast Asian Refugees*, SEATTLE TIMES, Feb. 8, 1994, at A1.

[104] Id. (citing Seattle University professor Lane Gerber, who volunteers at refugee clinic at Harborview Medical Center).

[105] Id.   [106] Id.

[107] Id.

[108] See Bill Ong Hing, *Refugee Policy and Cultural Identity: In the Voice of the Hmong and Iu Mien Young Adults*, 1 HASTINGS RACE AND POVERTY L. J. 111 (2003); Madhavi Sunder, *Cultural Dissent*, 54 STAN. L. REV. 495 (2002).

and the effects of PTSD on many, along with language challenges and poverty, make it very difficult for the parents to provide guidance for their children.[109] The parents have difficulties assimilating into U.S. life themselves, and concern for the social adjustment of their children takes a back seat.[110]

As with most immigrant and refugee children, Cambodian youngsters acculturate much more quickly than their adult counterparts.[111] As this "differential acculturation" gap grows, greater discord occurs as parents adhere to their native culture and the children gravitate toward the new.[112] Communication between parents and children decreases, and correspondingly, family bonds are weakened.[113] As relationships suffer, the child's self-esteem is challenged.[114] Many Cambodian refugee parents simply do not possess the child-rearing skills necessary to grapple with these new cultural issues.

Conflicts within families are all too familiar. As roles are reversed, children can use their English proficiency as an advantage over their limited-English-speaking parents. In one instance, a young man, who police picked up and drove home for criminal behavior, incredibly told his parents that the police chauffeured him home as a special prize for good performance in school.[115] A young girl's parents rewarded her with $10 for getting two As. Her proud mother was in for a surprise, however, when a community worker saw the report card and had to tell her the marks were for gym and art classes.[116] The daughter was actually flunking core subjects.[117] Disagreements or misunderstandings on matters such as American dating customs arise as well.[118]

---

[109] Cahn and Stansell, *supra* note 83, at 5.   [110] Id.

[111] Ko, *supra* note 88, at 29.   [112] Id.

[113] Id. at 39.   [114] Id.

[115] Joyce Riha Linik, *Catching Kids before They Fall, Northwest Regional Educational Laboratory,* at http://www.nwrel.org/nwedu/spring_99/text8.html.

[116] Id.   [117] Id.

[118] Id. One researcher who has examined crime among Southeast Asian refugees and other immigrants looks at it this way:

> [W]aves of youthful crime in immigrant groups emerge out of intergenerational conflict, which, due to the dynamics of migration, can sometimes emerge with unusual suddenness and intensity. Youthful crime emerges, in other words, not out of a particular culture group, but out of the type of parent-child relationship that tends to be created by the process of migration. There are two general principles potentially involved, both of which are related to the relationship between parents and youth:
>
> 1. Migrant groups inherently have unusual demographics, which, in turn, pattern social reproduction independent of culture. This happens because migrant groups are never cross sections of the sending [countries], but rather selected groups that emerge out of

Some children refuse or fail to understand the significance of the post-traumatic stress from which their parents suffer. One counselor sees the family breakdown and sees the problem all the time, as parents withdraw or act out from PTSD.[119] Unfortunately, "[t]heir children think they are wacky," he laments. "They don't want to be around them."[120]

Poverty

Cambodian refugees are poor. They earned $5,120 per person in 1990, compared to $14,143 for all Americans, and $18,709 for other Asian Americans.[121] A decade later, there was little improvement, as 37 percent of Cambodian households were making less than $12,000 a year.[122] Lacking higher valued human capital skills in the U.S. labor market, many adults had to take on more than one minimum-wage job, at the expense of time to supervise their children.[123] Socioeconomic and immigrant status often combine to exacerbate the problem of delinquency as parents work long hours and are thus unavailable to their children.[124] The limited English-speaking ability, financial pressures, and traumatic effect of war on parents add up to serious emotional separation in families. "[R]efugee youth may feel reluctant to burden mothers and fathers with problems that seem unimportant compared with their parents' need to make a living in a strange country, and to deal with a past filled with suffering that the children only dimly comprehend."[125]

In places like Chicago, many Cambodian professionals and merchants are able to move out of the inner city, but those who have not been financially successful remain mired in the refugee experience.[126] Many

the dynamics between the sending and receiving countries. These dynamics, particularly in an industrial society like the United States, are also patterned by the socioeconomic situations in which the new social locations will develop.

2. Migration implies the shedding of one set of preexisting social norms in exchange for another. This is never a smooth process, and it inevitably involves misinterpretations and misunderstandings about the bases for normative action on the part of both immigrants and the receiving community.

Waters, *supra* note 74, at 199–200.

[119] James Willwerth, *From Killing Fields to Mean Streets,* TIME, Nov. 18, 1991, at 103.

[120] Id. (citing Buddhist monk Benton Samana).

[121] Cahn and Stansell, *supra* note 83, at 5 (citing Office of Surgeon General, 1999).

[122] Id. (citing Khmer Health Advocates, 2002).

[123] Id. at 5 (citing Hyman et al., 2000).   [124] Ko, *supra* note 88, at 34.

[125] Cahn and Stansell, *supra* note 83, at 6 (citing Hyman et al., 2000).

[126] Stuart H. Isett, *From Killing Fields to Mean Streets,* WORLD PRESS REV., at 34, reprinted in BANKOK POST (Dec. 1994).

were farmers back home, with little formal education. Therefore, with limited skills, they became dependent on public assistance.[127] Those who did find work usually ended up in minimum-wage factory jobs, struggling to support their families.[128]

Low-Income Neighborhoods

Because of refugee status, the resettlement process, and poverty, most Cambodian refugees live in low-income neighborhoods.[129] Not surprisingly, the neighborhood environment has a great impact on how children develop, especially when the neighborhood is dangerous.[130] When danger lurks, seeking out a strategy that provides protection is natural.[131] The poverty rate among Southeast Asians is comparable to that of blacks and Latinos, and the rate for Cambodians is the lowest.[132] Some researchers have identified the connection between poverty and delinquency: "socioeconomic status is consequential for violent offending primarily because it affects the cultural contexts encountered by youths (e.g., family and peer contexts) and thus indirectly shapes the learning of cultural definitions about violent delinquency."[133]

Lower class youth are considered the most likely to hold attitudes that favor delinquency, because of the joint contributions of social stratification and culture.[134] For example, in Chicago, Cambodian youngsters attend Chicago's notoriously violent public schools, where shootings are common and metal detectors serve as "greeters" at school entrances.[135] On the streets, as in the case of Kim Ho Ma, young Cambodians have had to confront a culture of guns and street gangs, and many have opted to assimilate into that culture.[136] In Long Beach, California, many Cambodian children live in the central part of the city and "learn American ways by copying the actions of Latino and black gangs around them."[137]

---

[127] Id.

[128] Id.

[129] Tizon, *supra* note 103.

[130] Ko, *supra* note 88, at 18.

[131] Id.

[132] Id. at 34.

[133] Id. at 34–35 (citing K. Heimer, *Socioeconomic Status, Subcultural Definitions and Violent Delinquency*, 75 SOCIAL FORCES 799–833 (1997)).

[134] Id. at 34.

[135] Isett, *supra* note 126.

[136] Id.

[137] Daryl Kelley, *Families Agonize as Children Go Astray; Culture Shock Hits Asians Hard*, LA TIMES, June 27, 1987, Metro, part 2, at 6 (citing Mory Ouk, junior high school principal in Cambodia and immigrant counselor for Long Beach Unified School District).

Poor Academic Performance

Youngsters who get bad grades, who are unenthusiastic about school, and who are truant are more likely to show signs of delinquency.[138] Little formal education was afforded to refugee children while they were in the camps. After arriving in the United States, few were provided with bilingual education or ESL classes in school.[139] Many Cambodian youth simply did not have happy experiences in school or in other social environments because they looked and sounded "foreign."[140] In addition, parents were clueless as to their children's experiences.[141] Kim Ho Ma put it this way:

> Many of the Asian youths was [sic] looking for a place of acceptance. A lot was [sic] very young, some was [sic] in their early teens, they had no understanding of their culture. Many came from poor living conditions and most was [sic] undereducated. Gangster life was a chance for them to build status in post modern America. . . . I spoke some English but not good enough, so I would get teased at school. Most of us got mocked for being different, taunted for being poor, and battered for being foreign. . . . We saw the gang as a congregation for strength and unity . . . there was no more intimidation at school.[142]

Youngsters from several groups say they join gangs because the routine of school, homework, and family is boring.[143] At refugee camps, Southeast Asian children were fortunate if any formal education was offered, putting them behind for their age when they entered the United States. Little wonder that one Cambodian girl would declare, "I'm lost," as her mother tried to make ends meet.[144] Many parents in that situation have not learned how to counsel their children.[145]

School officials are not always helpful. Classroom placement level is often determined without adequate consideration of English ability.[146] Many refugee children who may have done well academically in their native country perform poorly here.[147] As they lose their confidence and self-esteem, they start to cut class or even drop out.[148] Some turn to crime.

---

[138] Ko, *supra* note 88, at 85.
[140] Id.
[142] Id. at 7.
[143] Lena H. Sun, *For Area Cambodians, A Conflict between Young and Old*, WASHINGTON POST, Feb. 19, 1995, at A01.
[144] Long, *supra* note 76, at 94.
[146] Id. at 95.
[148] Id.

[139] Cahn and Stansell, *supra* note 83, at 6.
[141] Id.

[145] Id.
[147] Id.

The Gang as Family

The comradery of gangs offers a surrogate family for many Cambodian youngsters.[149] As many children reject their parents' culture but also do not find themselves a part of the American culture, they may become disillusioned.[150] They search for acceptance and often find a sense of common understanding with their peers who are experiencing similar feelings of ostracism from mainstream and Cambodian culture.[151] Once they find a place where they have a sense of belonging or feel comfortable, they may assume the ethics of their friends, rather than those of their elders.[152] Sometimes those values are not good and can lead to delinquency.[153] For many Cambodian teens, the popularity of gangs is a response to feeling isolated from their families as well as from their peers of other backgrounds:

> The gangs are mostly a way for us to be with other people who can understand, who have the same kind of background. Our families are pretty strict, so maybe some of the kids go wild when they get old enough to get out of the house. . . . Being in a gang was a way to feel that I wasn't so different from other kids in school. I never fit in at all. I think it was because I was so old when I got here [about ten years old]. . . . Maybe because we lived in too many different places – Thailand, Chicago, then Boston, then Providence – it didn't feel like home until I found other Cambodian kids and we just stuck together.[154]

Thus, for many kids, gangs provide a sort of family structure, a place to fit in.[155] The attraction of the "structure" that the gang offers is critical for the members, because they cannot find that in the families who remain traumatized by the killing fields.[156] These gangs are not motivated by economic gain; they come together for social reasons.[157] As one young gang member put it:

> [Why did I join a gang?] Everybody looks at us as "other." Our parents don't understand us. So where do we feel like we belong? With our friends. . . . Parents don't understand us. The world doesn't understand our parents. Everybody else seems to get attention. Nobody pays attention but our friends.[158]

---

[149] Ko, *supra* note 88, at 37–38.
[151] Id.
[153] Id.
[155] Linik, *supra* note 115.
[157] Sun, *supra* note 143.

[150] Id.
[152] Id.
[154] Cahn and Stansell, *supra* note 83, at 7.
[156] Mydans, *supra* note 89.
[158] Long, *supra* note 76, at 97.

The Gang as Protection

Often, young Cambodians cite the need for protection as a reason for joining gangs. For some in Southern California, that may have been a logical step. "You land in a gang neighborhood, it might seem natural to form a militia to defend yourself," explains Steve Valdivia, director of LA County's Community Youth Gang Services Project.[159] Street gangs throughout the state mimicked the Latino "cholo" (lowlife) styles.[160] Hassled by the East Side Longos, Cambodians responded with gangs named Tiny Rascals and Asian Boyz, imitating their enemies.[161] Protection is what motivated seventeen-year-old David Chum to hook up with the Asian Boyz: "On my first day of school I got beat up. I had to go and get an X-ray, and when I went back to school I got beat up again. So I joined a gang."[162] Joining for protection is common, according to social workers.[163] As early as 1981, Cambodian teenagers had formed a gang, the Black Cambodian Killers, or BCK.[164] One of the first gang members was an uncle of Gino's who helped carry him as an infant during their escape from Cambodia. "I joined the BCK to protect myself and my people," he says. "Others were fighting with us, and we fought back. In 1982, we had 20 people – they were my friends, and we were alone."[165]

Rehabilitation over Deportation of Immigrants

The deportation of convicted lawful permanent residents and refugees who entered as infants and toddlers implicates the general problem of our criminal justice system and resettlement/integration efforts.

Lock Them Up and Throw Away the Key

The United States chooses punishment through prisons as a means to control the social crisis of violence. Prisons are our substitute for more constructive and effective social policies. "A growing prison system was what we had instead of an antipoverty policy, instead of an employment policy, instead of a comprehensive drug-treatment or mental health policy."[166] The complex fear of crime leads the public and legislatures to call

---

[159] Willwerth, *supra* note 119.
[160] Id.
[161] Id.
[162] Mydans, *supra* note 89.
[163] Id.
[164] Isett, *supra* note 126.
[165] Id.
[166] Elliott Currie, CRIME AND PUNISHMENT IN AMERICA (1998).

for "tough" punishments. The basic ideology toward criminal justice in the United States rests on the erroneous belief that violent crime continues because of a "criminal justice system [that] is far too lenient with criminals."[167] Fear of violence is normal, and a civilized society should take the necessary precautions to implement a criminal justice system that protect its citizens and maintains social order. Yet, even with such a narrow-minded approach to violence and crime, the United States remains the most violent advanced industrial society.[168]

"We have been engaged in an experiment, testing the degree to which a modern industrial society can maintain public order through the threat of punishment."[169] In the year 2000, twenty-two states and the federal prison system operated at 100 percent or more of their highest capacity.[170] A key contributing factor is the tremendous growth of private prisons. According to the Department of Justice, privately operated facilities retain 5.5 percent of all state prisoners and 2.5 percent of all federal prisoners.[171] Many states continue spending their limited budgets on prisons rather than education. Job training and education programs are not available to inmates, because the American public resists an increase to the billions of dollars already spent annually on corrections. Prevailing punitive ideology applauds harsh prison conditions, mistakenly believing that individuals convicted and sentenced for crimes do not deserve the benefits of rehabilitation.[172] As a result, inmates receive little to no vocational training, education, substance abuse treatment, or counseling.

Over the past twenty-five years, prison populations grew 377 percent and prison budgets have grown 600 percent.[173] Recidivism is still a key issue, continuing to drive the explosion of the prison population and budget.[174] In the past three years, nationwide recidivism rates remain at approximately 62 percent to 65 percent.[175] The largest contributing factor to the cycle of recidivism is untreated substance addiction and abuse.[176] "It is foolish not to treat the addicted criminals while you have

---

[167] Id. at 4.   [168] Id. at 3.

[169] Id. at 21.

[170] Human Rights Watch, *U.S. Prisons*, at http://www.hrw.org/prisons/united_states.html.
[171] Id.   [172] Id.

[173] BC & A International, *The Economic and Social Burden with the Current Prison-Drug Addiction Cycle of Failure: A Review of Government Findings* 1 (Aug. 2003), at http://www.penalrehab.org/whitepapers/bcanda/PrisonDrug_BCandAInt.pdf.
[174] Id.   [175] Id.

[176] Id.

them under your control – or they will be back," said Dr. Alan Leshner, former director of the National Institute on Drug Abuse.[177] As a result of unanswered issues tying recidivism and drugs afflicting our criminal justice system, the United States pours approximately $95 billion a year into a recycling hole.[178] Only a small fraction of the addicted correctional population undergoes any kind of substance abuse treatment while incarcerated.[179] Fewer than 7 percent of these individuals receive formalized treatment, which provides some form of credential or counseling.[180] More somber, only 3.5 percent of the incarcerated with substance addictions break the cycle and are rehabilitated through effective treatment.[181]

In 2000, more than twenty thousand prisoners were confined to special super-maximum-security facilities.[182] Prolonged supermax confinement of prisoners is justified in an effort to increase control and safety. The objective is to confine the "most dangerous or disruptive inmates in facilities designed specifically for that purpose," believing this will increase safety and security.[183] However, these same goals could be attained by reducing the size of prisons and providing additional services and programs for prisoners with the cost savings from fewer or smaller prisons to help decrease the rate of recidivism.

Supermax prisoners spend twenty-three hours a day locked in small cells.[184] A couple times a week, prisoners are allowed to shower and solitary exercise.[185] Access to educational or recreational activities is almost nonexistent. The absence of social interaction and mental stimulus is emotionally, physically, and psychologically destructive.[186] Those in favor of supermax prisons stress that "exploding prison populations, meager budgets, and punitive political climates overwhelm the ability of corrections professionals to operate safe, secure and humane facilities."[187]

More than 100,000 children in the United States are confined in juvenile facilities. Rather than enter an environment of rehabilitation and

---

[177] Id.   [178] Id.
[179] BC & A International *supra* note 173, at 2.
[180] Id.   [181] Id.
[182] Human Rights Watch, *U.S. Prisons, supra* note 170.
[183] Id.   [184] Id.
[185] Id.
[186] Human Rights Watch, *Out of Sight: Super-Maximum Security Confinement in the United States* (2000), at http://hrw.org/reports/2000/supermax/Sprmx002.htm# P54_4600.
[187] Id.

counseling, these youth often experience abuse and neglect.[188] Increasingly, children are tried as adults. California adopted a measure that made transferring juveniles to the adult system mandatory in some cases, versus allowing the process only after a judicial hearing.[189] In addition, minority youth are more likely to end up in adult court. In California, for example, children of color are charged with violent crimes three times more than white children and are seven times more likely to be sentenced to prison when tried as adults.[190]

We are caught in an endless cycle of destruction and oppression. It begins with limited resources and budgets diverted to the correctional system; this aggravates the deterioration of troubled neighborhoods and decreases the economic opportunities for low-income individuals. High levels of crime in the United States remain steady despite enormous increases in incarceration, thus creating calls for more of the same "tough" on crime response.[191]

The myth of America's leniency on crime is perpetuated by misleading facts spread to the public by politicians and tough-on-crime advocates.[192] We are led to believe that the most violent crimes go unpunished, that convicted offenders are subject to shockingly short sentences, or that most violent criminals roam our streets on parole or probation.[193] The Council on Crime in America argues "that America needs to put more violent and repeat criminals, adult and juvenile, behind bars longer."[194] But in fact, the majority of crimes are not serious. Over half the crimes committed are "simple assaults without injury."[195] Furthermore, the majority of crimes do not ever enter the criminal justice system.[196]

The more fitting question is how many violent offenders are we catching and putting behind bars. California's three-strikes law, targeted at low-income property offenders and drug offenders, resulted in a higher number of people sentenced to prison.[197] However, the number of *violent* offenders sentenced is still relatively low. The three-strikes law mostly affects repeat offenders of nonviolent crimes. Thus, the real issue is whether we are allowing the wrong people to remain free, not whether we need to lock up more.

---

[188] Human Rights Watch, *U.S. Prisons, supra* note 170.
[189] Id.
[190] Id.
[191] Id. at 34.
[192] Id. at 39.
[193] Id.
[194] Id.
[195] Id. at 40.
[196] Id. at 41.
[197] Id. at 48.

Proponents of the prison "works" ideology want the public to believe that prisons are the *most* effective way to control crime.[198] However, individuals committing less serious crime are incarcerated for longer sentences. Again, the critical issue is whether the most effective way to cut crime is by putting more people in prison.[199] The choice is between prevention and strategic social investment versus simply increasing incarceration. An analogy using hospitals helps to illustrate the short-sightedness of the incarceration-only approach. Hospitals work wonders for treating existing diseases and illnesses. However, the services provided by hospitals cannot substitute for preventative measures over the long term. Relying solely on admitting sick people to hospitals ignores the real causes of the problem. Similarly, incarcerating more people every year, without an effort to address the real causes of the problem, leads nowhere.

Of course, arguing that prevention is better than incarceration is not enough. The role of rehabilitation in our current criminal justice system is critical but challenging given the multidimensional issues of crime, recidivism, and the failures of prison administration. But shifting the focus of criminal justice back to rehabilitation may provide a chance to regain control of a system gone awry. Rehabilitation gives inmates an opportunity to use their time in prison to better themselves. Thousands of inmates are wasting away mentally, emotionally, and psychologically. Rather than being educated in vocational training or through traditional university systems, today inmates receive little to no chance at preparing themselves to rejoin society upon release. Rather than receiving treatment for drug and alcohol abuse, inmates develop long-term addictions to harder drugs such as methamphetamine and heroin, worsening an already bad addiction.

In addition to revisions to the current criminal justice approach, when it comes to immigrants and refugees, the government's efforts at resettlement and integration need to be reexamined as well.

Government's Failure in Resettling

The environment in which many immigrants and refugees land can be challenging. The vast majority of refugees begin as public assistance recipients, mired in poverty, while many immigrants settle for low-wage

[198] Id. at 55.　　　　　　　[199] Id. at 64.

employment. Resettlement efforts have led to tough inner-city living environments for many, where they are surrounded by urban crime and gang activity. The resulting socioeconomic conditions for these immigrants and refugees explain much of the criminal activity that has created the pool of potential deportees.

In spite of what was and remains readily apparent, U.S. resettlement and integration efforts do not provide immigrant and refugee parents and communities with adequate tools or resources to address the challenges of parenting, guidance, and mentoring that youngsters need in what is for many a radically different cultural environment. Old country approaches and mechanisms fail or cannot be adapted, especially given the emotional, social, and economic challenges parents face. During the acculturation process, their initial needs may be addressed. For example, obtaining adequate housing and transportation is challenging, but most are able to meet those needs. But while basic survival needs may be addressed during the first period of acculturation, long-term issues are not. Stress on family relationships and mental health problems, especially among refugees, present special challenges.[200]

No government entity – not even the U.S. Office of Refugee Resettlement – provides much funding for newcomer programs that meet the needs for long-term parenting skills or support that would address the conditions that lead to criminality. The main purpose of the refugee resettlement program is to help refugees become employed and self-sufficient as soon as possible after their arrival in the United States.[201] Typically, the office helps to establish programs for job development and microenterprise development, not general social adjustment.[202]

---

[200] Id.

[201] Refugee Resettlement Program, Office of Refugee Resettlement, Administration for Children and Families, U.S. Department of Health and Human Services, 1992 ANNUAL REPORT TO CONGRESS 63 (1993).

[202] The vision from the director of the Office of Refugee Resettlement in 1993 is illustrative:

> The first year in this country defines a refugee's future experience; attaining employment as soon as possible following arrival in the U.S. is the best way to achieve stable, ongoing attachment to the labor force, to improve English language proficiency, and to gain familiarity with American customs and values. The strength of the family and the dignity of the parent role model within the family hinge upon a family's economic independence from public assistance. The growth and development of refugee communities, as well as communities as a whole, depend upon individual and family productivity.

Refugee Resettlement Program, Office of Refugee Resettlement, Administration for Children and Families, U.S. Department of Health and Human Services, 1993 ANNUAL

In spite of the failure of U.S. resettlement and integration processes, the response to lawful immigrant and refugee criminality is, essentially, "one strike and you're out." The result recalls Sir Thomas More's criticism of the English justice system of the 1500s, especially the law that subjected thieves to the death penalty, when he wrote:

> For if you suffer your people to be ill educated, and their manners to be corrupted from their infancy, and then punish them for those crimes to which their first education disposed of them, what else is to be concluded from this, but that you first made thieves and then punish them?[203]

In essence, the resettlement process has set up low-income immigrants and refugees to fail, and part of that failure is manifested in the relatively high incidence of criminality in the community. Furthermore, the process, which provides minimal long-term adjustment tools to newcomer families, is evidence of bad faith. Serious questions of morality are raised when we understand that the United States has set up an economic and social system that attracts low-income immigrants and, in some parts of the world, contributes to the creation of refugees.

Without a long-term view toward adjustment, the U.S. integration and resettlement efforts have neglected a responsibility that includes helping newcomers assimilate. Settling in a completely foreign environment, many face economic challenges (for some, poverty) and cultural barriers while suffering stress. Given little institutional support, the families essentially were left to fend for themselves in a strange new land. Those in low-income neighborhoods face a battleground for survival.

Even when criminality and its causes have become apparent, nothing is done to address the root causes; intervention is not provided in an attempt to break the cycle for the next group or generation of low-income immigrants and refugees. The communities are left to fend for themselves, as immigrants continue to settle in (and refugees are placed in) neighborhoods where they are least likely to get help. Instead, the government "solution" to the criminal problem is left to the deportation process. After we attract low-income workers and welcome refugees (for whom we bear

---

REPORT TO CONGRESS 67–68 (1993). One Office of Refugee Resettlement–funded program that does provide some assistance for parenting issues with a goal of decreasing the number of refugee youth joining gangs is the Outreach to New Americans program of the National Crime Prevention Council. See POWERFUL PARTNERSHIPS, at vi, 5 (1998).

[203] Thomas More, UTOPIA (1516), at http://oregonstate.edu/instruct/phl302/texts/more/utopia-contents.html.

some responsibility), we have a responsibility to ensure that they receive the assistance that they need to find their place here. If they or their children cannot succeed at that, then it is we who have failed and must be held accountable.

Rethinking Deportation

The removal of low-income immigrants and refugees who have committed crimes challenges us to rethink the purpose of deportation. On the one hand, you have the sentiment reflected in the statement of federal immigration official spokesperson Sharon Rummery: "If you haven't become a citizen, you are here as a privilege. And, if you commit a crime, you lose that privilege," and "[t]hese are people who have been convicted of serious crimes."[204] This hard line is reflected by a chief author of the 1996 reforms, Congressman Lamar Smith: "In 1996, Congress intended that all noncitizens who committed serious crimes should be deported. We should not give criminals who are not U.S. citizens more opportunities to further terrorize our communities."[205]

On the other hand, Cambodian refugee leaders like Meyer Kith argue: "[Deportation] is unfair to [the] Cambodian community. [Most of the] returnees are young and they [grew] up in [the United States]. This is not a Cambodian problem. It is a failure of the U.S. system. . . . To dump their problems back to Cambodia will not solve the problem."[206]

Irrespective of whether deportation or removal is punishment for the purpose of invoking the Eighth Amendment's cruel and unusual punishment prohibition[207] or for seeking aspects of procedural due process that

---

[204] Swilley, *supra* note 65.

[205] Randall Richard, *Deporting Controversy – No Second Chance: Jailed at 17, He Can Never Return to America*, SACRAMENTO GAZETTE, Oct. 31, 2003, at 1.

[206] E-mail from Meyer Kith, Bilingual Homeownership Project Coordinator, International District Housing Alliance, to Bill Ong Hing, Professor of Law and Asian American Studies, University of California, Davis (Oct. 29, 2003) (on file with author).

[207] Courts have consistently rejected assertions that deportation constitutes cruel and unusual punishment under the Eighth Amendment, on the grounds that deportation is civil, rather than criminal, in nature. See, for example, *Bassett v. INS*, 581 F.2d 1385 (10th Cir. 1978); *Chabolla Delgado v. INS*, 384 F.2d 360 (9th Cir. 1967); *Santelises v. INS*, 491 F.2d 1254 (2d Cir. 1974). In one instance, a federal district court held that the deportation of a young man, based upon the sale of three marijuana cigarettes to a former roommate, violated the Eight Amendment. However, the Seventh Circuit Court of Appeals quickly overturned that decision. See *Lieggi v. INS*, 389 F. Supp. 12, 20–21 (N.D. Ill. 1975), rev'd, 529 F.2d 530 (7th Cir. 1976).

attach to criminal proceedings,[208] we know that deportation results in banishment, the loss of "all that makes life worth living."[209] Removal is a "life sentence of exile from what has become home."[210] After 1996, the current statute provides no realistic relief for long-term lawful residents or refugees who have committed aggravated felonies.

The tension between the Rummery/Smith view that those who commit crimes must be deported and the Kith perspective that removal is unjust because the U.S. system has failed is a debate about whether justice is served. The concern about being too soft on immigrants who have committed serious criminal offenses, which led to the termination of Section 212(c) relief for aggravated felons, is a manifestation of the reformers' sense of making sure that justice is served.[211] Of course, justice is a concept that can be pondered through a range of meanings and definitions. An "antiseptic" construction of justice would emphasize "objectivity, impartiality, and the fair application of rules," while a "passionate" construction would emphasize "love, compassion and the vindication of the weak."[212] But, shouldn't justice combine both objective and compassionate qualities?

The "icon" of criminal justice, the statue of Justicia, symbolizes the antiseptic vision of justice.[213] Blindfolded, armed with sword, and balancing her scales, she symbolizes "neutrality" and "impartiality."[214] One could argue that, in theory, this antiseptic vision requires that the state and the judge "must always act rationally" and never "show mercy," because being merciful is not rational, as it allows individuals to be "specially treated."[215] Uniformity is the goal of this antiseptic vision of justice.[216]

---

[208] See Robert Pauw, *A New Look at Deportation as Punishment: Why at Least Some of the Constitution's Criminal Procedure Protections Must Apply*, 52 ADMIN. L. REV. 305, 337–345 (2000).

[209] *Ng Fung Ho v. White*, 259 U.S. 276, 284 (1922).

[210] *Jordan v. De George*, 341 U.S. 223, 243 (1951) (Jackson, J., dissenting).

[211] Congressman Smith, who was behind the 1996 reforms, acknowledged that deportation may not always be appropriate. But he was concerned with a large number of "hardened criminal" aliens who were "still slipping through the cracks" and not being deported. See Anthony Lewis, *Cases that Cry Out*, NY TIMES, Mar. 18, 2000, at A15.

[212] Jonathan Burnside, *Tension and Tradition in the Pursuit of Justice*, RELATIONAL JUSTICE: REPAIRING THE BREACH 42, 42–43 (Jonathan Burnside and Nicola Baker eds., 1994).

[213] Id. at 43.

[214] Id.

[215] Id. at 44.

[216] Id.

Mandatory minimum federal sentencing guidelines and three-strikes legislation are examples of this antiseptic uniformity. Strict formulas and sentencing grids are employed in the interest of "consistency."[217] The focus is on process, rather than on the meaning of the final results.[218]

An approach that joins the antiseptic vision with elements of compassion and understanding is essential. We need aspects of both approaches to achieve a sense of "social well-being."[219] Certainly, our aim is for the state to behave rationally and to be accountable for its actions toward the people over whom it has power.[220] Taking into account the individual features of particular cases and responding accordingly, however, is an important quality of a civil society. Great Britain's move to eliminate its mandatory life sentence for murder is a good example: A wide range of cases had been included in the common-law definition of murder, from "mercy killings" to abused wives who were provoked to premeditated murder.[221] Greater flexibility and discretion were needed to respond to this variance.[222]

The criticism of mandatory sentencing in the United States is also centered on its "tendency to negate the value of individualized justice."[223] These sentencing schemes take discretion out of the hands of trial judges, who would otherwise be able to assess defendants face to face; instead, the legislature makes a blanket decision.[224] The problem is that the legislature's judgment simply cannot differentiate between defendants who continue to pose a threat and those who might not.[225] To make matters worse, that legislative judgment likely is skewed by a "few highly publicized offenses" or outrage against crime in general.[226] In effect, an across-the-board regime of "majoritarian oppression" is established where some are appropriately punished at the expense of others who are overly punished.[227]

As the argument goes, more discretionary, indeterminate sentencing is preferred because

> the judiciary is in a superior position to the legislature to act as sentencer because its proximity to the offender allows for the "carefully individualized, retrospective evaluation of the offense and the offender" that is

---

[217] Id.

[218] Id. at 42–43.

[219] Id.

[220] Id.

[221] Id.

[222] Id.

[223] Kristin K. Sauer, *Informed Conviction: Instructing the Jury about Mandatory Sentencing Consequences*, 95 COLUM. L. REV. 1232, 1239 (1995).

[224] Id. at 1240.

[225] Id.

[226] Id. at 1240–1241.

[227] Id.

necessary to achieve equity in sentencing. Furthermore, where the judge has sentencing discretion, she can act as a check on possible legislative excesses in fixing penalties.[228]

So Justicia, as a symbol of justice, is insufficient. Justice is not simply about meeting the elements of procedural due process.[229] Arguably, deportable aggravated felons are not even given due process because they are effectively foreclosed from introducing evidence of their rehabilitation. Justice is about wanting to live in strong and meaningful relationships and, as the ancient Greeks put it, "to bring order into our cities and create a bond of friendship of union."[230] In the case of immigrants, we should be committed to bringing them into our American family. As part of that process, if they become caught up in the justice system, that system ought to be designed in a way that continues the actualization of their incorporation into society rather than giving up on them. The challenge is to become more committed in our investigation of how to best bring them into our family, indeed "to maintain a dialectic between antiseptic and passionate constructions of justice."[231]

Given the adjustment challenges that immigrant and refugee families confront, the relationship between the individuals facing deportation and their families and new communities should be given greater attention. Justice should not be approached as simply a "cold virtue" that calls for "*dispassionate* judgment."[232] Rather, "doing justice" is very much about building and strengthening relationships between individuals and their communities, which connotes the "language of emotion, care, [and] affective ties."[233]

Make no mistake. In the context of deportable immigrants, the more passionate view of justice could lead to an approach that emphasizes

---

[228] Id. at 1241. Many of those who support the move toward a more predictable, determinate system, including the U.S. Sentencing Commission, have nevertheless assailed mandatory sentences as too inflexible to distinguish between offenders and thereby achieve just punishment. See U.S. Sentencing Commission, SPECIAL REPORT TO THE CONGRESS: MANDATORY MINIMUM PENALTIES IN THE FEDERAL CRIMINAL JUSTICE SYSTEM 2634 (1991), at http://www.ussc.gov/r_congress/MANMIN.pdf (criticizing mandatory sentences as inflexible and overinclusive and maintaining that a guided sentencing system can achieve the same goals with more just results).

[229] Burnside, *supra* note 212, at 45. [230] Id.

[231] Id.

[232] Anthony Bottoms, *Avoiding Injustice, Promoting Legitimacy and Relationships*, RELATIONAL JUSTICE: REPAIRING THE BREACH 53, 53 (Jonathan Burnside and Nicola Baker eds., 1994).

[233] Id.

mutual responsibility between the state and the individual, rather than simply the right of the individual to remain free from monitoring by immigration officials. This is a rejection of a concept of liberalism that has come to rely on a belief in "freedom of the individual from arbitrary external authority," where the individual is the "source of his or her own moral values" – a concept that has "shaped the Western world over the past several hundred years."[234] For immigrant adjustment in the United States, liberalism's focus on the individual, at the expense of relationships that can nurture human well-being, is misplaced. Describing liberalism as a system that promotes a view that "people do not need other people," where "all they need is a system of rules that will constitute procedures for resolving disputes as they pursue their various interests," may be an over-statement.[235] Liberal visions of justice, however, definitely have a strong bias toward individualist values.[236]

The weakness of the liberal approach, especially in the refugee con-text, is its emphasis on the individual's autonomy "at the expense of the communal relationships."[237] The family and community, however, tradi-tionally are big parts of Cambodian and Mexican cultures, for example, as well as what we aspire American society to reflect. People need more than a system of rules. We need a tradition of "historical bonding and sense of continuity" as part of our approach to justice.[238] That requires a community-oriented approach. Community building and the tools for fostering relationships in a radically different culture have been missing from the immigrant and refugee resettlement process for many newcom-ers. Presenting alternatives to deportation offers one method to begin providing the ability to reconnect.

Alternatives to Deportation

The current deportation process should include alternatives to auto-matic removal from the United States. Rehabilitation of individuals with criminal convictions was a critical issue in Section 212(c). Immigration judges were able to consider the testimony of friends, family, employers, probation officers, and counselors to decide if the person had sufficiently rehabilitated his or her life. Naturally an individual's crime, time spent

---

[234] Burnside, *supra* note 212, at 47.
[236] Id.
[238] Id. at 48–50.

[235] Id. at 47.
[237] Id. at 48.

in prison, current living situation, character, family support, employment, and personal efforts at rehabilitation came into consideration. Unlike their U.S. citizen counterparts, noncitizens face double punishment for their crimes. First, they must complete their sentence, and second, they are exiled from their home and family. Deportation is the most final and permanent punishment an individual can face.

To implement a more compassionate removal process, space should be provided, at the very least, for the voice of the respondent and his or her family and community to be heard. The reinstatement of Section 212(c)–type relief is a starting place.[239] In this way, the immigration judge, who is in a good position to assess the individual facts, can consider evidence of rehabilitation, remorse, family support, and prospects for the future.[240]

Those who supported eliminating Section 212(c) relief for aggravated felons in 1996 were frustrated with the way in which immigration judges exercised discretionary relief.[241] "The per se bar for some felons can be seen as a legislative attempt to control the exercise of discretion by saying that no circumstances could justify relief from deportation when the crime is one classified as an 'aggravated felony.'"[242] Much of that concern was overblown. In fact, obtaining Section 212(c) relief was not automatic.[243] Furthermore, immigration judges who granted Section 212(c) relief routinely warned respondents that if they recidivated, the exercise of favorable discretion again in the future was unlikely and deportation would be ordered.

---

[239] An argument might be made that the starting point in the context of Cambodian refugees is to altogether bar deportation of anyone who entered the United States as an infant or young child. One proposal for a "youth bar" to removal is the following:

> As a matter of public policy, any individual who fled their homeland for fear of persecution while under the age of six and was later admitted to the United States as a refugee or parolee or who was granted asylum shall be insulated from deportation proceedings. The reasoning behind the youth bar is that for all intents and purposes, such individuals no longer have attachments to their homelands. Their subsequent behavior and lifestyles purely are the product of refugee experiences and life in the United States.

Bill Ong Hing, *Legislative Proposals for a CARE Act* (July 21, 2003) (on file with author).

[240] See *supra* notes 27–42 and accompanying text.

[241] Nancy Morawetz, *Rethinking Retroactive Deportation Laws and the Due Process Clause*, 73 N.Y.U. L. REV. 97, 110–111 (1998) (citing *Mojica v. Reno*, 970 F. Supp. 120, 178 (E.D.N.Y. 1997)).

[242] Id. at 157.

[243] See *supra* notes 27–52 and accompanying text.

Yet, the concern that opponents of Section 212(c) relief had, that immigration judges were too lenient, should make us wonder if some other options ought to be available to immigration judges. Under the pre-1996 framework, the judge handling the case of a long-term resident (at least seven years) who was convicted of an aggravated felony had two choices: to deport or to grant Section 212(c) relief.[244] In either scenario, the respondent had no further contact with government officials after the order was enforced. One wonders whether something short of deportation could be created that would address concerns raised by both the proponents and opponents of deportation.

Given the special challenges faced by groups such as Cambodian refugees and other low-income immigrants, a system that adopts a rehabilitative approach to justice might be most appropriate. A relationship-building theme ought to be central to that approach, because their children need assistance with relationship-building in the family and with community.[245] What some term relational justice[246] – with the goal of

---

[244] When I handled Section 212(c) cases, both as a legal services attorney and in conjunction with law school clinical programs, occasionally judges who were not happy with these two extreme options would create an in-between option. They would do so by taking some evidence at an initial hearing and then later continuing the matter for several months (sometimes for more than a year) until eventually holding a final hearing. That way, the judge created an informal probationary period, during which time he could get a sense of how the respondent would behave. The experience of other immigration attorneys was similar:

> The award of a [212(c)] waiver depended not only on the nature of the criminal conduct, but also on the immigrant's life after committing the crime. Like a parole board, the immigration judge would look at whether the individual had genuinely rehabilitated. As in the case of an inmate who will face a parole board, the immigrant could conform his or her conduct to the expectations of the reviewing body. But unlike in the parole board context, where reviews take place during the course of a sentence, the waiver of deportation process could also serve as a forum for considering the long term record of those persons against whom deportation proceedings were initiated years after they had committed their crimes and served any criminal sentences. This waiver process protected the interests of the immigrant who may have built a life of work, family, and community based on the understanding that his or her past conviction would not lead to deportation. It also protected the interests of all of those whose lives were intertwined with that of the immigrant, including family members, employers, and the employees of immigrants who operated businesses. In practice, approximately half of the long time permanent residents who sought relief from deportation were granted such relief.

Morawetz, *supra* note 241.

[245] See *supra* notes 76–165 and accompanying text (discussing why youth turn to crime in the Cambodian community).

[246] See Burnside, *supra* note 212, at 42.

avoiding injustice and promoting legitimacy and good relationships – makes a good deal of sense as a set of guiding principles for the removal process. This set of principles is capable of being translated into practice. Experts in relational justice may approach criminal justice from diverse backgrounds and philosophies. They share an understanding, however, that problems result from relationships that have failed "between individuals, between individuals and institutions, and between individuals and communities" and that societal justice is all about repairing those relationships.[247]

A relational or restorative approach is premised on the goal of rehabilitating the individual, sometimes using group therapy, counseling, and even job training.[248] Studies have demonstrated that although socioeconomic factors such as poverty may lead to crime, families, schools, and "informal social bonds" could play important roles in changing individual paths:

> Consistent with a sociological theory of adult development and informal social control, . . . we found that job stability and marital attachment in adulthood were significantly related to changes in adult crime – the stronger the adult ties to work and family, the less crime and deviance occurred. . . . Despite differences in early childhood experiences, adult social bonds to work and family had similar consequences for the life trajectories of the 500 [identified juvenile] delinquents and 500 controls [i.e., non-delinquents in adolescence]. In fact, the parameter estimates of informal social control were at times nearly identical across the two groups.[249]

Focusing on restoring relationships apparently is time well spent in terms of reducing recidivism.

In contrast to the incapacitation view of justice as simply an "instrument of social control for protecting the innocent from the guilty," relational justice is premised on a belief that individuals are capable of change:

> to improve if they are given guidance, help and encouragement; to be damaged if they are abused or humiliated. It emphasizes respect for human dignity and personal identity. It looks more toward putting things right for the future and to make things whole than to punishing the past (although the latter may sometimes be part of the former).[250]

[247] David Faulkner, *Relational Justice: A Dynamic for Reform*, RELATIONAL JUSTICE: REPAIRING THE BREACH 159 (Jonathan Burnside and Nicola Baker eds., 1994).

[248] Bottoms, *supra* note 232, at 54 (internal citations omitted).

[249] Id. at 63 (internal citations omitted).   [250] Faulkner, *supra* note 247, at 160–161.

This philosophy seems quite relevant in the deportation context, where the respondent has already served and completed a sentence for the criminal offense. The deportation setting is all about the future. That is where guidance and encouragement to become reincorporated into the community makes so much sense.

Relational justice recognizes that conventional criminal justice institutions (i.e., courts, police, probation departments, community agencies), who, we hope, would understand the approach, are not solely responsible. "Informal networks," including family, friends, neighbors, employers, and perhaps even victims, must step up to make the process work.[251]

Proponents of relational justice point to an additional set of values that needs to be engrained in the system if it is to work properly:

> [A]ll those involved in the criminal justice process should treat people with whom they come into contact – in whatever situation or capacity – with courtesy, dignity and respect. This may seem obvious, but it is all too easily overlooked in practice. It requires people to be prepared to stop and listen, to answer questions and hear arguments or complaints, and to give reasons for decisions. . . . It seeks to preserve a sense of being valued as a human being, and of some hope for the future, even if the person has done something dreadfully wrong. . . . It tries to respond not only to situations as they present themselves, but also to look for unspoken signs that a person may need an explanation or reassurance, and to remember those who may be worrying unnoticed or unseen.[252]

The current removal process for aggravated felons who have grown up in the United States contains none of these components or values. Relief is altogether foreclosed for them. Information on their lives, their families, their community, and their rehabilitation is deemed irrelevant. The immigration laws have made deportation an extension of the criminal justice process.

Although a rehabilitative approach to deportable immigrants and refugees should inspire new, creative options, the criminal justice system itself provides some examples that might be considered. Some standard options are available prior to trial, while others may be considered after a finding of guilt. Consider the use of probation office reports and recommendations, pretrial diversion programs, group therapy, anger

---

[251] Id. at 162. [252] Id. at 162–163.

management, drug rehabilitation programs, and community service options. Some jurisdictions have adopted restorative justice or relational justice programs that have an underlying premise that may be particularly appropriate to consider as an alternative to the deportation of noncitizens. If one assumes that an immigrant and refugee-receiving country bears some responsibility to assist in the adjustment of newcomers to their new culture, then a program that responds to criminal behavior in a manner that seeks to repair damage to the community and/or to encourage the respondent to take responsibility for his or her actions on the road to rehabilitation is worthy of consideration.

Consider youth courts in Great Britain as an example of a program that has features worthy of emulating. The outcome in particular cases can range from dismissal to incarceration, or from a fine to a penalty that is more "community based" for those under eighteen.[253] Prior to sentencing, a probation officer or social worker prepares a report that includes information on the offense, the circumstances, and the youth's social background, with an eye toward preparing a plan of action in which the youth and the youth's family are included.[254] The option of performing community service has met with great success, especially when the offender sees how appreciative beneficiaries of the service are; the offenders regard the experience as "worthwhile" and "meaningful."[255] Older offenders have been placed in groups that focus on developing interpersonal and problem-solving skills that have also reduced recidivism.[256] In addition, an approach that involves family interventions seems particularly appropriate for the challenges that newcomer families from very different environments face in their new American neighborhoods. Parents are taught supervision and negotiation strategies with the intent of developing "behavioral contracts" with their children.[257] The interventions have been promising, as children's behaviors have been modified and the family system made more stable.[258]

Even the probation officer or department entity that is such a critical part of the criminal justice system offers ideas to consider. Probation is

---

[253] John Harding, *Youth Crime: A Relational Perspective*, RELATIONAL JUSTICE: REPAIR-ING THE BREACH 104–113 (Jonathan Burnside and Nicola Baker eds., 1994).
[254] Id.   [255] Id.
[256] Id.   [257] Id.
[258] Id.

a postconviction process that serves as an alternative to incarceration. Its fundamental raison d'être is the reformation of the defendant in the society in which he or she must eventually live. The defendant is released under the supervision of a probation officer and is subject to reasonable court-imposed conditions.[259] Probation officer reports are critical to the process: "A probation report is a written account of the probation officer's investigations, findings, and recommendations regarding the defendant's fitness for probation. The purpose of this report is to assist the sentencing judge in determining an appropriate disposition of the defendant's case after conviction."[260]

Besides information on the basic facts of the case and crime, the report can include information on prior criminal conduct, the defendant's social history, family, education, employment, income, military service, medical and psychological history, an evaluation of factors relating to the disposition, recommendations, and a reasoned discussion of aggravating and mitigating factors affecting sentence length or whether imprisonment is even necessary.[261] The use of probation-type reports may even satisfy the harshest enforcement supporters. Congressman Smith, one of the critics who dismantled the old Section 212(c) relief, subsequently acknowledged that deportation should not always result. He suggested that immigration officials exercise prosecutorial discretion and not seek deportation in hardship cases. Furthermore, he suggested that agents should identify hardship aliens who would not be deported.[262]

In diversion programs, criminal cases are "diverted" out of the criminal justice system. In such programs, courts generally require offenders to participate in a treatment or rehabilitation program in lieu of being incarcerated. Criminal charges are dropped upon successful completion of diversion programs, relieving offenders from being stigmatized with a criminal conviction. Either the prosecution or defense counsel may offer diversion to offenders. Defense counsel may wait until a defendant's first court appearance and ask the judge to order an "evaluation for diversion." Those referred to diversion meet with a probation officer, who conducts

---

[259] David. H. Melnick, *Comment, Probation in California: Penal Code Section 1203*, 50 CAL. L. REV. 651, 652–653 (1962).

[260] 5 CAL. CRIM. DEF. PRAC.: SENTENCING AND PROB., POSTTRIAL REMEDIES §90.03[3] (1)–(11) (2004).

[261] Id. [262] See Lewis, *supra* note 211.

an investigation and prepares a report regarding the suitability for diversion. The recommendation may specify the type of program most suitable for the offender.

Requiring offenders to perform community service is another alternative. Here, courts assign offenders to work, uncompensated, for nonprofit organizations or for governmental organizations instead of serving jail time. Requiring community service holds offenders accountable by making them repay society and encourages a more positive connection with the community. Local community service coordinators or probation officers administer community service orders. The orders often involve work in community centers. Community service is usually imposed in conjunction with other forms of punishment, such as probation, fine, or restitution.

In another option, courts order offenders out of their homes for a fixed term and place them in group living arrangements, such as a residential treatment facility. Under this scheme, clinical and counseling staff provide regular mentoring, counseling, and treatment for drug abuse to offenders. Clients receive treatment for substance addiction and alcoholism. The program may offer one-on-one counseling, group therapy, educational lectures, relapse prevention groups, and individualized treatment. The goal is for residents to learn to become self-sufficient, contributing members of society.

The idea behind many of these options is not simply that imprisonment may not be appropriate, but that rehabilitation is a real possibility. In the same vein, analogous options in the immigration enforcement context ought to recognize that rehabilitation is not only a possibility, but ought to be promoted given the background and circumstances of groups like Cambodian refugees and other noncitizens who resettled in challenging environments. Beyond the benefits to the individual, the family, the community, and the entire society stand to gain from a constructive rehabilitative approach. In contrast, the destructive forces of deportation wreak havoc on all the parties and their relationships.

Conclusion

In a review of the highly acclaimed film *The Boys of Baraka*, a documentary about a group of at-risk, inner-city boys from Baltimore who are transplanted to a rural two-year boarding school in Kenya, *Los Angeles Times* movie critic Kenneth Turan wrote:

> [The film's] greatest service is in shining a light on a problem many people don't want to talk about: our willingness to throw away the lives of kids who grow up in dangerous neighborhoods far from quality schools. The enormous potential of these children, how eagerly they respond to the kinds of educational opportunities more fortunate young people take for granted, should make us wonder how society let things get this bad.[263]

By deporting noncitizens who have grown up here, we essentially throw away their lives. Ridding the country of noncitizen criminals is an admirable goal; however, the policy overlooks several considerations when it comes to long-term residents. The first is the impact the policy has on family members and employers. Second, many deportable foreign nationals have resided in the United States since infancy. Third, the policy implies that the criminal justice system is a failure for noncitizen criminals who serve sentences imposed by U.S. courts and should be expelled from our borders immediately after release, to protect the public.

Rethinking removal and developing reasonable approaches to the challenges presented by criminality in immigrant communities from a community-based perspective is not an easy task. But something is terribly wrong with a system that results in the deportation of individuals who entered the country as infants and toddlers, when their criminality is the product of their U.S. environment. Short of a total bar on deportation, which may be difficult to achieve in a get-tough era of immigration enforcement, policymakers should be urged to provide an alternative to deportation – especially one that helps to build community. If we are interested in taking responsibility as a society for the environment that has resulted in high crime rates among certain immigrant and refugee communities, we have to roll up our sleeves and move forward, rather than remain paralyzed by the law and the difficulty of the task.

In our hearts, we know that deportation is not always appropriate, especially when our country bears culpability for creating the problem. In our souls, we know that when we repatriate refugees and immigrants who have

---

[263] Kenneth Turan, *The Light beyond the City's Dead End: "The Boys of Baraka" Examines How a Kenya School Is Used to Help African American Boys in Baltimore*, LA TIMES, Jan. 20, 2006, at E4.

grown up in our society, we further destroy a family at a time when the family needs, more than ever, to be whole. The right response requires the involvement of community, school, neighborhood and government institutions, and parents. But policymakers must first provide the opportunity for us all to assume our responsibilities by giving the potential deportees and their supporters a second chance.

3 . . . . . Promoting Family Values and Immigration

Promoting family reunification has been a major feature of immigration policy for decades. Prior to 1965, permitting spouses of U.S. citizens, relatives of lawful permanent residents, and even siblings of U.S. citizens to immigrate was an important aspect of the immigration selection system. And after the 1965 reforms, family reunification was the major cornerstone of the immigration admission system.

Although President Kennedy's reform goals initially envisioned a first-come, first-served egalitarian system, after his 1963 assassination the reform effort evolved into a category-oriented proposal that eventually was enacted. The 1965 immigration amendments allowed 20,000 immigrant visas for every country not in the western hemisphere. Of the 170,000 immigrant visas set aside for eastern hemisphere immigrants, about 80 percent were specified for "preference" relatives of citizens and lawful permanent residents, and an unlimited number was available to immediate relatives of U.S. citizens. The unlimited immediate relative category included spouses, parents of adult citizens, and minor, unmarried children of citizens. The family preference categories were established for adult, unmarried sons and daughters of citizens (first preference), spouses and unmarried children of lawful permanent resident aliens (second preference), married children of citizens (fourth preference), and siblings of citizens (fifth preference). Third and sixth preferences were established for employment-based immigration.

As Asian and Latin immigrants began to take advantage of the family-based immigration system in the 1970s and 1980s, somehow the emphasis on family reunification made less sense to some policymakers. Since the early 1980s, attacking family reunification categories – especially the sibling category – has become a popular sport played every few years. Often the complaint is based on arguments such as we should be bringing in *skilled immigrants*, a point system would be better, a system based on family relationships is nepotistic, and in the case of the sibling category, brothers and sisters are not part of the nuclear family or the category represents horizontal as opposed to vertical immigration.

Over time, Asian and Latin immigration came to dominate most of the immigration to the United States. By 1976, a new worldwide preference system (which now included the western hemisphere) was installed with a quota of 270,000 that continued to reserve 80 percent for kinship provisions; the category for immediate relatives of the U.S. citizens remained numerically unlimited. The effects of this priority were demonstrated vividly in the subsequent flow of Asian immigration, even though nations such as those in Africa and Asia, with low rates of immigration prior to 1965, initially were handicapped. The nations with large numbers of descendents in the United States in 1965 were expected to benefit the most from a kinship-based system. At the time, fewer than a million Asian Americans resided in the country when the total population was more than 194 million. Although the kinship priority meant that Asians were beginning on an unequal footing, at least Asians were on par numerically, in terms of the twenty thousand visas per country quotas. Gradually, by using the family categories to the extent they could be used and the labor employment route, Asians built a family base from which to use the kinship categories more and more. By the late 1980s, virtually 90 percent of all immigration to the United States – including Asian immigration – was through the kinship categories. And by the 1990s, the vast majority of these immigrants were from Asia and Latin America.

Attacking Families

Once Asian and Latin immigrants began to dominate the family immigration categories, the kinship system was attacked. Consider the following critique in 1986:

> Nowhere else in public policy do we say not "who are you and what are your characteristics?" but ask rather, as we do in immigration, "who are you related to?" Current policy says: "if you have the right relatives, we

will give you a visa; if you don't have the right relatives, well, it is just too bad."[1]

Arguing that the system was nepotistic or that the country would be better off with a skills-based system became popular. The following like-minded statement also from the mid-1980s about undocumented migration reveals the racial nature of the complaint:

> If the immigration status quo persists, the United States will develop a more unequal society with troublesome separations. For example, some projections indicate that the California work force will be mostly immigrants or their descendants by 2010. These working immigrants, *mostly nonwhite*, will be supporting mostly white pensioners with their payroll contributions. *Is American society resilient enough to handle the resulting tensions?*
>
> . . .
>
> The American economy will have more jobs and businesses if illegal alien workers are allowed to enter freely and work in the United States. But the number of jobs and businesses alone is not an accurate measure of the soundness of economic development or *quality of life*. Tolerating heavy illegal immigration introduces distortions into the economy that are difficult to remedy, while imposing environmental and *social costs* that must be borne by the society as a whole.[2]

Apparently, this perception of a good "quality of life" without "environmental and social costs" is one with minimal tension from the presence of "nonwhite" "immigrants or their descendants." As an observer at the time recognized, "It may be fair to conclude that the problem masquerading as illegal immigration is simply today's version of a continuing American – in fact, human – condition, namely xenophobia."[3] As in the Asian exclusionary era, the complaints were not simply about the economy; they were about keeping people out who did not fit the right image.

From the early 1980s to 1996, the leading voice attacking family immigration, especially the sibling category, was Republican Senator Alan

---

[1] Testimony of Barry R. Chiswick before the Joint Economic Committee, Congress of the United States, S. Hrg. 99-1070, May 22, 1986, at 236. Of course this statement was factually incorrect; even under the system at the time, prospective immigrants with skills needed by an employer could qualify for a labor employment category.

[2] Philip Martin, *Illegal Immigration and the Colonization of the American Labor Market,* Center for Immigration Studies, 1986, at 45 (emphasis added).

[3] Annelise Anderson, *Illegal Aliens and Employer Sanctions: Solving the Wrong Problem,* HOOVER ESSAYS IN PUBLIC POLICY, The Hoover Institution, 1986, at 21.

Simpson of Wyoming. Simpson had been a member of the Select Commission on Immigration and Refugee Policy that issued a report in 1981 calling for major changes in the immigration laws. After the Immigration Reform and Control Act of 1986 (IRCA)[4] was enacted to address the issue of undocumented migration through employer sanctions and legalization, Simpson turned his attention to legal immigration categories. At the time, although 20 percent of preference categories were available to labor employment immigrants (54,000), when the unrestricted immediate relative immigration categories were added to the total number of immigrants each year, fewer than 10 percent of immigrants who were entering each year were doing so on the basis of job skills.

In fact, soon after the Select Commission report, Senator Simpson proposed the elimination of the sibling immigration category. At the core of what became a long crusade, Simpson's complaint was that brothers and sisters are insignificant relatives for immigration purposes – that in U.S. culture, the sibling relationship is simply not close enough to justify providing an immigration preference. He ignored the many experts who testified in hearings before the Select Commission stressing the importance of family reunification – including between siblings – over employment-based visas. Demographer Charles Keely testified that

> We, as a nation, cannot only accept, but are enriched in countless ways, by traditions which honor the family and stress close ties not only within the nuclear family of spouses and children but also among generations and among brothers and sisters. Attacks on family reunification beyond the immediate family as a form of nepotism are empty posturing.[5]

The Mexican American Legal Defense and Education Fund, the League of United Latin American Citizens, the U.S.–Asia Institute, and others testified in favor of retaining the category. One organization opposing Simpson's proposal, the American Committee on Italian Migration, noted:

> For Italians and for many other ethnic groups, brothers and sisters, whether or not they are married, are an integral part of the family reunion concept. Elimination of this preference category would violate a sacrosanct human right of an American citizen to live with his family according to his own traditional life style.[6]

---

[4] Pub. L. No. 99-603, Nov. 6, 1986, 100 Stat. 3359.
[5] Select Commission on Immigration and Refugee Policy Report (SCIRP) 1981d, at 48.
[6] U.S. Senate Committee on the Judiciary 19a, at 19, 170.

Arizona Democratic Senator Dennis DeConcini, also a member of the Select Commission, added his voice to the debate:

> Proposals have been offered to eliminate the [sibling] preference. It is felt by some to be too generous, as it refers to horizontal rather than a vertical family concept. . . . But to deny that brothers and sisters are an integral part of the family is to impose upon many ethnic groups a narrow concept of family and one that especially discriminated against the Italian-Americans. We also should stress the rights of U.S. citizens by allowing them to bring their families to America. This view should precede the technical notion that we need certain types of specialist and skilled workers.[7]

In fact, the Select Commission overwhelmingly had endorsed the policy of keeping brothers and sisters as a preference category.[8] Proposals to eliminate family categories created by the 1965 amendments were rejected.

> The reunification of families should remain one of the foremost goals of immigration not only because it is a humane policy, but because bringing families back together contributes to the economic and social welfare of the United States. Society benefits from the reunification of immediate families, especially because family unity promotes the stability, health and productivity of family members.[9]

Simpson did not relent, and in the late 1980s, at a time when legal immigration continued to be dominated by Asians and Latinos even after "diversity programs" were being implemented to aid non-Asian and non-Mexican immigrants, he wanted the family immigration numbers reduced or at least managed. His legislation, S. 358, was approved by the Senate in July 1989, which would establish a ceiling of 630,000 legal immigrants for three years. Of the total, 480,000 would be reserved for all types of family immigration and 150,000 would be set aside for immigrants without family connections but with skills or job-related assets. After numerous markups and hearings, the House of Representative passed Democratic Congressman Bruce Morrison's H.R. 4300, a rather different bill, on October 3, 1990. This bill actually would reduce family immigration more dramatically – thereby reducing the number of Asian and Latino family immigrants,

---

[7] Address in 1978 to the American Committee on Italian Migration, reported in IMMIGRATION UPDATE NATIONAL SYMPOSIUM (1980).

[8] SCIRP 1981a, at 119. [9] SCIRP 1981b, at 357.

providing 185,000 family-based visas and 95,000 employment-based visas annually.

The Morrison bill was attacked for its wholesale elimination of temporary work visas for professionals. The concern was that the spigot actually might be closed on foreign workers. Also, the possible elimination of H-1 nonimmigrant status for certain professions outraged immigration lawyers, who called it a "must-kill" provision. Another one of Morrison's more controversial suggestions was to tax employers who use alien employees. One early proposal required businesses to pay 15 percent of an alien's salary into a federal trust fund used to train U.S. workers. As introduced, the bill would impose a flat user fee dependent on the size of the company. After furious negotiations, especially with fellow Democratic Congressman Howard Berman from Los Angeles, Morrison agreed to drop proposals that would have reduced the number of family-based visas, persuaded by Berman's argument: "To cut back on the ability of new Americans to be with their family members betrays the core American value and tradition of emphasizing the integrity of the family."[10]

As passed, H.R. 4300 would increase the number of legal immigrants to 775,000 a year from the prior 540,000. It would also speed the process of uniting families, attract more skilled workers, and create a new diversity category for immigrants from countries whose nationals have largely been excluded in the past. After passing the bill, the House changed the bill number to S. 358 to enable it to go to a joint House–Senate conference. However, many Senate conferees were opposed to the more liberal House bill and negotiated to cap legal immigration and place new measures to control illegal immigration, including tougher provisions against criminal aliens. The House conferees insisted on a sunset cap in the bill and wanted extra visas to go to relatives rather than to skilled workers. But Senator Simpson refused to agree, leading the *Wall Street Journal* to dub him a "one-man border control" and "Stonewall Simpson."[11] Eventually compromises were reached and Congress passed S. 358.

Enacted on October 26, 1990, the compromise bill would allow 700,000 immigrants from 1992 to 1994 and 675,000 annually in subsequent years.[12]

---

[10] Stewart Kwoh, *Family Unity Ranks First in Immigration*, LA TIMES, Sept. 14, 1989.

[11] 67 INTERPRETER RELEASES 1153–1155 (1990).

[12] The compromise included portions of S. 3055 sponsored by Simpson, which would speed deportations of criminal aliens. Section 501 expanded the definition of "aggravated felony" to include illicit trafficking in any controlled substance, money laundering, and

For the time being, proposals to cut back on family immigration were defeated, and the Immigration Act of 1990 had responded to lobbying efforts by American businesses. The act was a significant, and to some a revolutionary, revision of the focus of U.S. immigration law. After passage of the act, although the main thrust of immigration law continued to be family immigration, highly skilled immigrants would be deliberately encouraged to resettle in the United States more than ever before. In the long run, the annual number of employment-based visas would nearly triple from 54,000 to 140,000 per year.

Although Simpson was disappointed that he failed to reduce the Asian- and Latino-dominated family categories in 1990, he was able to install an overall numerical cap. Furthermore, for Simpson, the new employment categories and expanded diversity programs could attract *real* American stock – those who were not Asian or Latino: "we [now] open the front door wider to skilled workers of a more diverse range of nationalities."[13]

Up to his retirement in 1996, Senator Simpson fought to eliminate the sibling category. On the eve of the 1996 presidential election, Congress enacted rather heinous immigration reform relating to deportation, asylum, and procedural issues. Until the late spring 1996, the threat that the immigration legislation also would include cutbacks on legal immigration categories was real. Congressman Lamar Smith and Senator Simpson again took aim at the siblings-of-U.S.-citizens category as well as the category available to unmarried, adult sons and daughters of lawful resident aliens (category 2B). Their efforts ultimately were not successful, so the 1996 legislation did not reduce family immigration.

Pitting Family Visas against Employment Visas

More than a decade later, as so-called comprehensive immigration reform is debated, immigration policy experts once again seek to place the family immigration categories on the negotiating table. This attack on

---

any crime of violence with a five-year imprisonment imposed. The bill also included both federal and state crimes. Aliens convicted of aggravated felonies would have expedited deportation hearings and would not be released from custody while in deportation proceedings. 67 INTERPRETER RELEASES 1229–1231 (1990).

[13] 136 CONG. REC. S17,109 (daily ed. Oct. 26, 1990) (statement of Sen. Simpson).

family immigration is a variation on the wouldn't-it-be-better-to-chose-immigrants-based-on-skills theme, by positioning family visas in opposition to employment-based visas:

> There is an *inherent tension* in the immigration system between job and family-based admissions. In allocating visas between family and employment criteria, the goal of family reunification cannot be entirely reconciled with the problem of visas as a scare resource. The answers here are either to accept persistent family migration backlogs or limit the scope of family migration to nuclear, instead of extended, family relationships.[14]

Inherent tension? Of course there is only an "inherent tension" between employment- and family-based visas if we choose to accept the premise that visas are a "scarce resource" or if we insist on pitting the two types of visas as oppositional. If instead we view the two systems as complementary ways of achieving and reflecting our goals and values as a society, then we do not have a problem of tension. In other words, if, for the sake of argument, we use immigration to help our economy, to promote the social welfare of the country, and to promote family values, then family and employment categories together can meet those goals.

The Labor Force Picture

Placing employment visas in opposition to family visas implies that family immigration represents the soft side of immigration while employment immigration is more about being tough and strategic. The wrongheadedness of that suggestion is that family immigration has served our country well even from a purely economic perspective. The country needs workers with all levels of skill, and family immigration provides many of the needed workers.

A concern that the current system raises for some policymakers is based on their belief that the vast majority of immigrants who enter in kinship categories are working class or low skilled. They wonder whether this is good for the country. Interestingly enough, immigrants who enter in the sibling category actually are generally highly skilled. But beyond that oversight by the complainants, what we know about the country and its general need for workers in the short and long terms is instructive.

The truth is that we need immigrant workers of all skill levels today, and we will need them in the future. As of 2004, twenty-one million

---

[14] Memorandum from Doris Meissner, Nov. 30, 2005 (emphasis added).

immigrants were in the U.S. labor force, representing 14.5 percent of the total labor force. A majority of the immigrant workforce is Mexican or from other Latin countries; foreign-born Asians are one-fourth of the immigrant workforce. Roughly 6.3 million (30 percent of all foreign-born workers) are undocumented workers.[15] This represents about 4.3 percent of the total U.S. labor force.

In the past few years, the employment of immigrants actually grew while that of native workers was stagnant. This trend is expected to continue because without immigrants, demographers project that the number of workers between the ages of twenty-five and fifty-four over the next few decades will decline. This suggests a strong demand for immigrants in a broad variety of industries.[16] Immigrants represent 20 to 22 percent of farm and nonfarm laborers. Mexican-born workers are much more likely than native workers to be found in food preparation, building and grounds maintenance, construction, and production jobs. The 2001–2003 recessionary period also represented a restructuring period; immigrants were favored in the declining manufacturing industry, as well as in the leisure/hospitality and construction areas. Professional business services also hired a large number of immigrants, likely because of increased global competition.

Most projections of future immigration suggest that foreign-born workers will play a significant role in the growth and skill composition of the U.S. labor force. The Bureau of Labor Statistics (BLS) projects that the labor force will grow 12 percent (17.4 million) between 2002 and 2012, reaching a total of 162.3 million.[17]

Given projections of slow growth of the native workforce, the levels of immigration used in BLS and other projections imply that immigrants will remain significant drivers of labor force growth. The BLS's most recent projections assume that total immigration, both legal and unauthorized, will continue to bring between 900,000 and 1.3 million people to the country each year until 2012.[18] Barring truly restrictionist policy, immigrants likely will continue to constitute a significant supply of workers under any legislation that is passed. In fact, immigrants have been an important

[15] B. Lindsay Lowell, *Immigrants and Labor Force Trends: Past to Present* (Nov. 30, 2005) at 1, 3 (unpublished paper) (on file with author).

[16] Id. at 14.

[17] Julia Gelatt and B. Lindsay Lowell, *Immigrants and Labor Force Trends: The Future* (Nov. 30, 2005) at 2 (unpublished paper) (on file with author).

[18] Id.

source of labor force growth in the recent past, making up 48.6 percent of the total labor force increase between 1996 and 2000 and as much as 60 percent of the increase from 2000 to 2004.[19]

These projections imply that an immigrant workforce of nineteen million is projected to grow to twenty-five million by 2010, twenty-nine million by 2020, and to thirty-one million by 2030. Likewise the share of immigrants in the total labor force is predicted to climb from 13 percent in 2000 to 18 percent by 2030 and then remain little changed through 2050.[20] After 2030, the projections indicate little further growth of the immigrant workforce, while much of the ongoing growth of the native workforce is implicitly being driven by the children of immigrants or the second generation.

Calculations by the Urban Institute suggest that if no immigrants entered the country after 2000, the labor force would be nearly ten million workers smaller by 2015 than if immigration follows current projections. By 2050, the difference between the size of the labor force with immigration and without would be forty-five million.[21]

The skill levels demanded by occupations projected to grow over the next several years parallel the educational profile of the labor force, suggesting ongoing demand along the skill spectrum. Every two years, the BLS publishes projections about the future size and shape of the U.S. labor force and the number of net jobs that will be created or lost in each occupation. The latest projections are for the years 2002 to 2012, and they forecast a slowing in the rate at which the total labor force is growing.[22] However, substantial variation is evident in the fortunes of various occupational workforces.

Tomorrow's economy will generate demand for jobs that are different from today's, and the skills that workers need will likewise change. The BLS separates out fifteen occupations that are projected to have the largest numerical growth and another fifteen that are projected to experience the fastest rate of growth. Immigrants make up a significant share of the labor force in many large and fast-growth occupations. Importantly, the BLS further classifies occupations by the degree of skill required for the job, showing a high future demand for both low- and high-skilled immigrant workers.[23]

[19] Id.

[21] Id. at 4.

[23] Id.

[20] Id. at 3.

[22] Id. at 5.

For the forecast large-growth occupations, eleven out of the fifteen require only short- or moderate-term on-the-job training, suggesting lower skilled immigrants could contribute to meeting the demand for these types of jobs. According to the 2000 Census data, immigrants were overrepresented in four of these occupations. Immigrants made up 20 percent of janitors and building cleaners; 17 percent of nursing, psychiatric, and home health aides; 13 percent of waiters and waitresses; and 13 percent of cashiers. On the high-skill end, three large-growth occupations – general and operations managers, other teachers and instructors, and postsecondary teachers – require a bachelor's degree or higher, and immigrants are especially well poised to contribute to these.[24]

Immigrants are also found in jobs that are expected to be important in serving tomorrow's aging population. Seniors are expected to increasingly generate demand for medical, home care, and other services, many of which require workers with only on-the-job training. According to analysis of BLS data, eight of fifteen occupations projected to grow most rapidly and several of the occupations projected to have largest absolute growth are medical support occupations including medical records technicians, nursing and home health aides, registered nurses, occupational therapist assistants and aides, personal and home care aides, and the like.[25]

In summary, forecasts of occupational growth suggest continued strong growth in occupations requiring better educated workers. However, substantial growth will also occur in jobs requiring little training and in which immigrants are already well represented. Educational forecasts suggest that throughout the next decade, immigrants are likely to play an important role in restructuring the U.S. labor force.[26]

The aging of the baby boomer generation will slow labor force growth, increase the burden of older, retired persons on younger workers, and create a potential drag on productivity growth. Between 2002 and 2012, persons aged fifty-five and older are estimated to grow an average of 4.9 percent per year, or nearly quadruple the growth rate of the overall labor force. The number of workers aged twenty-five to fifty-four, in contrast, will grow by only 5.1 million workers, or at a rate of 0.5 percent per year.[27] These demographic trends slow the rate of growth of the total prime-age labor force.

---

[24] Id. at 6.
[26] Id. at 7–8.

[25] Id. at 7.
[27] Id. at 8.

The aging of the population will change the dependency ratio – the number of nonworking dependents compared to economically active workers. That ratio is expected to rise as the baby boomer generation enters retirement and as U.S. fertility rates remain low, leaving a greater number of elderly to be supported by each worker. The decreasing number of taxpaying workers supporting each retiree will strain public assistance programs for the elderly including Social Security and Medicare.[28] An infusion of young taxpaying immigrants can help address future shortfalls in these programs.

While immigration cannot be expected to solve the problem on its own, the evidence suggests that greater immigration could aid elderly assistance programs. Increased immigration can temporarily lessen the Social Security and Medicare burden on native workers, but immigrants are only 12 percent of the U.S. population, and current rates of immigration add about 1 million immigrants yearly to an existing base of about 34 million.[29] In the longer run, permanent immigrants will also age into retirement.

Interestingly, the employment of undocumented workers does create a windfall for the Social Security system. Some undocumented workers get jobs using fake Social Security numbers. Wages are withheld from their paychecks for Social Security and Medicare taxes. When the Social Security Administration gets W-2 forms from their employers, it cannot match their names and Social Security numbers with information in its records. The taxes these workers have paid go into the Social Security trust funds and their wage data goes into an electronic earnings suspense file. The undocumented workers cannot claim the Social Security benefits they have earned, creating a windfall for the system. For example, in 2003, $7.2 billion in taxes were credited to the trust fund based on wage items placed in the suspense file, according to the Social Security Administration. This represented about 1.3 percent of total payroll taxes credited to the trust funds. The $7 billion amount has been holding relatively steady in recent years. Standard & Poor analysts have concluded that the vast majority of wages in the suspense file are attributable to undocumented workers who will never claim their benefits. Their conclusion partly was based on a finding that 43 percent of employers associated with wages in the suspense file came from five out of eighty-three industry

---

[28] Id.   [29] Id.

categories. Two of the top five industries were restaurants and construction, which we know employ many undocumented workers. The Social Security Administration estimates that three-fourths of undocumented immigrants pay Social Security taxes and that without the flow of taxes from wages in the suspense file, the system's long-term funding gap over 75 years would be 10 percent worse.[30]

Immigration also boosts productivity, because immigrant workers tend to be younger and therefore generally more productive than older workers, but how significant of a boost is difficult to calculate. A National Academy of Sciences report in 1997 concluded that immigrants generate a small but positive boost to the gross national product by generating increased returns to capital that are greater than their adverse wage impacts. Some evidence suggests that innovation thrives when human capital is combined in areas with many specialists and skilled migrants. The booming economy of the late 1990s was fueled by historic productivity gains, one-third of which came from information technology (IT), and foreign workers fueled one-fourth of the IT labor force growth. Also, immigrants launched about a third of Silicon Valley's high-tech start-ups.[31] Potential problems created by the aging of the U.S. labor force cannot simply and entirely be solved by more immigration, but budget and productivity shortfalls at least will generate demand for generous numbers of skilled immigrant workers.

Some might argue that strategies other than immigration could be used to meet the country's coming economic needs. For example, the need for high-skilled labor could be met in ways other than increasing the numbers of high-skilled immigrants allowed into the country. High-technology jobs could be outsourced to rising centers of technological expertise such as Bangalore or other growing hot spots around the world. Or the United States could devote greater resources to raising the skill level of residents, retraining workers from sunset industries and improving the teaching of skills most relevant to the future economy of the country's youth.

Given the dynamic nature of the economy, the uncertainty of any attempts to predict the needs of tomorrow's economy, and the limited control any government can exert over demographic changes, how

---

[30] Kathleen Pender, *Losing Out on a Huge Cash Stash*, SF CHRONICLE, Apr. 11, 2006, at C1.

[31] Gelatt and Lowell, *supra* note 17, at 9–10.

immigration can or should be used to meet the needs of the country's coming labor markets may be difficult to say with precision. But clearly, immigration has been an important source of labor force growth in the past, and the skills required of the occupations important to the future, in both technology and health care industries, will likely match reasonably well with the skill profiles of immigrants today and the projected skill profiles of future immigrants. Immigrants currently play a large role in several of the occupations expected to have most growth both in terms of the rate of growth or growth in numbers of workers, and therefore can be expected to contribute to meeting the future demand of these industries.[32] Immigration is not the only answer to the country's future economic needs, but it could, and likely will, play an important part in a more comprehensive solution.

The Competition Charge

Immigrant workers have long contributed to the power behind the motor of the U.S. economy. However, concerns that immigrants compete with native workers to the latter's detriment still thrive in the public mind. A review of the literature about immigration's impact on native wages and job displacement is a starting place to resolve this question. But before doing so, any serious observer must acknowledge that immigrants positively affect the economy in ways that are not reflected by wage and job displacement studies.[33] Immigrant entrepreneurship creates jobs; immigrants are increasingly associated with further openings to international trade and other forms of exchange; high-skilled immigrants innovate in key sectors of the economy; immigrants make tax contributions; the presence of significant numbers of immigrants in a sector helps make that sector's products and services cheaper – and thus more affordable by all consumers; and immigrant workers both produce and, in turn, consume goods and services – thus having much wider ripple economic effects, including creating jobs through consumer demand.

Most economic competition discussions generally focus on the short- and medium-term impacts of immigration. When immigrant workers enter a labor market, there may be initial pains to accommodate them,

---

[32] Id. at 11.

[33] Julie Murray, Jeanne Batalova, and Michael Fix, *A Fresh Look at the Evidence: The Impact of Immigration on Native Workers* (Nov. 30, 2005), at 1 (unpublished paper on file with author).

and in response to those difficulties, the labor market may adjust, perhaps by creating more jobs that immigrants and/or natives could fill or by inducing natives to move. However, in the long term, the impact of an immigrant cohort depends on the degree to which immigrants assimilate into U.S. society (i.e., become like native workers in terms of the skills they have). If they, or perhaps more importantly their children, assimilate economically, a given immigrant cohort will tend to make the economy larger without putting downward pressure on natives' wages.[34] Also, keep in mind the possibility that immigrant employment often complements that of native workers.

Immigrants are an important and growing part of the U.S. labor force. Estimates indicate that one of every two new workers in the 1990s was foreign born. As a result of these flows, from 1990 to 2002, the immigrant share of the workforce rose from 9.4 to 14 percent. Immigrants are also disproportionately low-wage workers, comprising 20 percent of the low-wage population, though they also make up much higher proportions in several high-skill occupations and sectors.[35]

In 1997, the National Research Council concluded that immigration had a small effect on the wages of native workers. Evidence showed that immigration reduced the wages of competing natives by only 1 or 2 percent. Effects were also weak for native black workers, a group often assumed to be in competition with immigrant workers. Earlier immigrant cohorts were more significantly affected: They could expect 2 to 4 or more percent wage decline for every 10 percent increase in the number of immigrant workers. The report also noted that immigration, as a whole, resulted in a net benefit to the economy of between $1 and $10 billion annually, a small but still significant positive impact.[36] Certain groups within the economy, such as those with capital or high-level skills or those consuming immigrants' goods or services, benefited from immigration, even if low-skilled natives stood to lose in the process.

Although there is still general agreement that some native groups, particularly the high-skilled or those with capital, benefit from overall immigration flows, the assertion that immigrants do not significantly affect natives' wages is now more broadly contested. Many studies continue to find no effect or only weak negative effects of immigration on low-skilled

[34] Id. at 2.   [35] Id.

[36] Id. at 3–4.

workers or workers in general. Others suggest that newly arriving immi-grants do not have a statistically significant impact, but the degree to which immigrants substitute for natives increases with time spent in the United States. Still others contend that the negative wage effects are larger, per-haps on the order of a 3 or 4 percent wage decline for competing workers for every 10 percent increase in immigrants with similar skills. On the other hand, some research found that immigration actually had a slightly positive and statistically significant effect on all natives' self-employment earnings.[37]

Findings now are contested regarding immigrants' wage effects for highly skilled native workers. Some researchers estimate that immigration during the past two decades depressed wages by 4.9 percent for native col-lege graduates. In contrast, others have found that high-skilled immigrants actually raise native wages, for example that a 10 percent increase in high-skilled immigrants raised native skilled workers' earnings by 2.6 percent.[38]

In essence, the literature indicates that the impact of immigration on native workers is an issue that is still up for debate, perhaps now more than ever. Some researchers have found divergent, large negative, small negative to nonexistent, and positive impacts from immigration on native relative wages, even among the most vulnerable populations. Further-more, most research has found some job displacement or native exclu-sion within given sectors or cities as a result of immigration, but critics of those studies charge that the researches only look at niches where one would expect to find impacts.[39] Certainly, immigration's impact on the most vulnerable native workers is increasingly contested ground, which makes predicting future impacts doubly difficult.

In the end, whether immigrants actually depress wages or displace some workers deserves only weak consideration within a larger policymaking context. Whether the effects are slightly negative, somewhat positive, or tend toward zero, they may be far outweighed by other effects that immigrants have on the United States.[40] Over and over again, we hear the claim that immigrants definitely take jobs away from native workers or that native wages are severely depressed by immigrant workers. But the empirical data supplies no smoking gun for those claims, and in fact, the opposite may be true.

---

[37] Id. at 5–6.

[38] Id. at 6–7.

[39] Id. at 11.

[40] Id. at 12–13.

Without an empirical foundation for attacking the entry of immigrants with low job skills, some critics of the current family-based system simply argue that there is a better way of doing things. They are not satisfied that immigration fills needed job shortages and aids economic growth as a result of the entry of ambitious, hard-working family immigrants and their children, many of whom are professionals as well as unskilled workers with a propensity for saving and investment. I wish those critics would calm down and open their hearts to the benefits that family immigration brings to communities and the well-being of the entire nation.

The Benefits of Family Immigration

The economic data on today's kinship immigrants are favorable for the country. The entry of low-skilled as well as high-skilled immigrants leads to faster economic growth by increasing the size of the market, thereby boosting productivity, investment, and technological practice. Technological advances are made by many immigrants who are neither well-educated nor well-paid and by white collar immigrants. Moreover, many kinship-based immigrants open new businesses that employ natives as well as other immigrants; this is important because small businesses are now the most important source of new jobs in the United States. The current family-centered system results in designers, business leaders, investors, and Silicon Valley–type engineers. And much of the flexibility available to American entrepreneurs in experimenting with risky labor-intensive business ventures is afforded by the presence of low-wage immigrant workers. In short, kinship immigrants contribute greatly to this country's vitality and growth.

Beyond the obvious economic benefits of the current system, a thorough consideration of the benefits of the family-based immigration system must include the psychic values of such a system. The psychic value of family reunification is generally overlooked by empiricists perhaps because of difficulty in making exact calculations. Yet the inability to make such a calculation is no reason to facilely cast aside the idea or ignore the possibilities.

Perhaps as a first step in getting a sense of the unquantifiable psychic values of family reunification, we could begin by thinking of our own families and what each one of our loved ones means to us. How less productive would we be without one or more of them? How less productive would we be, having to constantly be concerned about their sustenance, safety, or general well-being? How more productive are we when we know that we can come home at the end of the day and enjoy their company or share our days' events with them?

Ask Ming Liu, a design engineer for a U.S. telephone and electronics equipment company from China. Liu was doing fine, better than his boss expected, and always had his nose to the grindstone. But he became an even better worker after his wife and child rejoined him following a two-year immigration process. Liu's productivity skyrocketed. His boss observed Liu's personality opening up after his family arrived, and Liu came up with a completely new, innovative concept that helped the company change direction and increase sales. In Liu's words, after his family immigrated, he could "breathe again."

Or ask Osvaldo Fernandez, a former pitcher for the San Francisco Giants. He had defected from the Cuban national baseball team, leaving his wife and child back in Cuba. After a mediocre first half of the 1996 season, his wife and child were allowed to leave Cuba and join Fernandez in the United States. Overnight, his pitching performance radically improved. He attributed this turnaround to reunification with his wife and child.

Consider the Ayalde sisters. Corazon became a U.S. citizen several years after she immigrated to the United States as a registered nurse to work in a public hospital devoted to caring for senior citizens. When her sister Cerissa, who had remained in the Philippines, became widowed without children, the two sisters longed to be reunited – especially after Cerissa became ill. Corazon filed a sibling petition, and after years of waiting, Cerissa's visa was granted. Corazon felt her "heart being lifted to heaven" as the sisters reunited to live their lives together once again. I think of the Ayalde sisters often in the context of my own mother's inability to successfully petition for her sister's immigration out of mainland China to be reunited. First there was the paperwork for the application, complicated by the difficulty in obtaining documents from China. Then there were the backlogs in the sibling category, and finally the hurdles of getting travel documents out of China in the 1970s. When my mother received word that her sister had passed away, the tears she shed were only a fraction of the pain she had endured being separated from her sister for decades.

The truth is that the family promotes productivity after resettlement in the United States through the promotion of labor force activity and job mobility that is certainly as important – perhaps more important – than the particular skills with which individuals arrive. Family and household structures also are primary factors in promoting high economic achievement, for example, in the formation of immigrant businesses that have revitalized many urban neighborhoods and economic sectors.

Those who would eliminate family categories contend that family separation is a fact of life (sometimes harsh) that we can get over or live with. Yes, most of us live without someone whom we love dearly either because of that person's death or because the person lives across the country. Yes, we can get over this separation and perhaps become as productive as ever. Yet to take this ability to recover, place it in the context of immigration policy, and say to someone who wants to reunify with a brother, sister, son, or daughter, "No, your relative cannot join you; you cannot reunify with this person on a permanent basis," is cruel. That policy choice places the burden and challenge of recovery on the person unnecessarily. The policy prevents voluntary choice by adults who are capable of making important life decisions relating to very private family matters. As such, the policy can affect life-altering circumstances that the individuals involved should have been permitted to control.

Conclusion

I once had a debate over lunch with a retired federal immigration judge about the sibling category. He could not understand the need for the category because, after all, he loves his sister just as much even though she lives in New York rather than next door in San Francisco. On further discussion, he acknowledged that he might feel differently if she was living in a different country where visa requirements made simple visits complicated or where political or economic circumstances were stressful for his sister. Family separation across national boundaries must be viewed differently from separation within the same country.

The opponents of the current system that favors many family categories contend that unending chain migration has resulted from this system. They present a picture of a single immigrant who enters, who then brings in a spouse, then each spouse brings in siblings who bring in their spouses and children, and each adult brings in parents who can petition for their siblings or other children, and the cycle goes on and on. Certainly for a period of time, family categories result in the arrival of certain relatives. However, the purveyors of the image of limitless relatives forget that throughout the course of immigration history to the United States, these so-called family chains are invariably broken. Thus, although virtually limitless numbers of western Europeans have been permitted to immigrate to the United States throughout the past two hundred years, at a given point, decisions are made – some slowly and gradually – by families about who is willing or wants to come to the new country and who does not. As a result, immigration numbers from western European countries have dramatically fallen off. Hundreds of thousands of immigrants from the United Kingdom, Germany, and Ireland immigrated to the United States in each decade of the first part of the twentieth century. The figures continued to be substantial for Germans and British nationals through 1970, but then the figures diminished significantly after that.

In reality, the proponents of the unending chain migration image are simply engaging in scare tactics that have serious racial overtones. Their proposal to cut off family categories comes at a time when three in four immigrants are Latino or Asian. Perhaps most reprehensible is the fallacy upon which these attacks are being made. In fact, the picture of ever-expanding immigration fueled by chain migration is a fabrication. Consider individual countries: the number of Koreans who entered in 1988 was thirty-four thousand, but by 1993, the figure was reduced by half, and in 2004 fewer than twenty thousand Koreans immigrated. The number of Filipinos who immigrated in 1990 was more than seventy-one thousand, but by 1993 the figure was about sixty-three thousand, and around fifty thousand by 2004.

In further twisted reasoning, supporters of family category reductions argue that because the categories are backlogged many years (especially the sibling category), they should be eliminated because they are useless and do not achieve any family values. However, the categories certainly are not useless for those who have waited their turn and who are now immigrating. And if there is real sympathy for those on the waiting list, then providing extra visa numbers for a while to clear the backlog is in order. In fact, the bipartisan Select Commission recommended extra numbers to address the backlogs more than a quarter century ago.

Clearing the backlogs is not novel and would send an important message. In 1962, for example, extra visas were made available to clear backlogs for Italian and Greek immigrants. Reducing backlogs is more consistent with the broad goals of immigration policy and democratic values of best practices in governance. Immigration policy helps define the United States in the eyes of the world, and clearing the backlogs would send a positive message about how much America values families. A message of relative openness also would create important linkages and opportunities for exchange.

Easing the worldwide backlogs by providing favored treatment for Mexican immigrants also is worthy of consideration. Expanded legal access for Mexican immigrants provides a great opportunity to reduce unauthorized flows to the United States by addressing the greatest source of migration demand. Expanding the number of legal immigrant visas to Mexicans or taking Mexican migration out of the worldwide quota would increase the number of available worldwide visas to other countries, thereby reducing backlogs per se. We stand at a crossroads in world history when we need to think regionally in terms of politics and economics. Providing favored treatment for Mexican immigrants would constitute an important gesture of goodwill and understanding to our contiguous neighbor, promoting greater economic and security cooperation between historically linked societies.

As to the attack on the sibling category in particular, for many citizens and residents of the United States, including those of Asian or Latin descent, the argument that brothers and sisters are a family relationship of limited importance is puzzling. The backlog in the sibling category is evidence itself that brothers and sisters are important to many families. Many U.S. citizens have filed immigration petitions for siblings rather than for their own parents. Parents, the older generation, are often deeply entrenched in the country of birth, more comfortable in their native surroundings, and reluctant to emigrate and face adjustments to a new society as seniors. On the other hand, contemporary siblings are more adventurous and eager to emigrate. Being of the same generation as the citizen sibling, they, more than the parent, often have a closer relationship because they tend to share the same goals, interests, and values. Siblings are among the easiest immigrants to resettle and the most likely to become immediate contributors to the economy.

The importance of the sibling category has been long recognized in U.S. immigration laws. Section 2(d) of the first quota act of 1921 stipulated that "preference shall be given as far as possible to wives, parents, brothers, sisters, and children under eighteen years" of U.S. citizens.[41] Preference

---

[41] Quota Act of May 19, 1921, 52 Stat. 6.

for brothers and sisters was included after World War II because siblings were in many cases the only surviving members of families. Thus, this preference for siblings was continued in the basic nationality act of 1952. Brothers and sisters of U.S. citizens were placed in the same category of importance as sons and daughters of citizens. And, of course, in the 1965 amendments, Congress assigned the sibling preference the highest percentage of visas – 24 percent.

The Select Commission on Immigration and Refugee Policy defended the family reunification system in its 1981 report:

> The reunification of families serves the national interest not only through the humaneness of the policy itself, but also through the promotion of the public order and well-being of the nation. Psychologically and socially, the reunion of family members with their close relatives promotes the health and welfare of the United States.[42]

After all, the system resulted in the entry of "ambitious, hard-working immigrants and their children" who provided a disproportionate number of skilled workers with a propensity for saving and investment.[43]

In an era of promoting family values, proposals to eliminate family immigration categories seem odd. What values do such proposals impart? What's the message? That brothers and sisters are not important? Or (in the case of the proposal to limit children of lawful permanent residents) that once children reach a certain age, the parent–child bond need not remain strong? Eliminating such categories institutionalizes concepts that are antithetical to the nurturing of family ties, that ignore the strong family bonds in most families, and that discourage ideals that should be promoted among all families. Indeed, the proposals send a strong antifamily message.

The preamble to the Universal Declaration of Human Rights highlights the unity of the family as the "foundation of freedom, justice and peace in the world" for good reason. Our families make us whole. Our families define us as human beings. Our families are at the center of our most treasured values. Our families make the nation strong.

---

[42] UNITED STATES IMMIGRATION POLICY AND THE NATIONAL INTEREST, FINAL REPORT OF THE SELECT COMMISSION ON IMMIGRATION AND REFUGEE POLICY 112 (1981).

[43] Id. at 103.

4 . . . . . Misusing Immigration Policies in the Name of Homeland Security

Perhaps we should have expected a crackdown on noncitizens after 9/11. After all, the nineteen hijackers were foreigners who somehow made it into the country to commit evil. Implementing new procedures and reorganizing administrative institutions to ensure that all immigration visa processes and enforcement were screened through the lens of national security appeared to be in order.

And because the villains were adherents of Muslim extremism as advocated by Osama bin Laden, focusing the crackdown on Arab and Muslim noncitizens made sense – ethnic and religious profiling seemed to be acceptable.

But did these responses really make sense? Had the changes been in force prior to 9/11, would the profiling and immigration-specific modifications have prevented the attacks? What do we have to show for the changes that have been made? At what price has the new regime been implemented?

The answers may be frustrating. In fact, we would not have caught the hijackers if the new systems were in place prior to 9/11. There is little to show for the profiling that has occurred, and the country has paid a tremendous price in terms of civil liberties and relations with noncitizen communities – particularly Arab, Muslim, and South Asian communities. Profiling may make us feel more secure, but we are not. Actually we may be making matters worse. Any real advances in homeland security that have been made are due more to efforts in place before 9/11 coupled with greater cooperation between agencies and better policing practices than with crackdowns on noncitizens.

Legislative and Executive Response to 9/11

Since 9/11, Congress and the president have screened immigration policy proposals and enforcement procedures through the lens of national security. For anti-immigrant forces in the United States, 9/11 provided a once-in-a-lifetime opportunity to use the tragic events to draw linkages with virtually every aspect of their nativist agenda. But this is a neo-nativist agenda born of old hate cloaked in suggestions of international intrigue.

The Bush White House helped lay the foundation for the neo-nativist agenda in its legislative proposals that led to the USA PATRIOT Act, authorizing broad sweeps and scare tactics. The Bush White House epitomized its philosophy in words such as these in its July 2002 National Strategy for Homeland Security:

> Our great power leaves these enemies with few conventional options for doing us harm. One such option is to take advantage of our freedom and openness by *secretly inserting terrorists into our country* to attack our homeland. Homeland security seeks to deny this avenue of attack to our enemies and thus to provide a secure foundation for America's ongoing global engagement.[1]

A restrictionist organization like the Center for Immigration Studies (CIS) takes these words and argues that in the Department of Homeland Security's

> expansive portfolio, immigration is central. The reason is elementary: no matter the weapon or delivery system – hijacked airliners, shipping containers, suitcase nukes, anthrax spores – operatives are required to carry out the attacks. Those operatives have to enter and work in the United States. . . . Thus keeping the terrorists out or apprehending them after they get in is indispensable to victory.[2]

Thus, CIS used the opportunity presented by 9/11 to argue against issuing driver's licenses to undocumented workers and to advocate for sweeps and apprehensions. Apparently, the idea is to make it hard for potential terrorists (i.e., foreigners) to move around or make a living, so they will become discouraged and leave. And who can argue against keeping terrorists out or apprehending them after they arrive?

---

[1] *President Releases National Strategy for Homeland Security*, July 16, 2002, at http://www.whitehouse.gov/news/releases/2002/07/20020716-2.html (emphasis added).

[2] Mark Krikorian, *Keeping Terror Out – Immigration Policy and Asymmetric Warfare*, NATIONAL INTEREST (Spring 2004).

Congress and the Bush administration heeded the appeals to implement harsh immigration policies. The events of 9/11 and the ensuing call to action from many quarters – including the anti-immigrant lobby – resulted in far-reaching legislative and enforcement actions. These enforcement actions had implications not only for suspected terrorists but also for immigrants already in the United States and noncitizens trying to enter as immigrants or with nonimmigrant visas.

The USA PATRIOT Act is the most notable enactment.[3] The act passed Congress with near unanimous support, and the president signed it into law a mere six weeks after 9/11. The vast powers embodied in the law provide expanded authority to search, monitor, and detain citizens and noncitizens alike, but its implementation since passage has preyed most heavily on noncitizen Arabs, Muslims, and Sikhs. Authority to detain, deport, or file criminal charges against noncitizens specifically is broadened. Consider the following noncitizen-related provisions in the law:

- Noncitizens are denied admission if they "endorse or espouse terrorist activity" or "persuade others to support terrorist activity or a terrorist organization," in ways that the State Department determines impede U.S. efforts to combat terrorism.
- The act defines "terrorist activity" expansively to include support of otherwise lawful and nonviolent activities of almost any group that used violence.
- Noncitizens are deportable for wholly innocent associational activity, excludable for pure speech, and subject to incarceration without a finding that they pose a danger or flight risk.
- Foreign nationals can be detained for up to seven days while the government decides whether to file criminal or immigration charges.
- The attorney general has broad preventive detention authority to incarcerate noncitizens by certifying there are "reasonable grounds to believe" that a person is "described in" the antiterrorism provisions of the immigration law, and the individual is then subject to potentially indefinite detention.

---

[3] The clumsy, complete title is the Uniting and Strengthening America by Providing Appropriate Tools Required to Intercept and Obstruct Terrorism Act, voila the USA PATRIOT Act (Pub. L. No. 107-56).

- The attorney general can detain noncitizens indefinitely even if the person prevails in a removal proceeding "until the Attorney General determines that the noncitizen is no longer a noncitizen who may be certified [as a suspected terrorist]."
- Wiretaps and searches are authorized without a showing of probable criminal conduct if the target is an "agent of a foreign power," including any officer or employee of a foreign-based political organization.

To further emphasize how future visa issuance and immigration enforcement must be screened through the lens of national security, the Immigration and Naturalization Service (INS) was subsumed into the Department of Homeland Security (DHS) on November 25, 2002. Previously, the INS was under the control of the attorney general's Justice Department – an enforcement-minded institution, but now the administration has institutionalized the clamping down on noncitizens in the name of national security. The new cabinet-level department merged all or parts of twenty-two federal agencies, with a combined budget of $40 billion and 170,000 workers, representing the biggest government reorganization in fifty years. DHS placed INS functions into two divisions: U.S. Citizenship and Immigration Services (USCIS), which handles immigrant visa petitions, naturalization, and asylum and refugee applications, and the Under Secretary for Border and Transportation Security, which includes the Bureau of Customs and Border Protection along with Immigration and Customs Enforcement units, for enforcement matters.

Before and after the creation of DHS, and presumably using preexisting authority and newfound power under the PATRIOT Act, the administration implemented, in the name of national security, a number of policies and actions aimed at noncitizens.

- Amending its own regulations on September 17, 2001, INS is authorized to detain any alien for forty-eight hours without charge, with the possibility of extending the detention for an additional "reasonable period of time" in the event of an "emergency or other extraordinary circumstance."
- On September 21, 2001, the chief immigration judge orders new procedures requiring all immigration judges to hold "secure" hearings separately from all other cases, to close the hearings to the public, and to

avoid discussing the case or disclosing any information about the case to anyone outside the immigration court.[4]

- On October 31, 2001, Attorney General John Ashcroft asks the secretary of state to designate forty-six new groups as terrorist organizations pursuant to the PATRIOT Act.

- On November 9, 2001, Attorney General Ashcroft calls for the "voluntary" interviews of up to five thousand aliens from countries suspected of harboring relatively large numbers of terrorists; interviewees may be jailed without bond if the attorney general finds they are violating immigration laws.

- On November 9, 2001, the State Department slows the process for granting visas for men, ages sixteen to forty-five, from certain Arab and Muslim countries by about twenty days.

- On November 13, 2001, President Bush issues an executive order authorizing the creation of military tribunals to try noncitizens on charges of terrorism.

- On December 4, 2001, U.S. Senator Russ Feingold holds hearings on the status of detainees. Attorney General Ashcroft suggests that those who question his policies are "aiding and abetting terrorism."

- On December 6, 2001, INS Commissioner James Ziglar announces that the INS will send the names of more than 300,000 aliens who remain in the United States, despite prior deportation or removal orders, to the FBI for inclusion in the National Crime Information Center database. This becomes known as the Alien Absconder Initiative.

- On January 8, 2002, the Department of Justice adds to the FBI's National Crime Information Center database the names of about six thousand men from countries believed to be harboring al-Qaeda members who have ignored deportation or removal orders.

- On January 25, 2002, the deputy attorney general issues instructions for the Alien Absconder Initiative to locate 314,000 people who have a final deportation order, but who have failed to surrender for removal. The deputy attorney general designates several thousand men from "countries in which there has been al-Qaeda terrorist presence or activity" as

---

[4] A subsequent proposal by the National Association of Immigration Judges (NAIJ) is noteworthy. In January 2002, NAIJ proposed the creation of a separate executive branch agency to house the trial-level immigration courts and Board of Immigration Appeals, citing "disturbing encroachments on judicial independence" taken by the president, the attorney general, and the Department of Justice in the aftermath of 9/11.

"priority absconders" and enters them into the National Crime Information Center database.

- On March 19, 2002, the Department of Justice announces interviews with three thousand more Arabs and Muslims present in the United States as visitors or students.

- In June 2002, the INS proposes broadening special registration requirements for nonimmigrants from certain designated countries.

- On July 15, 2002, the Department of Justice announces a surveillance pilot program whereby U.S. citizens, including truckers, bus drivers, and others, can act as informants to report "suspicious activity." The program is to be called Operation TIPS (Terrorism Information and Prevention System).

- On July 24, 2002, the Department of Justice authorizes any state or local law enforcement officer – with the consent of those who cover the jurisdiction where the law enforcement officer is serving – to perform certain functions of INS officers during the period of a declared "mass influx of aliens."

- On August 21, 2002, the INS deports approximately one hundred Pakistanis arrested on immigration violations.

- On September 16, 2002, Attorney General Ashcroft orders the INS to launch a "prompt review" of political asylum cases to identify any immigrants who have admitted to accusations of terrorist activity or being members of any terrorist organizations.

- On November 6, 2002, INS expands the special registration or National Security Entry–Exit Registration System (NSEERS) by requiring certain male nationals and citizens of Iran, Iraq, Libya, Sudan, and Syria admitted to the United States prior to September 10, 2002, to register with INS. Failure to report to an INS office for fingerprinting, a photo, and an interview will result in deportation. On December 16, 2002, nonimmigrant males sixteen years or older from Saudi Arabia and Pakistan are added to this list. On January 16, 2003, five more countries – Bangladesh, Egypt, Indonesia, Jordan, and Kuwait – are added to the list of twenty whose male citizens must register with INS.

- On November 18, 2002, the Foreign Intelligence Surveillance Act (FISA) Court of Review rules that the USA PATRIOT Act gives the Department of Justice broad authority to conduct wiretaps and other surveillance on terrorism suspects in the United States.

- On March 17, 2003, the Bush administration launches Operation Liberty Shield to "increase security and readiness in the United States." As part of this effort, DHS implements a temporary policy of detaining asylum seekers from three countries where al-Qaeda is known to have operated.

- On March 20, 2003, the attorney general reveals that since December 18, 2002, FBI agents and U.S. marshals have detained foreign nationals for alleged immigration violations in cases where there is not enough evidence to hold them on criminal charges.

- In late 2005, President Bush confirms that the United States has engaged in secret wiretapping of telephone calls of U.S. citizens with others from abroad without going to the FISA court for authorization.

As though the PATRIOT Act did not provide enough authority to target certain noncitizens, Congress used the backdrop of 9/11 to enact even more enforcement-related immigration laws in early 2005. In 2002, Congress created the National Commission on Terrorist Attacks Upon the United States (the 9/11 Commission) charged with investigating the circumstances surrounding the 9/11 terrorist attacks and recommending responses. Its final report and recommendations were released in July 2004, and in response, Congress drafted legislation to implement the recommendations. During debates on the legislation, several members of Congress, most notably Representative James Sensenbrenner (R-Wisconsin), the Chair of the House Judiciary Committee, argued for the inclusion of a number of contentious immigration measures. These measures went beyond the Commission's specific recommendations, nearly preventing the 9/11 Commission legislation's passage. The immigration-related proposals would expand the government's authority to arrest, detain, and deport immigrants; restrict judicial review and oversight; and reduce the number of documents immigrants may use to establish their identity. Sensenbrenner also wanted to include a provision barring states from issuing driver's licenses to undocumented aliens. But commission members and 9/11 victims' relatives spoke out against these provisions, arguing that the debate was delaying legislation and would not make any significant contribution to public safety and security. Congress removed Sensenbrenner's proposal and the other anti-immigrant measures from the final version of the commission's legislation, and the Intelligence Reform and Terrorism Prevention Act of 2004 was enacted.

However, in early 2005 Representative Sensenbrenner quickly reintroduced the controversial provisions (dubbed the REAL ID Act) that had been removed as a separate bill, and on February 10, the House of Representatives passed Sensenbrenner's full package.[5] One month later, the same legislation was attached to a huge emergency appropriations bill – a must-sign piece of legislation – to fund U.S. military efforts in Iraq and Afghanistan. The House passed this massive funding bill without any public debate or hearings. When the appropriations issue shifted to the Senate, the bill passed by that body did not include the REAL ID Act. But when the legislation went to the House–Senate conference committee to resolve differences in the two bills, House supporters pushed strongly for the Sensenbrenner provisions to be included. During debates legislators removed a few of the unsavory provisions, including one that would have rewarded private bounty hunters for enforcing immigration laws. But the basic REAL ID Act provisions remained, and the act was part of the package signed into law.[6]

The REAL ID Act will affect all Americans and has essentially provided the basis for making driver's licenses de facto national identity cards. Sensenbrenner's initial stated purpose of simply denying driver's licenses to undocumented aliens became buried in the onerous provisions required of all states. By 2008, states must issue driver's licenses that include a "common machine-readable technology" in order for the license to be accepted for federal purposes, such as boarding airplanes, entering federal courthouses, or using the services of private entities such as banks. To get a new approved license, people will have to produce several types of documentation. Those records must prove their name, date of birth, Social Security number, principal residence, and that they are lawfully in the United States. Although states will be responsible for verifying these documents, states receive no funding under the law. The IDs must include the information that appears on state-issued driver's licenses and non-driver ID cards – name, sex, address, and driver's license or other

---

[5] REAL ID Act of 2005, Pub. L. No. 109-13.
[6] The REAL ID Act affects everyone in the United States. Beginning in 2008, anyone living or working in the United States must have a federally approved ID card to travel on an airplane, open a bank account, collect Social Security payments, or take advantage of nearly any government service. Practically speaking, every driver's license likely will have to be reissued to meet federal standards. The REAL ID Act hands the Department of Homeland Security the power to set these standards and determine whether state drivers' licenses and other ID cards pass muster.

ID number and a photo. The act requires photos to be digital so authorities can include them in the multistate database. But the IDs must also include additional features that driver's licenses and nondriver ID cards do not incorporate. For instance, the ID must include features designed to thwart counterfeiting and identity theft. Once REAL ID is in effect, all fifty states' departments of motor vehicles will share information in a common database and may also verify information given to them against various federal databases.

The "machine-readable technology" requirement and perhaps DHS add-ons raise serious risk that the REAL ID Act will cause privacy violations. A radio frequency identification (RFID) tag may be placed in our licenses. (Other alternatives include a magnetic strip or enhanced bar code.) In the past, the DHS has indicated a preference for the RFID chips. These tags emit radio frequency signals that would allow the government to track our movement. Private businesses may be able to use remote scanners to read RFID tags as well, adding to the digital dossiers they already compile on consumers. The act requires no safeguards against such intrusions.

The Results

Given the implementation of immigration-related laws and policies, the question is whether the changes have actually helped in achieving the goals of apprehending terrorists. The answer is no.

Perhaps the failure and ill-advisedness of the use of immigration policies to catch terrorists is best illustrated by the results of the special registration (or NSEERS) program. The call-in program required male noncitizens from twenty-five mostly Arab and Muslim countries to register with immigration authorities between November 2002 and April 2003. About eighty-three thousand men came forward, and nearly thirteen thousand were placed in deportation proceedings. Many (the actual number is unknown) were in fact deported for minor immigration violations, but no one was charged with crimes related to terrorism. DHS officials, who inherited the program from the Justice Department, suspended the program, saying that resources could be better used on other counterterrorism initiatives.[7] The INS held closed hearings for

---

[7] Rachel L. Swarns, *Program's Value in Dispute as a Tool to Fight Terrorism*, NY TIMES, Dec. 21, 2004, at A26.

more than six hundred immigrants because the government designated the detainees to be of "special interest" to the government – the detainees were Muslim. Again, the call-in program uncovered no actual terrorists.

James Ziglar, appointed by President Bush as INS commissioner before INS became part of DHS, raised doubts about the benefits of the special registration program when Justice Department officials first proposed it. He questioned devoting significant resources to the initiative because it was unlikely that terrorists would voluntarily submit to intensive scrutiny.

> The people who could be identified as terrorist weren't going to show up. This project was a huge exercise and caused us to use resources in the field that could have been much better deployed. . . . As expected, we got nothing out of it. To my knowledge, not one actual terrorist was identified. But what we did get was a lot of bad publicity, litigation, and disruption in our relationships with immigrant communities and countries that we needed help from in the war on terror.[8]

Ziglar, who eventually left the Bush administration, had expressed doubts about linking immigration law with homeland security a month after the 9/11 attacks when he recognized, "We're not talking about immigration, we're talking about evil."[9]

Certainly, the selective enforcement – racial profiling – program provided the government with fingerprints, photographs, banking, and credit card records about Arab and Muslim immigrants that were previously unavailable, but the government did not apprehend a single terrorist. The sweeping roundup diverted resources from more pressing counterterrorism needs, strained relations with some Arab and Muslim nations, and alienated immigrants who might otherwise have been willing to help the government hunt for terror cells in this country. The roundups simply were not smart police work.

In its report, the 9/11 Commission noted that one detainee from al Qaeda implied that the special registration program had made al Qaeda operations more difficult. The commission said that if the detainee was credible, the program might have had a deterrent effect, but measuring the success of operations that include deterrence as a goal was difficult.

---

[8] Id.

[9] *Attorney General Briefing on New Anti-Terrorism Immigration Policies*, Oct. 31, 2001, at http://usinfo.state.gov/eap/Archive_Index/Attorney_General_Ashcroft_Briefing_on_New_ AntiTerrorism_Immigration_Policies.html.

The commission also made it clear that concerns about the program extended beyond the INS. Some State Department officials feared that the program would offend Arab and Muslim nations that were cooperating with the United States in the global campaign against terrorism. Robert Mueller, director of the FBI, echoed those concerns in testimony before the commission, acknowledging that the program came at a cost to American relations with important allies.[10]

Other profiling programs aimed at ensnaring terrorists were equally unsuccessful. In 2002, the Department of Justice reported on its project of interviewing approximately 5,000 Arab and Muslim men. About half – 2,261 – of those on the list were actually interviewed and fewer than twenty interview subjects were taken into custody. The Department of Justice charged most of those taken into custody with immigration violations, and the department arrested three on criminal charges. The department linked none to terrorism.[11]

The absconder initiative, as a general immigration enforcement measure, may have been legitimate and important. But after 9/11, the government changed the program's character to make it nationality specific. The change had marginal security benefits and further equated national origin with dangerousness.

Examples of even highly publicized immigration-related arrestees illustrate the ineffectiveness of the policies. Four brothers – Mohsen, Mojtaba, Mohammed, and Mostafa Mirmehdi – were detained for almost four years under the preventive detention policies used by the Bush administration after 9/11 for suspected terrorist links. Their chief offense appeared to be that they once attended a rally held in the United States in support of the Mujahedin-e Khalq (MEK). The State Department designated MEK as a terrorist organization in 1997 despite the group's long campaign to overthrow the fundamentalist Iranian regime, which the Bush administration, ironically, labeled as part of an "axis of evil." They remained in custody until March 2005, even though in the summer 2004 a court cleared them of terrorism-related charges. The rally they attended took place before the MEK was placed on the State Department terrorist list and featured Congressman Gary Ackerman (D-New York) as one of the speakers. At

---

[10] Swarns, *supra* note 7, at A26.

[11] Migration Policy Institute Staff, *Immigration and National Security Post–Sept. 11: Updated Chronology*, May 1, 2003, at http://www.migrationinformation.org/Feature/display.cfm?ID=78.

the time, Missouri Senator John Ashcroft (who later became President Bush's attorney general) also was a MEK backer.[12]

Noor Alocozy, a pizzeria owner, was arrested under the USA PATRIOT Act. He was charged with participating in an unlicensed money transfer operation that transferred funds for militants or terrorists in Pakistan and his native Afghanistan. But none of the terrorist support allegations were true. In fact, Noor and his wife fled Afghanistan nine years earlier during the civil war that brought the Taliban to power. Religious extremists killed Noor's brother and mother, making the allegations of sending money to the people that he hated absurd. Noor actually had state and county business permits to engage in a money transfer business, but he did not know that a federal license also was required. A federal judge eventually dropped all the allegations of terrorist support, fined Noor $5,000 for lack of a federal license, and sentenced him to home detention for four months. Federal prosecutors supported the outcome because Noor had cooperated fully.[13]

The wrongheadedness of these immigration-related security policies has another unfortunate effect. By creating an atmosphere where "immigrants who look like terrorists" are fair game, private citizens feel licensed to engage in racial profiling. The incarceration of many detainees was a result of profiling by ordinary citizens who called government agencies about neighbors, coworkers, and strangers based on their ethnicity, religion, name, or appearance. For example, the Migration Policy Institute (MPI) found that in "Louisville, Ky., the FBI and INS detained 27 Mauritanians after an outpouring of tips from the public; these included a tip from a suspicious neighbor who called the FBI when a delivery service dropped off a box with Arabic writing on it."[14] Private citizen tips to authorities resulted in arrests of well over a quarter of the detainees.

Of course, these tips were completely unreliable when it came to finding terrorists. Immigration arrests based upon tips, sweeps, and profiling resulted in no terrorism-related convictions against detainees.

---

[12] Robert Collier, *Exonerated in Terror Case, 4 Brothers Still Locked Up: Supporters Say Iranians Pawns in Post-9/11 Chess Game*, SF CHRONICLE, Jan. 25, 2005, at A1.

[13] Jim Herron Zamora, *Man Sentenced in Money-Transfer Case*, SF CHRONICLE, Aug. 27, 2005, at B3.

[14] Testimony of Muzaffar A. Chishti, Director, Migration Policy Institute at New York University School of Law, before the Committee on the Judiciary, United States Senate, Nov. 18, 2003 [hereinafter Chishti Testimony].

Four detainees with terrorism-related charges were interviewed by MPI researchers; their arrests resulted from traditional investigative techniques, not immigration enforcement initiatives. One detainee has since been convicted and two have been acquitted; charges were dropped against the fourth individual, and he was deported.

In general, noncitizen detainees have suffered exceptionally unfair treatment. The government conducted a determined effort to hide the identity, number, and whereabouts of its detainees, raising First Amendment questions related to the public's right to be informed about government actions. Many had severe problems notifying or communicating with their family members and lawyers or arranging for representation. The government held others for extended periods of time before charging them with immigration violations. Some had exceptionally high bonds imposed, and the government denied more than 42 percent of detainees the opportunity to post bond. The INS subjected many to closed hearings. Others suffered solitary confinement, twenty-four-hour lighting of cells, and physical abuse. Of the detainees for whom MPI could obtain information, they believed approximately 52 percent were subject to an FBI hold. The FBI hold prevented their repatriation for weeks or months even after the INS ordered them to be deported. In the view of MPI researchers, the immigration measures imposed are the type "commonly associated with totalitarian regimes."[15]

Vigilantism by private citizens has had other ugly ramifications. At one point after 9/11, hate crimes against Muslims soared, rising more than 1,500 percent. And discrimination in the workplace climbed after September 11. So overwhelming was the number of complaints it received that the Equal Employment Opportunity Commission (EEOC) created a new category to track acts of discrimination against Middle Eastern, Muslim, and South Asian workers after 9/11. In the fifteen months between September 11, 2001, and December 11, 2002, the EEOC received 705 such complaints.[16]

What is the result of the immigration-related, antiterrorism initiatives? Certainly not the capture of terrorists. Instead the initiatives have "created an atmosphere which suggests that it is okay to be biased against Arab-Americans and Muslims."[17]

[15] Id.
[16] Id.
[17] Id.

What We Really Need and Why

Better Intelligence Strategies

Treating law-abiding Arab, Muslim, and South Asian noncitizens already in the United States as suspects is not smart police or intelligence work. In fact, this type of profiling may actually be harming our efforts to combat terrorism by alienating communities that could help our efforts to learn about dangerous extremists. To understand what strategies might make sense, one place to begin is by learning what we can about the terrorists who did us harm on 9/11.

The 9/11 Commission's investigation revealed much about the hijackers.[18] The nineteen hijackers entered the United States a total of thirty-three times, using either tourist or student visas. They arrived through ten different airports, though more than half came in through Miami, JFK, or Newark. All but two of the hijackers obtained admission with tourist visas good for the customary six-month visitor's period. One hijacker had a student visa and was admitted for a stay of two years, while another sought and obtained admission for twenty days. Although U.S. law allows nationals of certain countries to enter without visas on a reciprocal basis under the visa waiver program, none of the 9/11 hijackers were nationals of a visa waiver country. Also, none of the 9/11 hijackers entered or tried to enter without inspection across the land borders with Mexico or Canada.

Of the five hijackers who entered the United States more than once, three of them violated immigration law. Ziad Farrah entered in June 2000 on a tourist visa and then promptly enrolled in flight school for six months. He never filed an application to change immigration status from tourist to student. Had the INS known he was out of status, it could have denied him entry on any of the three subsequent occasions he departed and returned while he was a student. Marwan al Shehhi came in through Newark in late May 2000, followed a week later by Mohammed Atta. Both gained admission as tourists and soon entered flight school in Florida. In September they filed applications to change their status. Before 9/11, regulations allowed tourists to change their status at any time, if they were in compliance. But both overstayed their periods of admission and completed flight school to obtain commercial pilot licenses. Both then left

---

[18] THE 9/11 COMMISSION REPORT: FINAL REPORT OF THE NATIONAL COMMISSION ON TERRORIST ATTACKS UPON THE UNITED STATES 383–384 (2004).

within a few days of one another and returned within a few days of one another in January 2001, while their change in visa status from tourist to student was still pending. When they lied upon being questioned about their student status on their reentries in January 2001, and when another hijacker failed to show up for the school for which the INS issued him a visa in December 2000, a student tracking system for informing immigration inspectors or agents was not available.

The entry and actions of the 9/11 hijackers have to be kept in context. U.S. consular officers annually process about ten million applications for visitors' visas at more than two hundred posts overseas. More than 500 million individuals (citizens and noncitizens) cross U.S. borders at more than two hundred designated crossing points every year; about 330 million of them are noncitizens, and some of that group may remain in the country longer than their visas permit. These numbers represent millions of important transactions daily. Of the noncitizens, 85 percent enter at land ports with Mexico and Canada, and the vast majority cross and return regularly, often daily. Perhaps another 500,000 or more enter without inspection across land borders.[19] We know that these entrants are vital to our continent's interdependent economies. We also know from experience that the overwhelming numbers of those arriving to our shores – even those who enter surreptitiously or who overstay their visas – are not entering to engage in terrorism. So the challenge for us in terms of national security is to prevent the very few people who may pose risks from entering or remaining in the United States undetected.

Prior to 9/11, critics viewed the immigration system as dysfunctional. Files were lost, delays were common, and INS employees were unnecessarily rude. At that time the system focused primarily on keeping individuals intending to immigrate from improperly entering the United States. In the visa process, the most common form of fraud is to get a visa to visit the United States as a tourist and then to stay to work and perhaps become a resident. Consular officers concentrated on interviewing visa applicants whom they suspected might not leave the United States. In national security terms, the pre-9/11 strategy focused on the possibility of smuggling of weapons of mass destruction, not the entry of terrorists who might use such weapons or the presence of associated foreign-born terrorists.[20]

[19] Id. at 383.   [20] Id.

The events of 9/11 have clarified matters. For terrorists, travel documents are as important as weapons. Terrorists must travel clandestinely to meet, train, plan, case targets, and gain access to attack. To them, international travel presents great danger, because they must surface to pass through regulated channels, present themselves to border security officials, or attempt to circumvent inspection points.

Apparently al Qaeda chose the 9/11 hijackers carefully to avoid detection – all but two were educated young men from middle-class families with no criminal records and no known connection to terrorism. Al Qaeda's strategy was to introduce "clean operatives" who could pass through immigration controls. Yet two of the hijackers' passports that survived were clearly doctored and manipulated in a manner that was suspicious and associated with al Qaeda. The 9/11 Commission believed that six more of the hijackers presented passports that had some of the same clues to their association with al Qaeda.

In their travels, terrorists use evasive methods, such as altered and counterfeit passports and visas, specific travel methods and routes, liaisons with corrupt government officials, human smuggling networks, supportive travel agencies, and immigration and identity fraud. These can sometimes be detected. Before 9/11, no agency of the U.S. government systematically analyzed terrorists' travel strategies. Had they done so, the 9/11 Commission concluded that analysts could have discovered the ways in which terrorist predecessors to al Qaeda had been systematically but detectably exploiting weaknesses in our border security since the early 1990s. As many as fifteen of the nineteen hijackers were potentially vulnerable to interception by border authorities. Analyzing their characteristic travel documents and travel patterns could have allowed authorities to intercept four to fifteen hijackers, and more effective use of information available in U.S. government databases could have identified up to three hijackers.[21]

Given this information and after serious study, investigation, and reflection, the 9/11 Commission did not recommend the types of ethnic profiling and nativist actions that anti-immigrant groups advocated and Congress implemented (e.g., the PATRIOT and REAL ID Acts):

Our investigation showed that two systemic weaknesses came together in our border system's inability to contribute to an effective defense against the 9/11 attacks: a lack of well-developed counterterrorism measures as a

---

[21] Id. at 384.

part of border security and an immigration system not able to deliver on its basic commitments, much less support counterterrorism.

. . .

Recommendation: Targeting travel is at least as powerful a weapon against terrorists as targeting their money. The United States should combine terrorist travel intelligence, operations, and law enforcement in a strategy to intercept terrorists, find terrorist travel facilitators, and constrain terrorist mobility.[22]

Thus the findings and immigration-system recommendations of the 9/11 Commission focused on the need for better counterterrorism measures, travel intelligence, and assessment of terrorist mobility.

In fact, under the Clinton administration, INS officials were taking steps to implement policies and systems at ports of entry that would manage the flow by segmenting populations, so that travel by the large, law-abiding majority could be certified in advance through biometric and other reliable techniques and safely facilitated. In this way, valuable law enforcement resources, expertise, and attention could be devoted to more careful screening of high-risk or unknown travelers. In the words of former INS Commissioner Doris Meissner, "Control and facilitation of movement are not contradictory. Rather, they constitute two sides of the same coin."[23]

The major entry–exit system stumbling block was the land borders. In 1998, INS tested available technologies for land border entry–exit in a simulation but was unable to recommend an approach that did not delay cross-border traffic. Widespread opposition to an entry–exit system from border communities in Canada and Mexico, cross-border commerce business representatives, and many others, including the administration, led Congress to delay implementation until 2001 and again until late 2004. Today, the land border problem remains unresolved.[24]

We would be deluding ourselves if we thought that databases are all we need to catch terrorists. But what good information systems can do is give a comprehensive picture of an individual's compliance with immigration requirements, travel to and from the country, applications for changes in status, and other information from which to validate proper

---

[22] Id. at 384–385.

[23] Testimony of Doris Meissner, Senior Fellow, Migration Policy Institute, before the National Commission on Terrorist Attacks Upon the United States, Jan. 26, 2004 [hereinafter Meissner Testimony].

[24] Id. The Enhanced Border Security and Visa Entry Reform Act of 2002 has tightened visa screening, border inspections, and tracking of foreigners.

or question suspect behavior. Such information is important when issuing visas, admitting individuals to the country, deciding applications for immigration benefits, and following investigative leads. Any of these actions can contribute to thwarting terrorism. Such information also can yield important insights into trends and patterns of possible criminal or terrorist activities.[25]

In short, the goal for DHS is to have the systems and structures in place to prevent wrongdoers from getting into the country. DHS should press for strong, comprehensive border controls, modern information systems, and interagency and international coordination. Major technology and systemic improvements must be a high priority. Many policy options are available that DHS can implement without excessive executive powers and with minimal intrusions on important civil liberties. A fundamental review of our country's intelligence infrastructure, better coordination of intelligence gathering, more focus on monitoring the tools of terrorism, better use of technology, improved training of screeners, and enhanced recruitment of translators and informants are among the policies that DHS has initiated and needs to expand.

Indeed, the government's major successes in apprehending terrorists have not come from post-9/11 immigration initiatives but from other efforts such as international intelligence gathering, law enforcement cooperation, and information provided by arrests made abroad. A few noncitizens detained through these immigration initiatives have been characterized as terrorists, but the only charges actually brought against them were for routine immigration violations or ordinary crimes.

Thus the primary domestic security responses to terrorism should be strengthened intelligence and analysis, compatible information systems and information sharing, and vigorous law enforcement and investigations. Improved immigration controls and enforcement can support good antiterrorism enforcement, but they are not enough by themselves. More than anything else, 9/11 demonstrated the need to dramatically improve the nation's intelligence capabilities. The immigration system captures voluminous amounts of data that can be important in "connecting the dots" about individuals under investigation.[26] But for this to be effective, information from visa and immigration data systems must be fully linked to establish complete immigration histories of visitors and residents.

[25] Meissner Testimony, *supra* note 23.   [26] Chishti Testimony, *supra* note 14.

Government agencies also must greatly improve both their information sharing and their systems for maintaining watch lists.

Legalizing the Undocumented

As discussed in Chapter 1, providing a path for undocumented immigrants to regularize their status is in the national interest. The argument is clear; legalizing undocumented workers coupled with a large worker program would promote our national security and constitutes a step that would aid our country in its efforts to combat terrorism. By offering a program that encourages undocumented workers to come forward, we can conduct background checks on a large group that currently lives underground while freeing up investigative resources to concentrate on real threats of terror at the border and within our shores. These new community members would be more inclined to participate in civic society and aid law enforcement efforts directly. Legalization would promote family reunification, and individuals would enjoy the psychological benefits derived from the comfort of family. With more definite status, wages and working conditions for the new Americans and all Americans would improve.

What We Don't Need

In recognition of the overwhelming numbers of law-abiding, hardworking immigrants in our midst, the 9/11 Commission reminded Americans:

> Our borders and immigration system, including law enforcement, ought to send a message of welcome, tolerance, and justice to members of immigrant communities in the United States and in their countries of origin. We should reach out to immigrant communities. Good immigration services are one way of doing so that is valuable in every way – including intelligence.[27]

What we do not need in the name of national security are immigration policies and administrative actions that send a "you're not one of us" message to immigrant and other ethnic communities. Following the London subway suicide bombings on July 7, 2005, by "home-grown" Muslim terrorists, some commentators were quick to give the United States credit for purportedly being more welcoming to our own Muslim minorities. For example, Boris Johnson, a member of the British Parliament, noted

---

[27] Id. at 390.

that Americans did not grow their own suicide bombers who volunteered to slaughter their neighbors. The simple reason, according to Johnson, is that America takes immigrants and makes them into Americans. Pledging allegiance to and proudly flying the flag is a way of showing that every citizen "is not only American but equally American, and has an equal stake in society. . . . We [Brits must], in a way that is cheery and polite," insist that our Muslim communities "acculturate to our way of life."[28] Similarly, Fareed Zakaria, the editor of the international edition of *Newsweek*, says that the difference is that in the United States Muslims advance and find economic and social acceptance.[29] Johnson and Zakaria overstate both the welcome and the assimilation of Muslims into U.S. society, but their point is well taken. Creating a welcoming environment can only be beneficial.

The immigration policy approach to homeland security actually used by the Bush administration and the Department of Justice did not follow this philosophy. To apprehend individuals like the 9/11 hijackers before they attack requires "laser-like focus" on the gathering, sharing, and analysis of intelligence, working hand-in-glove with well-targeted criminal and immigration law enforcement.[30] Instead, the government conducted roundups of individuals based on their national origin and religion. These roundups failed to locate terrorists and damaged one of our great potential assets in the war on terrorism – the communities of Arab and Muslim Americans.

The government's use of immigration law as a primary means of fighting terrorism has substantially diminished civil liberties and stigmatized Arab and Muslim American communities in this country. These measures, which primarily target Muslims, have diminished the openness of U.S. society and eroded national unity. As a result, Arabs and Muslims in America feel under siege, isolated, and stigmatized.

For example, the so-called voluntary interview program greatly alarmed Arab and Muslim American communities. In some places, the Federal Bureau of Investigation (FBI) worked to establish good relations with the community and conducted the program in a nonthreatening manner. But problems occurred when the FBI tasked poorly trained police officials

---

[28] *How They See Us: Britain's Response to Terror Beats America*, THE WEEK, July 29, 2005, at 13.

[29] Interview of Fareed Zakaria, *The Daily Show*, July 21, 2005.

[30] Chishti Testimony, *supra* note 14.

to implement the program. Moreover the goals of the program (investigating the 9/11 terrorist attacks, intimidating potential terrorists, recruiting informants, and enforcing immigration violations) were contradictory. The immigration enforcement focus and public fanfare that surrounded the program worked against its potential for intelligence gathering.

In its research, MPI also discovered an important international "echo effect" from domestic immigration policy. By targeting Muslim and Arab immigrants, the U.S. government has deepened the perception abroad that the United States is anti-Muslim and that its democratic values and principles are hypocritical. This echo effect is undermining U.S. relationships with exactly the moderate, pro-Western nations and social groups whom we need in our fight against terrorism.[31]

In effect, the administration has engaged in offensive ethnic profiling of these communities by specifically targeting Muslims and Arabs in the United States. Adding an ethnic or racial component to the "profiles" used to screen people for visas abroad or when seeking admission at the port of entry is problematic but may be justifiable. But extending that approach to U.S. neighborhoods and communities is very troubling. Rather than relying on individualized suspicion or intelligence-driven criteria, the government has used national origin as a proxy for evidence of dangerousness.

The effectiveness of profiling is questionable because it casts too wide a net around a community without providing any information about individual behavior. Many law enforcement professionals view profiling as a crude and ultimately inadequate substitute for behavior-based enforcement and effective intelligence gathering. They also maintain that profiling leads to less rigorous scrutiny of individuals who may be dangerous but do not fit the profile.[32] In fact, profiling can give a false sense of security – it would not catch Atlanta Olympics bomber Eric James Rudolf, Oklahoma City bomber Timothy McVeigh, American Taliban fighter John Walker Lindh, or al Qaeda recruit Jose Padilla. Consider also the speculation in the law enforcement community that the person responsible for the anthrax mailings in the fall 2001 was a trusted U.S. citizen with security clearance. In addition to being ineffective, profiling stigmatizes, intimidates, and alienates immigrant communities and makes their members less eager to cooperate with law enforcement agencies.

[31] Id. [32] Id.

The passage of the REAL ID Act also is problematic in the fight against terrorism. The Sensenbrenner provision that bars states from issuing driver's licenses to undocumented aliens actually threatens rather than assists law enforcement officials. Critics raised legitimate concerns that undocumented workers may drive their cars despite the bar, putting the public at risk through the absence of driver regulation and the inability of such drivers to obtain car insurance. But more serious effects on law enforcement are at stake. West Point Professor Margaret Stock points out that "the collective DMV databases are the largest law enforcement databases in the country, with records on more individual adults than any other law enforcement databases."[33]

Denying driver's licenses to undocumented immigrants will hurt our national security by depriving law enforcement officials of critical information on substantial numbers of adults who are physically present in the United States. Law enforcement officials may be unable to find persons who may be security threats, and they will have less information with which to prevent and solve crimes. When a terrorist incident happens, determining what happened and when will be more difficult.[34]

In the wake of 9/11, law enforcement officials needed the driver's license data after the fact to figure out where the terrorists had been, how they moved, and who helped them. The importance of the DMV database following 9/11 was confirmed by the American Association of Motor Vehicle Administrators in its October 2003 report:

> Law enforcement agencies, federal, state and local, use the driver license image on a frequent basis to identify victims, criminal suspects, missing children and the elderly. *Digital images from driver records have significantly aided law enforcement agencies charged with homeland security. The events of September 11, 2001 clearly demonstrate the value of the driver record photograph.* The 19 terrorists obtained driver licenses from several states and *federal authorities relied heavily on those images for the identification of the individuals responsible* for the horrific criminal acts on that fateful day.[35]

---

[33] Margaret D. Stock, *Driver Licenses and National Security: Myths and Reality* (2004) (unpublished paper on file with author).

[34] Id.

[35] American Association of Motor Vehicle Administrators, *Access to Drivers License and Identification Card Data by Law Enforcement*, October 2003, at http://www.aamva.org/Documents/idsIDSecurityFrameworkAppendices278303.pdf (emphasis added).

Conclusion

The MPI (which included former INS Commissioner Doris Meissner on its research staff) conducted a comprehensive study of U.S. immigration policies after 9/11, interviewing Arab and Muslim community leaders and senior intelligence and law enforcement officials while analyzing the profiles of more than four hundred post-9/11 detainees. Not surprisingly, the researchers concluded that harsh government measures against immigrants in the name of homeland security failed to make the nation safer, violated fundamental civil liberties, and undermined national unity. The MPI determined that

- the U.S. government overemphasized the use of the immigration system;
- as an antiterrorism measure, immigration enforcement is of limited effectiveness; and
- arresting a large number of noncitizens on grounds not related to domestic security only gives the nation a false sense of security.[36]

In calling for better intelligence strategies rather than targeting innocent immigrants – especially those of a particular ethnic or religious group – MPI researchers noted:

> It is crucial for law enforcement to engage Arab- and Muslim-American communities as it works to identify terrorism-related conspiracies, recruitment, and financial networks. This requires cultivating new relationships and building trust. The government should also embrace these communities as bridges of understanding to societies and peoples around the world who are deeply alienated from the United States.[37]

Our nation must take the smart approach to national security to avoid another 9/11. A smart approach to national security is one that reaches out to noncitizen communities not simply because they are part of the United States but because they are allies in protecting our homeland. A smart approach to national security recognizes the economic and social benefits that newcomers bring to our nation so that strengthened security strikes a balance between our need for those contributions and investigative intrusions into their lives.

[36] Muzaffar A. Chishti et al., *America's Challenge: Domestic Security, Civil Liberties, and National Unity after September 11* (June 2003) (published report available from MPI).
[37] Chishti Testimony, *supra* note 14.

Sadly, when government takes the lead in unreasonable profiling and private citizens follow, the targets are de-Americanized – told that they are not *real* Americans, not part of us. The de-Americanization process is capable of reinventing itself generation after generation. We have seen this exclusionary process aimed at Jews, Asians, Mexicans, Haitians, and those of other descent throughout the nation's history. De-Americanization is not simply xenophobia because more than fear of foreigners is at work. This is a brand of nativism cloaked in a Eurocentric sense of America that combines hate and racial profiling. Whenever we go through a period of de-Americanization like what is currently affecting South Asians, Arabs, and Muslim Americans, a whole generation of Americans sees the following: that exclusion and hate are acceptable, that the definition of who is an American can be narrow, and that they too have a license to profile. Their license is issued when others around them engage in hate, and the government engages in its own profiling. This is one regrettable process of racism that haunts our country.

Targeting noncitizens of a certain ethnic, religious, or racial background or closing our borders to newcomers or visitors is a national security strategy that does not make our country safe. In fact, those strategies may diminish the opportunity to engage newcomer communities in assisting with smarter law enforcement approaches to public safety. Because the 9/11 hijackers were foreign born, cracking down on noncitizens – especially those who looked like or were of the same religion as the hijackers – made sense to some. But the crackdown apprehended no terrorists. By falling for the temptation of profiling, we actually sacrificed the fundamental values and principles of openness and inclusion that we ought to have been guarding. Those who would do us harm won an important battle when we chose to target Arab, Muslim, and South Asian members of our communities. We damaged a part of America, shaming ourselves in the process.

5 . . . . . A Welcome Wagon
for New Americans

Reports that the July 7, 2005, London subway suicide bombings were perpetrated by "home-grown" Muslim terrorists, "born and brought up in respectable suburbs of northern England, rather than medieval religious fanatics,"[1] came as a surprise to many observers. Three were born in Great Britain, went to British schools, raised children there, worked in local shops, and were part of a community. Sometime, somehow they were inculcated with a message of hate, revenge, and contempt.[2] In recalling Timothy McVeigh, no one doubted that the United States has its own brand of home-grown terrorists. But when it came to Muslims in our communities, the United States received stellar marks for being welcoming to people of different backgrounds. British Parliament member Boris Johnson praised the United States for giving its immigrants "an equal stake in society." Fareed Zakaria of *Newsweek* gave similar credit to the United States:

> In a sense it was always too simple to say that we would spread democracy in the Arab world and that will change things. It's true that there's a lot of dysfunctions built up in the Arab world and spreading democracy or helping them become more democratic and open up their systems will help. [But] this is a virus that developed over 30 or 40 years, and it spread [as a] part of globalization. Radical Islam spread from Saudi Arabia and got globalized. And there are people, disaffected young men in Europe, particularly in Europe because they tend to not get assimilated very well,

[1] Anatole Koletsky, *The Act of Small-Time Losers,* THE TIMES (London), July 14, 2005.
[2] *Confronting Terrorism's New Face,* COURIER MAIL (Queensland, Australia), July 16, 2005.

who search around for some grand theory, kind of ideology, of protest. Forty years ago it might have been Marxism or Maoist ideology; now, particularly for Muslims, it's this kind of Islamic protest. And they get seduced by it.

. . .

The fundamental cause is this radical strain of ideology, that's feeding this kind of hatred and a cult of death [that is] seducing, particularly some small segment of European Muslims, because they feel disaffected. They feel like they're not part of the society. One of the things to notice – maybe it's that we've gotten lucky in America, but I think that one part of why we haven't had a knapsack bomber here, is because the *American Muslim community is actually pretty well integrated into America*. If you look at average income, the professions they're in, they're doing well; they are actually very much part of the classic immigrant success story of moving up, getting integrated, they're not in ghettos. So that alleviates the problem somewhat. It means you don't have this pool of potentially radicalized youth.[3]

Although I believe Johnson and Zakaria give the United States too much credit, their premise makes sense. Integrating minority groups can only be beneficial to our national security. The 9/11 Commission also recognized the security and intelligence benefits of sending a "message of welcome, tolerance, and justice" to immigrant communities.[4] In fact, we benefit from the integration of newcomers into our society for reasons far beyond the important matter of national security.

Every day we are reminded that the United States is a land of immigrants. For most of us, we need only walk outside our front door and travel to work to notice the diverse ethnic backgrounds, languages, cultures, customs, and foods that make up America. The 1965 amendments to the nation's immigration selection system, refugee policies, family ties, economic opportunities, and political tensions abroad have all come together to fuel the increased diversity that immigrants and refugees have brought to this country in the past thirty to forty years.

The reaction to newcomer diversity is itself diverse. Many native-born Americans welcome the economic, social, and cultural contributions that new Americans bring, while others fear or even resent the social and economic impact of new arrivals. For some native born, the reaction varies, depending on the particular immigrant or refugee group considered. Still

---

[3] Interview of Fareed Zakaria, *The Daily Show*, July 21, 2005 (emphasis added).
[4] THE 9/11 COMMISSION REPORT: FINAL REPORT OF THE NATIONAL COMMISSION ON TERRORIST ATTACKS UPON THE UNITED STATES 390 (2004).

others may be concerned about being overwhelmed by too many newcomers. A more negative or hostile reaction may also ensue when native-born Americans perceive newcomers as unwilling to learn English or to adopt "American" customs or values.

Immigrants and refugees themselves have different reactions to their new environment. The vast majority are grateful to be in the United States and appreciate the opportunities available to them. Many seek out programs to learn English, to learn about their new country, and to participate actively in civic life. Others are overwhelmed by their new foreign environment (especially those refugees who may be suffering from post-traumatic stress) and fall back on the comfort or familiarity of enclaves where they are able to speak their native language in a familiar culture. Most are focused on getting their feet on the ground.

Given the varying attitudes of and about newcomers and demographic trends, the integration of newcomers into civic life is critical, from the perspectives of both the receiving communities and the newcomers themselves. The early integration and civic involvement of newcomers should be a high priority because that involvement is a key to better social, economic, and cultural integration of the newcomer and his or her family. And after the events of 9/11 and the London subway bombings, we know that integration is also good for national security. In short, the integration of newcomers is good for local communities and good for the nation.

Governmental institutions can and should play a lead role in integration efforts. The influence of local leaders and government agencies on integration programs can have an overwhelmingly positive and immediate effect on the lives of newcomers. Important forms of civic engagement are not predicated on citizenship. Schools, neighborhoods, community groups, and public service programs can all benefit from the immediate involvement of newcomers. Voting may be an aspect of civic participation, but civic participation is a broader concept than voting and should be encouraged soon after arrival into the country.

Demographic Data

As economic conditions in western Europe improved in the late nineteenth and early twentieth centuries, immigration from Germany, the United Kingdom, and Ireland declined. But at the same time, immigration from southern and eastern Europe rapidly increased. During the first decade of the twentieth century, which remains the decade that witnessed the greatest immigration to the United States, 1.5 million immigrants entered from Russia and another 2 million from Italy and Austria-Hungary. The constant flow of Italians, Russians, and Hungarians fueled racial nativism and anti-Catholicism. This culminated in passage of the Act of February 5, 1917, which contained a controversial literacy requirement that excluded aliens who could not "read and understand some language or dialect."

The reactionary, isolationist political climate that followed World War I, manifested in the Red Scare of 1919–1920, led to even greater exclusionist demands. The landmark Immigration Act of 1924, opposed by only six senators, once again took direct aim at southern and eastern Europeans whom the Protestant majority in the United States viewed with dogmatic disapproval. The arguments advanced in support of the bill stressed recurring themes – racial superiority of Anglo-Saxons, that immigrants would cause the lowering of wages, and the unassimilability of foreigners – while citing the usual threats to the nation's social unity and order posed by immigration.

The act restructured criteria for admission to respond to nativist demands and represented a general selection policy that remained in place until 1965. It provided that immigrants of any particular country be limited to 2 percent of their nationality in 1890. The law struck most deeply at Jews, Italians, Slavs, and Greeks, who had immigrated in great numbers after 1890 and who would be most disfavored by such a quota system.

The 1965 immigration amendments finally abolished the quota system after successive criticism of the 1924 framework by Presidents Truman, Eisenhower, Kennedy, and finally Johnson. The new law allowed twenty thousand immigrant visas for every country not in the western hemisphere. This framework provided the foundation for expansive immigration from Asia and Latin America that has dominated immigration totals since the 1970s.

Not surprisingly, Nathan Glazer's 1985 description of the United States as the "permanently unfinished country" continues to be apt.[5] With the number of foreign-born residents in the United States increasing by

[5] Nathan Glazer, ed., CLAMOR AT THE GATES: THE NEW AMERICAN IMMIGRATION 3 (1985).

15 million in the past ten years, a primary lesson from demographic data is that our nation continues to be a land of immigrants. The foreign-born population numbers thirty-six million, about 11 percent of the total. In particular, the census story reveals changes in the past dozen years that reflect increasing numbers of residents of Latin and Asian descent in new parts of the country. Asians and Latinos have reached a stunning 58 percent in population growth rate over the past ten years nationwide.[6]

The rise in Latinos outstripped overall population growth throughout the country.[7] Data from the 2000 Census showed explosive growth in the Latino population outside the nation's urban areas as Latinos helped to fill increasingly available low-wage jobs in the 1990s. They came in large numbers to work in meatpacking plants in Minnesota and Nebraska, tend crops in Kentucky, and manufacture carpets in Georgia mills.[8] The numbers are further evidence of how thirty-plus years of massive Latino immigration continues to alter the nation's demographic landscape. Half of all Latinos live in Texas and California, and 77 percent (27.1 million) live in seven states: California, Texas, New York, Florida, Illinois, Arizona, and New Jersey, listed in order from the largest to the smallest Latino populations. In fourteen other states scattered throughout the country, the percentage of Latinos as part of the overall population doubled in the 1990s. Those states are Alabama, Arkansas, Delaware, Georgia, Indiana, Iowa, Kentucky, Minnesota, Mississippi, Nebraska, North Carolina, Oregon, South Carolina, and Tennessee.[9] The dramatic surge in the nation's Latino population was due mainly to a 53 percent increase in the number of people of Mexican heritage. Mexican Americans made up 63 percent of the nation's 40.4 million "Hispanics" in 2005, by far the fastest-growing segment of the U.S. Latino population.[10]

The Asian American rate of growth almost has matched Latino growth. The Asian American population increased from seven million in 1990 to

---

[6] Mercedes Tira Andrei, *Asians Soar in Number in Big American Cities*, BUSINESS-WORLD, Apr. 6, 2001, at 27.

[7] Laurent Belsie, *Hispanics Spread to Hinterlands*, CHRISTIAN SCIENCE MONITOR, Mar. 26, 2001, at 1.

[8] Genaro C. Armas, *Hispanic Population Surges in Small Towns, Rural Communities*, SOUTH BEND TRIBUNE, Apr. 1, 2001, at A7.

[9] Tony Pugh, *U.S. Hispanic Population Surges to 20.6 Million*, KNIGHT RIDDER WASHINGTON BUREAU, May 10, 2001.

[10] Pew Hispanic Center, *Hispanics: A People in Motion* (2005), at 2–3, available at http://pewhispanic.org/files/reports/40.pdf.

twelve million in 2000, and to fourteen million in 2004. Asian American presence is most visible in the big states of Texas, New York, New Jersey, Virginia, Maryland, Illinois, Ohio, and Pennsylvania, where they cluster in huge numbers in the capital cities where jobs are available and generally recession proof.[11] Between 2000 and 2004, the Asian American population grew by 25 to 37 percent in states like Nevada, Georgia, New Hampshire, Delaware, Florida, Arizona, North Carolina, and Connecticut. Even in a place like Kentucky, the 2000 Census found a 75 percent population increase in Asian Pacific Americans since 1990 and an even greater 173 percent increase in the Latino population.[12] In Louisville, more than a third of the residents will likely be foreign born by the year 2010.[13]

The type of diversity that immigration has engendered is not limited along racial lines. Consider the religious diversity that has developed in a traditional "Bible Belt" city like Nashville, Tennessee, where one can now find six Buddhist communities, five Jewish congregations, five Islamic mosques, a Baha'i center, a Hindu temple, and a Hindu ashram, or teaching abode, plus assorted Sikhs and Jains. In Nashville, two categories of new religious expression are apparent: the Christian and the non-Christian variety. Enclaves of Laotian Buddhists and Kurdish Muslims and a scattering of Jains, practitioners of an ancient Indian philosophic tradition, can be found, but also four thousand Korean Protestants, Armenian Christians, and an Eastern Orthodox coffeehouse/chapel.[14] In Bowling Green, Kentucky, the population of fifty thousand includes four thousand Muslims.[15]

Immigration-driven growth is not limited to a few states. In fact, in reccent years the foreign-born population grew far more slowly in states with the largest immigrant populations, such as California, New York, and Texas, than in a group of nineteen new-growth states.[16] The nineteen new-growth states – those with the fastest-growing immigrant populations in the 1990s – include Alabama, Arizona, Arkansas, Colorado, Georgia,

---

[11] Andrei, *supra* note 6.

[12] Butch John, *Asian Populations Surge in Kentucky and Indiana*, COURIER-JOURNAL, May 20, 2001, at 4a.

[13] Id.

[14] Ray Waddle, *Bible Belt Getting Stretched: City Known as "Protestant Vatican" Now Includes Variety of Religions, Study Shows*, TENNESSEAN, Apr. 1, 2001, at 1B.

[15] Id.

[16] *Growth of California's Foreign-Born Population Slows as Immigrants Move to Other States*, News Release, the Urban Institute, Jan. 11, 2001.

Idaho, Iowa, Kansas, Kentucky, Maryland, Mississippi, Nebraska, Nevada, North Carolina, Oklahoma, Oregon, South Carolina, Utah, and Virginia. During the 1990s, the foreign-born population grew by a dramatic 95 percent in the new-growth states, compared to only 23 percent in traditional immigrant destination states of California, New York, Florida, Texas, New Jersey, and Illinois.[17]

Even traditional immigrant destinations have become more diverse. For example, in New York City, while Chinese Americans remained the largest Asian Pacific American group, Asian Indian Americans grew 80 percent (to 170,899) in the 1990s, while Bangladeshi Americans surged 285 percent to 19,148.[18] The city's Mexican American population grew from 62,000 in 1980 to about 200,000 in 2000.[19]

Information pertaining to particular states suggest that issues pertaining to cultural pluralism, race relations, and defining who is an American are real questions in many communities across the nation. Consider these examples.

Colorado's Latino population nearly doubled in the past decade. They make up more than a third of Denver's population.[20] Roughly one-fourth of the state's 724,000 students are Latino, many of them Mexican immigrants.[21] In Denver, Latino and Asian American communities are booming, and businesses in thriving immigrant enclaves do well.[22]

---

[17] Id. The South also gained a record number of African Americans during the 1990s, an increase that made it the only region in the country where more blacks arrived than left. The departure of blacks from the rest of the country and migration to the South represents a historic pattern that has come full circle: African Americans spent most of the past century fleeing the South's racial oppression and lack of economic opportunity. The pattern of flight slowly began to change three decades ago and accelerated dramatically in the 1990s, when the South's black population grew by nearly 3.6 million through births, immigration, and migration. That was twice the increase of the 1980s and the result of a combination of attractions: family ties, the region's improving fortunes, and easing racial prejudice. D'Vera Cohn, *Reversing a Long Pattern, Blacks Are Heading South*, WASHINGTON POST, May 5, 2001, at A1.

[18] *New Census Data Gives a More Detailed Portrait of Asian Americans in New York City*, June 27, 2001 (news release) (on file with author).

[19] *Immigrants Frustrated by Laws that Take Kids from Home*, 37 NATIONAL CATHOLIC REPORTER 6 (June 29, 2001).

[20] Tina Griego, *Hispanics a Multicultural Nation of Our Own*, DENVER POST, Mar. 21, 2001, at B1.

[21] Jorge Amaya, *Mexican Immigrants Need to Get Involved*, DENVER POST, Feb. 21, 2001, at B11.

[22] Louis Aguilar, *Language of Business Binds Cultures; Latino, Asian Markets Thrive*, DENVER POST, May 29, 2001, at C1.

Merchants and workers in some neighborhoods find it increasingly necessary to use three languages – English, Spanish, and an Asian language, often Korean.[23] Jeremiah Kong, a native of Seoul, South Korea, owns La Plaza Mexicana, a 26,000-square-foot building with eighteen shops that sell everything from auto parts to furniture and cater to Spanish-language immigrants. Eight of the shop owners are Korean; the others are Latino, both U.S. born and Mexican immigrants. His workers are also Spanish-language immigrants. So, for Kong to deal with his employees, he tends to use "Spanglish" – a combination of English and Spanish. Estella Jaime, a native of Mexico who works for Kong, also understands a few Korean phrases.[24] Smaller Colorado towns also experienced significant increases in their immigrant population. Known for their proximity to world-class skiing, the counties of Garfield, Eagle, and Summit saw increases of 568 percent, 389 percent, and 722 percent, respectively, as immigrant families came to fill jobs in ski ressorts, hotels, and other service industries. The state's Latino population grew 73 percent and Asians by 68 percent in ten years.

Iowa's Latino population grew by roughly 29,000, a leap of roughly 90 percent, in the 1990s. The 61,500 Latino residents are the state's largest minority group. Iowa's Asian population grew by 11,300, an increase of 44 percent.[25] In all of Iowa's ninety-nine counties, Latino population growth during the 1990s outpaced the overall population rise (or declined more slowly in counties that lost people). Latino growth ranged from Clarke County (up 1,842 percent) to suburban Dallas County right outside Des Moines (up 1,112 percent).[26]

North Carolina led the country in Latino growth, up 394 percent in ten years, followed by Arkansas, Georgia, Tennessee, and Nevada. In Siler City, North Carolina, Latinos made up 4 percent of the town's 4,808 people in 1990. By 2000, they constituted 39 percent of the city's 6,966 residents, drawn by jobs at chicken-processing plants and textile mills.[27]

Oklahoma's Latino population doubled in the 1990s; Mexicans make up three-fourths of the total.[28] In Oklahoma City, schools experienced

---

[23] Id.   [24] Id.

[25] Thomas Beaumont, *What Is Abuse? Cultures Vary*, DES MOINES REGISTER, Jan. 2, 2001, at 1.

[26] Belsie, *supra* note 7.   [27] Armas, *supra* note 8.

[28] Ginnie Graham, *Jump in Hispanics Has Advocates Busy; Recent Arrivals Need More Assistance*, TULSA WORLD, May 18, 2001.

an eightfold increase in the number of students who consider English a second language.[29]

Kentucky's population increased by nearly 10 percent during the 1990s, topping four million for the first time at 4,041,769.[30] The Asian American and Latino growth in the state was even greater: 75 percent for Asian Americans (to almost 30,000) and 173 percent for Latinos (to approximately 60,000).[31] In Louisville, more than a third of the residents soon will be foreign born.[32]

Consider these other immigrant-driven statistics: One of every four residents of Arizona are now Latino. In Tennessee, the Latino population nearly tripled in ten years and now accounts for 2 percent of the state population. The number of Asians almost doubled, though the state remains 80 percent white and 16 percent black. The Latino population also tripled in Alabama, Georgia, and Minnesota, while at least doubling in states like Utah, Idaho, Indiana, Oregon, Kansas, South Carolina, and Mississippi. In New Hampshire, the Latino population grew by 81 percent and the Asian Pacific Islander community by 74 percent. In Utah, Asians are the second-largest minority group following Latinos. In Massachusetts, the Asian population increased nearly 70 percent, while Latinos grew almost 50 percent. The Asian population doubled in South Dakota.[33] The appendix sets forth related data on several other states.

The effect of immigration on the census is obvious; the population throughout the country is becoming more diverse. And this immigration-driven growth in diversity will likely continue.

Resentment and Misunderstanding

Misunderstanding and resentment between newcomers and native-born Americans often arise when groups know little about each other and have

---

[29] Charisse Jones, *New-Timers' Lives Revive Old Cities; Immigrants Feed a Population Boom, and Help Communities that Need to Fill New Jobs and Positions Left Vacant by Retirees,* USA TODAY, Apr. 20, 2001, at 3A.

[30] *Population Shifts during the 1990s: State-by-State Breakdown of Ups and Downs,* SEATTLE TIMES, Apr. 1, 2001, at A20.

[31] Within the Asian American population, Vietnamese grew at the highest rate. John, *supra* note 12. Joseph Gerth, *Bridging a Language Gap; Need for Court Interpreters Grows Quickly,* COURIER-JOURNAL, July 31, 2001, at A1.

[32] John, *supra* note 12.

[33] *Population Shifts during the 1990s, supra* note 30, at A20.

few opportunities to meet and intermingle. A typical example might be Hamblen County, in the northeastern section of Tennessee, where the Latino population became 6 percent of the county's residents within a ten-year span (outnumbering the small but long-standing black population). Already bitter about the movement of local jobs to other countries, including Mexico, many white working-class residents viewed the entry of Latinos into the local labor markets as an aggressive threat that added insult to injury. Letters to the editor of local papers decried the Latino presence. A white woman recounted:

> [S]omeone decided to come up and start telling me – and she didn't even know me, that was the first time I had met her – that she had just lost her job because of the immigrants. I said, "How do you know that?" She couldn't give me an answer, but I think what it came back to is that the job she had before this, . . . that plant had shut down to relocate to Mexico. Then the place where she lost her job just last week had a few immigrants employed there, and when she lost her job she just naturally assumed that was why.

One Latino expressed concern about her white coworkers: "They view me badly, they don't want me; they hate me."[34]

Latino immigrants also unsettled the dualistic white–black racial hierarchy in Hamblen County. Most residents sense intense hostility that some white workers hold toward new immigrants, and black and white residents have observed that Latinos have replaced African Americans as the chief target of white racism. Actually, this has engendered sympathy, rather than competition, between many African Americans and Latinos.

Although some long-term residents are negative about immigrants, others are not. In January 2002, the Morristown-based chapter of the Ku Klux Klan organized a rally at the courthouse to protest "the growing non-white flood of illegals into our communities." Literature promoting the event called for closing the nation's borders "before American-hating foreigners pollute and destroy our community. We must secure the existence of our people and a future for white children." The rally attracted more than fifty supporters. However, a counterdemonstration, organized by the NAACP, Jewish anti-defamation groups, and others drew eight hundred to one thousand people. In addition, a celebration of diversity at the local

---

[34] Barbara Ellen Smith, *Across Races and Nations: Toward Worker Justice in the U.S. South* (Center for Research on Women, University of Memphis, 2003) (unpublished paper on file with author).

high school, supported by the mayor and district attorney, was held to counter the Klan's message of hate. Many people in Hamblen County have sought to welcome new immigrants; health professionals and other service providers have organized to meet the needs of Spanish-speaking clientele, and some local churches have begun to offer services in Spanish.

Yet, the resentment toward immigrants can be chilling, as epitomized by the sentiments of a local labor leader:

> I don't think [residents of Hamblen County] are actually against the people because they are Mexican. I think it is sort of a complex deal where they are mad at the government for opening the doors. They know they are losing their jobs to foreign competition, and [the Mexicans] don't really care about the jobs that much; . . . they are just here on a free ride. They don't . . . really care about America . . . .
>
> I'll tell you what I hear through the grapevine: we are going to have a real problem here in America. It will probably wind up being racial. I'm not saying anything against the Latino, but I hear there are groups here in the South and the Midwest that are just ready to roll if things don't change. I'm not a fanatic, and I'm not reading this out of any kind of lunatic magazine, but I'm thinking people are really getting down on the politicians more and more . . . . [T]here is not going to be any kind of move made . . . to change anything to benefit the working people. And I think the NAFTA thing and losing jobs – if this economy drops down, I believe [America] is going to be a violent place.[35]

When Things Go Seriously Wrong

Unfortunately, cultural pluralism is under seige in many quarters. The rise in hate violence directed at law-abiding Arab Americans, Pakistani Americans, American Muslims, and those of Sikh descent following 9/11 demonstrates that things can go terribly wrong in some neighborhoods. Misguided individuals act in an emboldened manner against Americans who do not fit a particular, European-descent image.

Within two weeks of 9/11, these hate incidents were reported:

- A gunman drove to a Mesa, Arizona, gas station and fired three shots, killing its Sikh owner, Balbir Dingh Sodhi.
- In a wild rampage, the gunman drove to another gas station and shot at the Lebanese clerk, and then fired shots into the home of an Afghan family.

[35] Id.

- In Los Angeles, a Pakistani man parked his car at the Glendale Galleria Mall and returned to find it scratched across the right side with the words, "Nuke 'em" written all over.
- In San Francisco, vandals threw a bag of blood on the doorstep of an immigration center that serves Arabs and the city's large Asian population. They also threw a large plastic bag labeled "pig's blood" on the front door of Minority Assistance Services in the primarily Latino Mission District.
- An Indian American walking in the South of Market area of San Francisco was beaten and stabbed by a gang of individuals yelling antiblack and anti-Arab epithets.
- A Huntington, New York, man screamed, "[I am] doing this for my country" as he attempted to run down a Pakistani woman with his car.
- A 7–11 shop owned by a Sikh was burned down in Ronkonkoma, Long Island.[36]

Unfortunately, examples of other anti-Asian hate crimes in the United States have been chronicled at a significant rate in the past two decades. One of the most highly reported killings was that of Vincent Chin, a young Chinese American who was beaten to death with a baseball bat by two unemployed autoworkers in Detroit who first thought Chin was Japanese American.[37] The pattern of a more recent example has become all too familiar.

Richard Labbe was upset that he was being evicted for nonpayment of rent. He had confronted the property manager, Sam Chan, who lived in the same complex, about the matter. An intoxicated Labbe punched an exterior wall and gutter and began talking about the Vietnam War, stating that he "hated Vietnamese people." During the confrontation, Labbe noticed Thung Phetakoune, who was of Laotian descent, walking toward a dumpster to throw away garbage, and Labbe said he wanted to kill Phetakoune. Uttering an epithet, Labbe approached the much smaller Phetakoune and pushed him powerfully with his hand. Phetakoune fell backward, knocking his head on the pavement and later died of severe head trauma. A police officer who responded to the scene asked Labbe what happened, and Labbe replied, "What's going on is that those Asians killed Americans, and you won't do anything about it, so I will. . . . Nothing

---

[36] *Asian American Legal Defense and Education Fund's Partial List of Reported Incidents of Anti-Asian, Bias-Related Incidents,* ASIANWEEK, Sept. 20–26, 2001, at 9.

[37] See *United States v. Ebens,* 800 F.2d 1422 (6th Cir. 1986).

happened, but those Asians killed my brother and uncle in Vietnam, call it payback." Ironically, in Laos, Phetakoune had fought alongside Americans as a soldier in that nation's army during the Vietnam War.

Hate crimes directed at Latino immigrants are also common. As the number of immigrants soared in North Carolina, for example, many have become walking targets for crime and exploitation. In one of the most outrageous cases, private security guards in one town were accused of systematically terrorizing Latino residents of several apartment complexes they were supposed to be protecting. They kicked residents in the ribs, maced their genitals, and warned, "I'm going to throw your Spic ass out of the country." The owner of the security firm encouraged the assaults. "I'm bored," he told his staff. "Let's go down to taco city and f – with the Mexicans."[38]

Hate crimes directed at immigrants of color are fueled, and perhaps inspired, by anti-immigrant rhetoric. Hatred fomented by anti-immigrant sentiment is not hard to find.

A New York–based group has put up billboards in twelve states that blame immigrants for inflating the U.S. population. The Washington-based Federation for American Immigration Reform (FAIR) goes further with ads that blame immigrants for urban sprawl. According to the group's political calculus, immigrants cause population growth and population growth causes urban sprawl. So immigrants cause sprawl.[39] FAIR also blames immigrants for a rise in the number of cases of rubella in North Carolina.[40] A typical ad from FAIR reads: "They come in and undercut jobs that natives have always worked in." Immigration also is blamed for severe overcrowding of many New York schools.[41]

A few years ago in Phoenix, the residents of once solidly white neighborhoods grumbled about Mexican taco trucks and inspired city officials to try to use regulations to create a "taco-free zone." In Texas, an armed group called Ranch Rescue rode down to the U.S.–Mexico border to help

---

[38] Barry Yeoman, *Hispanic Diaspora – Drawn by Jobs, Latino Immigrants Are Moving to Small Towns like Siler City, North Carolina, Bringing with Them New Diversity and New Tensions*, 25 MOTHER JONES 34 (July 1, 2000).

[39] Ruben Navarrette, *Immigrants Are Our Most Precious Import*, DENVER POST, Dec. 17, 2000, at L-02.

[40] Laura Parker and Patrick McMahon, *Immigrant Groups Fear Backlash Rhetoric, Actions Have Intensified Coast to Coast since Release of Data from Census 2000, Activists Report*, USA TODAY, Apr. 9, 2001.

[41] Jones, *supra* note 29.

ranchers fend off trespassing border crossers. The group was a prede-
cessor to the Minuteman Project and other border vigilantes helping
Arizona ranchers who picked up Winchester rifles to fend off the "invasion" there.[42]

Dave Gorak, director of media relations for the Midwest Coalition to
Reform Immigration, chimes in with similar attacks:

> American businesses and their allies in Congress have been conning you
> into believing that immigrant labor is key to a strong economy. . . . This
> greed-driven scam began in earnest in 1990, when Congress had an oppor-
> tunity to reduce immigration. Enticed by campaign contributions, an irre-
> sponsible leadership in Washington agreed there was a labor shortage,
> and, in so doing, contributed to the quadrupling of our annual immigra-
> tion levels from what they were 30 years ago. . . . Simply increasing the size
> of the economic pie is irrelevant if we also increase the number of peo-
> ple eating the pie. It is only by increasing productivity that we increase
> per capita income. If increased population were important, China, India,
> South America and Africa would be leading the world in standard of living
> instead of languishing at the bottom of the economic heap.[43]

At a David Duke rally in Siler City, North Carolina, signs read: "To hell
with the wretched refuse," and "No way, Jose!" "Ladies and gentlemen,
you are all here today because you share a deep feeling about what is
happening to your city," declared Sam van Rensburg, a leader of a neo-
Nazi group called the National Alliance. "Your city is being sold out for
a quick buck by unscrupulous corporations, who are willing to ruin the
town your fathers founded. Folks, there is no such thing as cheap labor.
You and I will pay for this labor for the rest of our lives." He went on
about "mongrels" and the "sewer of immigration." "Siler City is at a crossroads," declared Duke, the former Ku Klux Klan grand dragon. "Either
you get the INS to kick the illegal aliens out, or you'll lose your community
and your heritage." County commissioners in Burlington, North Carolina,
unanimously called for a halt to all immigration – legal and illegal. In one
poll, 79 percent of white North Carolinians said their neighbors would
oppose living among Latinos. The Siler City police chief agreed: "A lot of
the older people, they will never accept them."[44]

---

[42] Navarrette, *supra* note 39.
[43] Dave Gorak, *High Immigration Hurts*, CHICAGO SUN-TIMES, Jan. 3, 2001, at 50.
[44] Yeoman, *supra* note 38.

In Bybee, Tennessee, more than two-thirds of the town's residents tried to block the opening of a Head Start center for Latino children. And in Lexington, Kentucky, residents circulated a petition opposing efforts to make the city "a safe place for Hispanics."[45] In Marietta, Georgia, a suburb of Atlanta, the city council passed an ordinance prohibiting day laborers and contractors from gathering on city streets to arrange for work.[46]

Whether such incidents could have been avoided completely by integration efforts is, of course, subject to debate. But certainly, integration efforts could have helped.

Why Civic Integration Programs Are Necessary

For all the reasons that native-born Americans should be encouraged to participate in civic life, newcomers should be encouraged as well. Engaging Americans in working to better our communities, schools, and neighborhoods – to work for the common good – is a goal that we must constantly pursue. In the case of newcomers, an added need to encourage civic participation and integration flows from the need to address the misinformation that abounds about them, which at times leads to misunderstanding, tension, and even hate.

Integration policies "generally refer to helping immigrants understand, navigate and participate in the social, economic and political aspects of society."[47] These may include efforts to help newcomers understand U.S. law and cultural practices or to assist in starting a business, finding a job, or otherwise becoming self-sufficient, while encouraging them to participate in civic organizations and community groups. When it comes to the integration of immigrants and refugees, state and local governments should help lead the way. Immigration and naturalization policy largely falls in the hands of the federal government. However, while federal policies determine how many immigrants and refugees enter the country, state and local governments are presented directly with the challenges and opportunities that newcomers present. With newcomers settling into their neighborhoods and cities, local and state entities have the most

---

[45] Id. [46] Parker and McMahon, *supra* note 40.

[47] Little Hoover Commission, *We the People: Helping Newcomers Become Californians*, June 2002, at 23 (report available from Little Hoover Commission).

direct contact with immigrants and much to gain for developing integration policies. And governmental leadership can set the example for
social and community groups to follow. Traditionally, given their location,
community-based organizations (CBOs) play an important role in integration efforts. Of course, CBOs must and should continue assisting with
integration efforts, but compared to CBOs, governmental entities have
more resources.

The importance of state and local government leadership in promoting
the civic integration of newcomers is appreciated by many governmental
entities. California's bipartisan Little Hoover Commission (LHC) recognizes that the state has a responsibility to ensure that public programs,
including education and training, public health and welfare, and economic development services effectively serve immigrants, enabling them
to contribute to the state.[48] Understanding the importance of investing in
immigrants is critical. Many immigrants are young, and others come to the
United States with limited formal educational. The LHC knows that "high
quality education and training programs can improve [immigrants'] earning potential and enhance their self-sufficiency."[49] The LHC emphasizes
the importance of this investment, because education and skills, more
than any other factor, determine the earning capacity of immigrants.[50]
The LHC offers the example that Latinas who have bachelor's degrees,
on average, earn 82 percent more than those with only a high school
degree.[51] Further, adult immigrants without high school educations, "over
their lifetime, draw more from public services than they pay in taxes at a
cost of about $13,000 each, while more educated immigrants contribute
about $198,000 more than they cost."[52] In short, the LHC believes that
investment in immigrants is necessary to ensure that they are able to make
lasting contributions.[53]

To emphasize the importance of promoting civic integration, the LHC
proposed the creation of a California Commission on Immigrants, charged
with initiating statewide dialogues on immigration, advocating for effective programs, and monitoring progress in immigrant integration. The

---

[48] Id. at 37.   [49] Id. at 37–38.
[50] Id. at 38.
[51] Id. (citing Angela Ginorio and Michelle Huston, *¡Si Se Puede! Yes, We Can* 13 [American
Association of University Women Educational Foundation]).
[52] Id.   [53] Id.

statewide dialogues would "promote public awareness of the contributions of immigrants and how immigration can support community goals."[54]
The commission would advocate for improvement in public programs
that promote "immigrant responsibilities to their communities and community responsibilities to immigrants"[55] and "pay particular attention"
to community-based organizations that promote integration and citizenship. Further, the commission would "identify ways to define and measure
immigrant integration and self-reliance and report progress to policy mak-
ers and the public."[56]

Fundamental to the LHC's position is the understanding that California's continued prosperity is dependent on the opportunities and
achievements of all its residents – including its immigrants. In short, all
of California benefits when immigrants are successful. Conversely, when
immigrants are trapped in poverty and isolation, the state bears a higher
tax burden for providing these immigrants services. Thus, "California's primary goal [is] to support the ability of all residents, including immigrants,
to be safe, healthy and law abiding, as well as live in safe affordable housing
and be economically self-sufficient."[57] Immigrants should participate in
self-governance and feel they belong and are responsible to their community. The state also should try to influence federal policies to better align
federal immigration practices with community goals. The reason is clear.
"Public policies that hinder immigrants' ability to become self-reliant,
responsible community members hinder the success of all Californians."[58]

Given immigrant-driven demographic changes occurring throughout
the country, lessons from California are worth reviewing. In Santa Clara
County (home to San Jose and Silicon Valley), officials have recognized the
importance of newcomer integration: "Our collective need to integrate,
improve, and transform the lives of all residents of Santa Clara County
depends upon our ability to integrate, improve, and transform the lives of
immigrants and the need to re-think planning, policies, and practices."[59]

The improvement and transformation of our lives in Santa Clara County
is integrally inter-wound with the improvement and transformation of the

---

[54] Id. at 53.
[55] Id.
[56] Id.
[57] Id. at 65.
[58] Id.
[59] *Bridging Borders in Silicon Valley: Summit on Immigrant Needs and Contributions,*
Santa Clara County Office of Human Relations Citizenship and Immigrant Services
Program, Dec. 6, 2000, at 21.

lives of immigrants in Santa Clara County. To the extent that immigrants are not provided the opportunities to integrate into existing structures, improve their lives, and help transform our lives and structures into a meaningful, productive, well-rounded existence, to that extent our economy, society, and culture will decline. We will slide into a Silicon Valley culture less rich in diversity, in knowledge, in growth, and in meeting human needs and potential. If we seek to blame those who look different than ourselves, act different than ourselves, or immigrated to this area at different times and are therefore seen as competitors rather than adding value, we could spiral downward as a county.[60]

With such a large number, percentage, and diversity of immigrants and a mandate to meet the human needs of all its residents, Santa Clara County needs to engage in long-term, strategic, sustainable, human-needs based planning. In many respects, if the county doesn't have a vision for meeting the human needs of immigrants in the county and individuals in the world, then the county cannot have a vision for meeting the needs of county residents. More than ever, immigrants and US-born county residents have an interlocking common fate.[61]

Santa Clara County also knows that speaking about immigrant families in a vacuum is impossible. Not only is the interrelationship with the native-born population significant, but families that comprise both immigrant and native-born members are quite common:

> [W]hen you include children born in the United States who have immi-grant parents to the number of immigrants in Santa Clara County, almost 1.1 million county residents (61% of the county's population) constitute . . . "immigrant stock", or direct immigrant lineage. . . . The implications of adding 27% of the county's US-born children of immigrants with approxi-mately 15% of the county's foreign-born children of immigrants are stag-gering. The impacts in schools and neighborhoods alone – the challenges of teaching and learning and of healthy multi-cultural co-existence – provide the county and its 15 cities with rich barriers and benefits unfore-seen until the recent past. Under what conditions will these children enter the workforce? Mixed status households of US-born and immigrants means that when we address immigration policies and practices, we are in fact addressing issues that affect vast numbers of people in our county, many more than those who are foreign born.[62]

After its own study of demographic and workforce changes in its own state, the Colorado Trust, a grantmaking foundation based in Denver, also

[60] Id. at 30.   [61] Id. at 31.

[62] Id. at 22.

recognizes the need for serious immigrant integration initiatives. By being proactive, the trust believes that Colorado institutions and community members will be much more likely to find themselves in strong, cohesive communities in the years to come. The trust encourages local governments to help take the lead in integration efforts and partner with businesses and CBOs. In addition to endorsing a philosophy and set of recommendations similar to those of LHF and Santa Clara County, California, the trust also recommends creating safe and welcoming environments within public institutions, encouraging public institutions to conduct outreach to immigrant communities, providing opportunities to share stories and develop relationships between newcomers and native residents, and supporting language learning, which includes supporting learning English for immigrants and refugees and learning foreign languages for the native born.

Thus the best interest of the community (and consequently the country) is served when all residents, native born and foreign born alike, are integrated into civic culture. Marginalization leaves people out; inviting them in encourages contributions and understanding that benefits everyone.

Examples that Work

Support for immigrant integration and cultural diversity has provided the impetus for a variety of efforts across the country that assist immigrants in their adjustment to American life. In recognition of the mutual responsibility of civic integration shared by the community and the newcomer, these efforts are not simply about providing services to immigrants and refugees, but also about encouraging newcomers to uphold their responsibilities to the community as well. Clear expectations can speed immigrants to personal success by supporting their desire to learn English, developing social networks, and expanding access to education and training programs that lead to more opportunities.

Consider Nebraska. Metropolitan Area Transit in Omaha has installed informational signs in Spanish and English in the advertising trays of all transit buses, in recognition of the area's growing Latino population. Bank and cash machines now offer information in two languages, and the state of Nebraska prints several information brochures, including the driver's manual, in Spanish. Sister Angela Erevia, director of a local Catholic ministry, said the effort follows the policy of the region's archbishop in assisting the growing Spanish-speaking population "to become an integral part of the community." "Many of the new Hispanic immigrants are looking for jobs. They haven't enough money to buy cars, and they are dependent upon public transportation."[63]

Omaha is becoming a U.S. Sudanese refugee population center where many refugees find better work, housing, and refugee support than in their first destination, Des Moines, Iowa. Refugees in Omaha have found opportunities and a sense of belonging that was missing in Iowa. Perhaps most important is Omaha's Sudanese association, which former Des Moines refugees say provides the assistance needed for those whose transition to American life is a constant challenge. The Omaha center, which is supported by a mix of grants, offers refugees transportation, interpreters, and daily English classes taught by fellow Nuer tribespeople, the southern Sudanese natives most common in the United States. Nebraska gives refugees a few additional months of state assistance (compared to Iowa) to help them get on their feet. The Omaha Sudanese association attempts to create a family atmosphere, translating mail, accompanying them in court, filling out immigration paperwork, and searching for jobs. Those advantages are alluring. The community's goal is to help the Sudanese achieve self-sufficiency.[64]

---

[63] James Ivey, *MAT Gets Rolling on Bilingual Effort,* OMAHA WORLD-HERALD, Jan. 17, 2001.

[64] Lee Rood, *Sudanese Refugees Abandon Iowa; They're Drawn to a More Viable Support System in Omaha,* DES MOINES REGISTER, June 3, 2001, at 1. The aid that hundreds of Sudanese refugees received upon coming to Iowa largely disappeared within months. Refugees felt stranded by the state agency established to help them as they struggled to adapt to a radically different culture. The Sudanese are not the first group of refugees to flee Iowa after attempts to resettle them. The Hmong of northern Laos, among more than twenty thousand Southeast Asians who came to Iowa in the 1970s and 1980s, also have dwindled in numbers, many migrating to Minnesota. Sudanese leaders say a little support and understanding would go a long way toward keeping the new Iowans here. "If people continue not to understand us, then more people will move," said David Kier, executive director of Des Moines' South Sudanese Friendship Association. "We need American friends to help us become more independent." Many of those living in Des Moines have joined Sudanese from elsewhere across the country in a pilgrimage to Omaha. Leaders there say people have found opportunities and a sense of belonging that was missing in Iowa. In Iowa, refugees were pressured within weeks of arriving to get jobs, often at wages too low to support their families. Some lost all state welfare assistance after they began to earn a paycheck or after they failed to

As part of an initiative to attract more immigrants to Iowa championed by Governor Tom Vilsack, the Sioux City New Iowans Center and a similar one in Muscatine gives immigrants a foothold by helping them find jobs, homes, English classes, and even rides to the doctor. The president of the chamber of commerce notes: "We're going to have some way to integrate people into our society quickly." (Although Nebraska does not operate anything similar to the New Iowans Centers, an immigration task force supports such centers in Nebraska as well.[65]) In June 2005, the federal government assisted. The Department of Labor awarded an $850,000 grant to Iowa Workforce Development to place New Iowan Centers in cities like Waterloo, Cedar Rapids, Des Moines, and Council Bluffs, Iowa. The goal of the project was to help speed transition of new Americans into communities, promote stability and employment with good wages, and increase local economic development.

Arkansas has a similar program. The Northwest Arkansas Multicultural Center started several years ago, which provides education and information to new immigrants in the areas. "We don't want you to forget your culture, we want you to become part of our culture," said Fred Patton, Fort Smith Multicultural Commission chairman. Arkansas political leaders promote such programs. In his welcoming remarks at a multicultural conference, Senator Tim Hutchinson (R-Arkansas) acknowledged the strength that flows from cultural diversity and from the common desire for freedom. To Hutchinson, bigotry, prejudice, and violence usually are the result of ignorance.[66]

In Kentucky, where the Latino population increased by more than 50 percent in the 1990s, Project PLOW (People Learning Each Other's

understand requirements in letters from the Iowa Department of Human Services. Others had problems obtaining education, drivers' licenses, or Social Security cards, or had difficulty with the law. Men occasionally got in trouble because they didn't know that beating their wives, commonplace in Sudan, was illegal. The Des Moines association wants to do more – provide English classes, job training services, and other services. Wayne Johnson, head of Iowa's refugee services, says, "One thing we're proud of in Iowa is that the refugee population works. We've never had a problem with large numbers of refugees on welfare." Id.

[65] Dave Morantz, *Helping Immigrants in the Midlands; Iowa and Nebraska Are Debating How Far They Should Go in Providing Services for Newcomers; Services at New Iowans Centers*, OMAHA WORLD-HERALD, June 28, 2001, at 1.

[66] Dave Hughes, *Fort Smith Panel Teaches New, Old Residents; Conference Addresses Matters on Immigration, Diversity*, ARKANSAS DEMOCRAT-GAZETTE, Aug. 9, 2000, at B1.

Ways) was instituted to bring together white farmers and Latino immigrants to learn each other's language and culture.[67] Pressed by a growing local need for teachers who can work with foreign students, the University of Louisville has held a special six-week English as a Second Language (ESL) institute during the summer. Up to twenty teachers from the Jefferson County Public Schools hone skills needed to teach students with limited English and diverse cultural backgrounds. The teachers can take more courses in the fall and spring. University teachers programs also are stepping up efforts to prepare future teachers to deal with the community's growing diversity by revising curricula. Other programs are tailoring courses to reach adults with special language needs. Barbara Thompson, assistant professor of elementary education, thinks local universities soon will have to actively recruit Latino high school students to train as teachers. At Jefferson Community College, there was one full-time and one part-time ESL instructor in 1992; now there are two full-time and seventeen part-time instructors, with evening courses to accommodate immigrants' work schedules. Several years ago only classes in grammar and writing were offered; now courses cover conversation, reading, speech, real estate, human services, philosophy, and American history and government.[68]

Non-English language services are needed in other areas of Kentucky life. When Chuk Chiu's Chinese restaurant was robbed, he was unable to find the words to tell police what happened. He does not speak English. When Jose Rodriguez's car was stolen from outside his apartment, he could not understand the officers' questions. He does not speak English either. Rodriguez said police treated him well and did not expect officers to speak Spanish. He wants to learn English, but finding time is difficult while he holds two jobs to make ends meet. When police ask a victim's friends or family members to act as interpreters, the situation can get awkward. In one homicide case, for instance, the suspect spoke only Korean, and police had to ask their initial questions through the suspect's relatives. In an attempt to deal with the problem, Louisville police circulated a questionnaire to learn who on the force was bilingual. Of 718 officers, just 6 are listed as speaking at least two languages. Two are fluent in Spanish. In

[67] Navarrete, *supra* note 39.

[68] Linda Stahl, *U of L Offers English Help for Teachers: Rise in Foreign Students Prompts Special Course,* COURIER-JOURNAL, May 22, 2000, at 1b.

Jefferson County (with the fast-growing migrant student population), police have been prompted to place pocket Spanish guides in every cruiser and to require each officer to take several hours of basic Spanish classes.[69] The city of Louisville, working with several private agencies such as Catholic Charities and Kentucky Refugee Ministries, plans to identify a bank of potential interpreters and help train and certify them. The interpreters would work through the agencies for a fee – allowing hospitals, medical clinics, home health providers, legal services, government agencies, and other federally funded human services agencies to contract for interpreters. This coordination would be a particularly useful resource in cases where the language in question is not widely spoken.[70]

Taking advantage of immigrant talent and energy is also viewed as important to the community. Louisville business leaders and academics also realize that many immigrants are highly skilled, in some cases with professional backgrounds, who should be provided tools to resume their professional talents to benefit their new community.[71] Louisville also offers a Center for Microenterprise Development program, which provides a ten-week course that teaches business start-up skills to refugees and other immigrants. The participants have come from strife-torn countries such as Zaire, Russia, Bosnia, Cuba, Vietnam, Sierra Leone, and Haiti.[72]

In Oklahoma, the bulk of jobs held by black and Latino workers are in service industries, while white workers are concentrated in executive, professional, administrative, and sales positions.[73] Yet, the need for developing a positive attitude toward newcomers and encouraging integration is being promoted:

> Workplace diversity doesn't stop with hiring. The concept extends to forging relationships with people of different cultures, backgrounds, races and gender. It takes understanding that diversity goes beyond what a person

---

[69] Shannon Tangonan, 'It's Really a Challenge for Us'; Crisis Workers Hit Language Barrier, Immigrants Often Can't Speak English, COURIER-JOURNAL, Mar. 13, 2000, at 1b.

[70] Butch John, Breaking the Language Barrier; Pool of Interpreters Being Formed; Federal Law Requires Communication Aid, COURIER-JOURNAL, Sept. 23, 2000, at 1a.

[71] Butch John, Tapping Immigrants' Skills Could Boost Area's Growth; Newcomers Often Can't Use Their Talents, COURIER-JOURNAL, June 29, 2001, at 1A.

[72] Sonja Sherrer, Immigrants Get Helping Hand; Center Offers Language Help, Advice, Money to Start Business, COURIER-JOURNAL, July 25, 2000, at 1C.

[73] Ginnie Graham, Celebrating Diversity at Work, TULSA WORLD, Feb. 16, 2001.

can see. It reaches into accepting a person's economic status, religion, and even home life. Month-long celebrations at work related to education and diversity can help. "We find this one of the easiest and most enjoyable ways to educate people. . . . Rather than always having to go to a class, people can experience something new in their normal environment." Diversity is part of our foundation and core values, and it is the right thing to do. "I think Tulsa is beginning to do things and is engaging in the topic of diversity. . . . But wherever we are as a community, we need to be doing better. . . . What diversity boils down to is being a good neighbor – being good to each other. It's an attitude issue. The values and visions of company leaders are reflected in the work force. There are some companies that take on diversity as a corporate responsibility and don't feel it is a mandate. . . . Racism is not about black and white. It's about the haves and have-nots, the privileged and not-so-privileged and why that is. To help people understand diversity, we have to define it." To give diversity meaning, Radious Guess, a diversity consultant, talks about how people have innate prejudices and ways to recognize those. She wants people to talk about their differences, to start working in teams and to go outside their "comfort zones." This has to be ongoing.[74]

The increase in Tulsa's Latino population has stimulated businesses to search for ways to deal with language barriers.[75] Advocacy on behalf of Latinos in Tulsa began in 1979 when the city created the Greater Tulsa Area Hispanic Commission, an advisory board with no authority to set policy. A statewide initiative petition in 2000 to ban foreign languages from government services prompted the group to establish a foundation to serve as an official nonprofit advocacy group to address social issues brought to the foundation. According to Reverend Victor Orta, one of the founders, "[t]hat initiative petition made us realize there was no organization to speak on behalf of political issues. . . . When we established the Hispanic American Foundation, we never dreamed we were going to be faced with so many issues."[76] According to Orta, the organizations bring together people in the community to understand reasons for immigration and the challenges facing immigrants. "The established Hispanic community has opened up to receive the newcomers," Orta said. "We're responding with what we can to make assimilation or resettlement here easier. A newcomer needs to learn the language to pursue their profession or vocation and know the laws and issues facing them. But first and foremost is getting a job."[77]

[74] Id.

[76] Graham, *supra* note 28.

[75] Id.

[77] Id.

Maryland and Wisconsin also have newcomer centers. The Maryland Office for New Americans promotes English literacy and civics education by funding English and civics classes. The curriculum encourages students to explore different service agencies and report on the information gleaned from their site visits. In 2001, in Montgomery County, Maryland, the county opened the Gilchrist Center for Cultural Diversity, a referral and activities center for new immigrants and others. At the center, residents can study English, obtain legal advice and learn how to use computers. The center also offers classes on citizenship, provides information on housing, and helps individuals find health care services. Integration in this county is important. Rene Antonio Leon, El Salvador's ambassador in Washington, called the county "the epicenter of economic activity for Salvadorans and Hispanics in the eastern U.S."[78] The Sheboygan County Job Center, in Wisconsin, welcomed three hundred new Hmong immigrants from Thailand in 2004 by launching its Refugee Resettlement Program. In a combined effort with Sheboygan County Health and Human Services and ACS, a company that works for the county running employment workshops at the job center, the resettlement program includes a simple curriculum for new refugees, teaching them the very basics – how to measure, count money, and make a budget. In addition, refugees receive job training and skills development. To help newcomers get settled in a new job, the center provides a Hmong translator for a few days.

Some short-term integration initiatives by several states in the late 1990s were launched to help legal immigrants adversely affected by the 1996 federal welfare law's restrictions on federal public benefits. For example, the Massachusetts legislature passed a three-year $2 million initiative in 1997 to fund a Citizenship Assistance Program for low-income immigrant residents. The program matched state funds with contributions from private organizations, foundations, and federal agencies. A statewide network of more than one hundred community-based organizations provided English and civics classes as well as assistance with citizenship applications. A twenty-four-hour hotline was created to provide information in nine languages on services such as civics and English classes, application assistance, and legal referrals. More than twenty-two thousand Massachusetts residents benefited from the program, and more than eleven thousand became new citizens. When asked their reasons

---

[78] Cameron Barr, *Counties' Diversity Leads Officials into Foreign Territory*, WASHINGTON POST, July 15, 2005, at C01.

for becoming U.S. citizens, most immigrants in the program said they wanted to vote and help their community. Massachusetts students were encouragd to participate in Immigrant's Day to get a firsthand look at how government works, meet with legislators, and discuss policies important to their community.

Through the Refugee and Immigrant Citizenship Initiative, Illinois' Bureau of Refugee and Immigrant Services expended $12 million over a seven-year period, contracting with thirty-two community-based organizations to provide lessons in U.S. history, civics, and instruction in English language. More than ninty thousand individuals were served. These contracts served members of the community through education and by stimulating civic participation. The Coalition of Limited English Speaking Elderly in Chicago developed and tested an innovative curriculum on daily life with a grant from the U.S. Department of Education. Immigrants and refugees from Bosnia, Cambodia, China, India, and Korea were given English language instruction and encouraged to participate in English conversations with their grandchildren, other relatives, and neighbors. The elderly decreased their social isolation and increased their civic participation, while they solved real-life problems and learned about their neighborhood and city.

The New Jersey Citizenship Campaign was a statewide naturalization effort led by a collaborative partnership of community-based organizations and state and federal agencies. The campaign began in 1997 with support from the governor and legislature, funded originally at $2 million and later increased to $3 million. Community-based organizations provided in-kind contributions of another $3 million. The campaign initially targeted low-income, elderly, and disabled lawful permanent residents and those eligible for New Jersey's State Food Stamp Program. By March 2000, the campaign provided services to 12,000 individuals, more than 7,100 of whom applied for citizenship.

The positive effect of integration programs on newcomers is readily apparent. Sia Thompson, an immigrant from Sierra Leone, participated in Santa Clara County's Immigrant Leadership course. With a strong interest in women's rights, she was able to bond with other women participants to lay the groundwork for collaboration during the course. The course also was helpful in providing information on resources available for immigrants generally. She also developed a sense of "where to go so that our voice will be heard." But even before she participated in this course, Sia had helped to form a Pan-African women's organization – African Refugee Women

Rebuilders (ARWR). She explained part of the reason for forming the organization this way:

> It was so difficult for me to adjust to the American system and I have been through high school. It must be extremely difficult for women [who have no education]. Having experienced trying to get a job, to get connected [to the community], to make myself useful, I wanted to try and continue to work with African women and human rights. When the African women come here and resettle, organizations like Catholic Charities, Jewish Family Services, and the International Rescue Committee work with the women for three months. In my view it is not a very long time. You are barely stepping your toes on the ground. So we are filling in the gap. Even on the very basic things like: the operation of vending machines, opening a savings account, where you can find the African food market – generally circumnavigating the system. We encourage the women to come in and get assistance.[79]

The church can also help promote civic participation and integration. Another participant in the Santa Clara County Immigrant Leadership course, Juventino Flores, an immigrant from Mexico, attributes his involvement in civic affairs to his church's leadership program.

> [It] made me aware of the need of the community and helped me become involved in church; to give back. Before I took the course, I went to church, prayed and went home. The course helps everyone take responsibility.
>
> I took the class by accident. There was one old lady who was working at the church and told me that the Diesis is offering the course, and asked if I wanted to take it.
>
> I didn't want to say yes or no – so I said maybe. Then the priest sent a letter telling me when the orientation was. [I went] and I liked it. I am fortunate. I have no regrets and [was] very happy to learn all the stuff.
>
> The course covered subjects including social justice, the community and things in the church. It discussed topics like why clothes can be cheap in this country and where they are made. I believe [that] it made you aware of many things. It was interesting and very helpful. It made me want to get more involved in the community and once you are there it is hard to get out. When are you sure that you have done enough – that you have solved all the problems? In this work, somewhere else there is a need. Once they [the instructors] make you an activist it is hard to get away and relax.

---

[79] Interview of Sia Thompson (on file with author).

In the course they related faith and the needs in the community. They make you strong in the faith and then you have to follow Jesus and Jesus is justice. Some times it is hard to sacrifice. It takes time – to make announcements [and there are] not many volunteers. [Sometimes] I think to myself that I can take more community college classes and get better pay and move somewhere else, but then I would never give anything else to the community. The volunteer work is part of the faith. I have to give to the neighbors; to my brothers and sisters; to the society; because according to our beliefs, if one suffers the other should suffer. It is hard to have more responsibilities, but you start growing and you take on more and more. Leadership for the community – helping the community [is] related to the faith that something better will happen, like Martin Luther King [and Dolores Huerta]. Now in the matter of such things as involvement with my children's school, I believe that the parents – we – should help the kids, not just teachers alone but also the parents need to be involved. It needs to be 50/50.[80]

Of course, while an ugly side of America has reared its head following 9/11 in the form of hate crimes and intolerance directed at Arab Americans, American Muslims, and Sikhs, efforts at immigrant integration and understanding have also occurred. In spite of the highly publicized prosecution of an alleged al Qaeda supporter there, the California central valley town of Lodi, California, is a good example of efforts at understanding. The town's population of fifty-seven thousand is more than a quarter Latino. Yet the community also has two thousand Muslims, mostly from Pakistan.[81] So Pakistani men playing cricket on a field across from their mosque and women wearing *hijabs* – head scarves – walking in the park are a common sight. But when the mosque was vandalized in the early 1990s, concerned citizens, led by a Japanese American mayor, came forward to form the Breakthrough Project to combat bigotry. High school students volunteered to help clean up the mosque and police started meeting regularly with mosque leaders. In the wake of 9/11, the pastor of the local United Congregational Christian Church conducted a four-part class on Islam for members of the community to gain better understanding of their Muslim neighbors. Isolated incidents of intolerance have occurred. However, one member of the United Congregational Christian Church who attended the Islam classes hoped that everyone across America was

[80] Interview of Juventino Flores (on file with author).
[81] Elizabeth Bell, *Fear and Suspicion*, SF CHRONICLE, Oct. 21, 2001, at A23.

reaching out: "I came to be supportive of our neighbors so they do not feel persecuted."[82]

The North Carolina Latino Initiative

North Carolina has engaged in noteworthy immigrant integration and understanding efforts. Between 1995 and 2000, North Carolina's Latino population increased by 73 percent, making North Carolina the region of the nation's fastest-growing Latino community.[83] In a state of seven million residents, Latinos now account for more than 4 percent of the population.[84] Well over half of the recent arrivals are from Mexico,[85] anticipating greater opportunities for themselves and their families in a state with plentiful work and inexpensive housing.[86] About half of the Mexican immigrants are undocumented.

The new diversity in North Carolina has presented challenges. The changing demographics immediately impacted schools, government agencies such as the Department of Motor Vehicles, and law enforcement. New students arrived with little or no English skills; personnel at different agencies were confronted with having to communicate information to Latino clients unable to speak English. Misunderstanding and frustration followed, and at one point a Democratic county commissioner from Chatham County sent a heated letter to the INS demanding help in either documenting the new arrivals or sending them back home. The commissioner felt that the county's resources were being "siphoned from other pressing needs . . . to provide assistance to immigrants with little or no possessions."[87]

Sensing the potential difficulties facing the state as the immigrant population expanded, the North Carolina Center for International Understanding (NCCIU) began a series of conversations in 1995 with key leaders from universities, foundations, the Latino community, and state government. A project of the University of North Carolina, the NCCIU had years of experience focusing on community exchanges. The early discussions led to the implementation of the Latino Initiative to address the potential conflicts

---

[82] Id.

[83] *The North Carolina Initiative: Helping Communities Understand Immigration,* 10 CLEARINGHOUSE ON STATE INTERNATIONAL POLICIES 2 (2000).

[84] Id.

[85] Id.

[86] Yeoman, *supra* note 38.

[87] Id.

and public policy needs relating to the burgeoning Latino population and the older residents of North Carolina.

One of NCCIU's primary concerns was the success of the school system in dealing with the change in its student population. To serve the new student population, educators and school administrators had to acquire an understanding of the immigrants' culture and family situations. NCCIU identified the twenty most affected counties across the state from census data and extended invitations to their teachers and administrators to participate in a two-week summer study abroad in Mexico. The program became an annual opportunity for twenty to twenty-five educators to spend two weeks in Mexico attending lectures, visiting museums and schools, and staying in the homes of Mexican educators. NCCIU collaborated with the Mexican organizations such as the Universidad Iberoamericana in Mexico City and Ipoderac, an orphanage for street children in Puebla.

NCCIU also invites community and state leaders to participate in the program. That way their contribution to emerging public policy will be informed by an understanding of political, social, and economic factors driving the decisions behind immigration as well as firsthand experience with the Mexican culture and family structure. The Latino Initiative also aims to assist leaders in recognizing the needs of Latinos and to distinguish the relevant agencies that address those needs so that the immigrants can become better incorporated into North Carolina life.

The annual program aims to provide a proactive, sabbatical approach, allowing educators and community leaders the opportunity to question their stereotypes as they travel. The program consists of a two-day pre-departure seminar, a two-week visit to Mexico that includes three days in Mexico City, three days in rural schools, and a weekend homestay. The group visits families who have sons, daughters, or husbands living in the United States; these families often reside in Mexican states known to be points of origin for many of the immigrants who have traveled to communities in North Carolina. Upon return to North Carolina, a follow-up planning meeting is held to consider appropriate forums for disseminating lessons learned on the trip. The Latino Initiative also holds annual seminars on Latino issues to encourage the development of a network of leaders who can guide public discourse and policymaking on issues surrounding Latino immigration.

Because of his concerns about the increasing misunderstandings and tension felt by the DMV's driver's license examiners while assisting clients with limited English proficiency, the director of the North Carolina licensing division participated in one of the Latino Initiative trips to Mexico. His experience led to the development of cross-cultural training for the state's 350 examiners. The North Carolina DMV then contracted with NCCIU to implement a program geared toward effective communication with Latino customers. The program was implemented through twenty-two group workshops across the state. As a result, the North Carolina DMV was awarded the profession's international award for excellence in customer service.

The first trip abroad for policymakers was scheduled for February 2000 and was originally intended exclusively for state-level leaders. NCCIU received a $20,000 grant from the Z. Smith Reynolds Foundation, one of the foundations who had participated in an earlier program. The foundation money fully funded ten participants including six state legislators, representatives of the Department of Public Instruction, the Administrative Office of the Courts, the Co-op Extension Service, and the Self-Help Credit Union, a community nonprofit. An additional five participants from the governor's office, AT&T, the North Carolina Rural Economic Development Center, the North Carolina Association of County Commissioners, and the University of North Carolina paid their own way to participate in the program. The trip was to be led by the director of the NCCIU, Millie Ravenel, and the director of the Latino Initiative, Winifred Ernst.

Unexpectedly, this first trip for state-level leaders was faced with a request that six civic leaders from Chatham County be included as well. Chatham County was one of the twenty most affected counties already targeted by NCCIU, and the county was in crisis. The county was embroiled in angry debate over the presence of immigrants sparked by the letter sent from County Commissioner Rick Givens to the INS asking for help in getting the undocumented workers documented or "routed back to their homes." The letter had been translated and distributed in the Latino community, and county meetings had turned into screaming matches. One of the cities in the county, Siler City, was 40 percent Latino. About 50 percent of the enrollment at Siler City Elementary School was children from Latino families. The county delegation to Mexico included Givens, another county commissioner, the Siler City chief of police, the sheriff, the vice-chair of the county school system, and a Mexican-born community educator from a local, Latino-focused community nonprofit organization. They joined the other state leaders at the last minute, funded partially by the county and partially through private foundation funds.

As in the case of educators and foundation members who participated in the earlier study abroad trips, the state leaders, including the Chatham County delegation, found the experience transforming, and their attitudes were turned around. After noting that he was "going to eat a lot of crow," Givens explained how the experience had changed his life and admitted that his earlier judgment of the Latinos was wrong; he also pledged to help the community in his area. That pledge was challenged only one week after Givens and the other members of the Chatham County delegation returned to Siler City from Mexico.

During the trip, the caustic letter Givens sent to INS had gained a strong backing, especially among local white supremacists. An anti-immigration rally was scheduled at the Siler City Hall, featuring the infamous ex-Klansman David Duke as one of the speakers. The organizers intended to use Siler City as a poster child that represented the negative effects of immigration. Givens, the sheriff, and the chief of police quickly mobilized to promote a boycott of the rally. Although the numbers at his rally were notably lower than expected, Duke was undeterred, and in his speech he chastised Givens' new commitment to the Latino community. Threatening to organize a recall of Givens' commission seat, Duke shouted that unless the law of the land is enforced, "America will be turned into another Mexico."

The delegation from Chatham County continues to meet to hear presentations about Latino issues, including speakers who are experts in Mexican politics. The county is focused on gaining state funding for more English-as-a-second-language programs as well as a soccer field. And law enforcement officials have participated in intensive Spanish language courses.

In 1999, the North Carolina General Assembly allocated $100,000 into the recurring budget to support the Latino Initiative. By the end of 2004, the total number of state and civic leader participants in the Latino Initiative totaled 250. An additional 100 educators participated in the parallel two-week educator trips.

The establishment of the Latino Initiative to help state and civic leaders understand the issues behind Latino immigration and to inform the development of sound policy is a model of a public–private–academic collaboration. The program has facilitated the integration of immigrants into

North Carolina communities and educated the communities about the new immigrants to encourage cooperation at the community level. As one participant commented upon returning to North Carolina from Mexico, "the most significant barrier facing [North Carolina] is the ability to live together and to nurture relationships across race, religions, and other kinds of diversity. That is the impact this program has had on me – it is making me know that it's possible."[88] The state's Senate president created an Office for Hispanic and Latino Affairs to act as a liaison with the Latino community and to improve outreach and education. The governor's office of Hispanic/Latino Affairs also is working to increase participation of Latinos on state and local boards and commissions and matches a database of qualified candidates to weekly postings of open positions.

Conclusion

What ever became of the Welcome Wagon tradition of hospitality when a local neighbor or hostess would show up at a new neighbor's home with a basket of goodies? A cursory Web surf discloses that the tradition came out of the pioneer days that seems to be practiced more in Canada today than in the United States. The practice could surely do much good today.

The time is ripe for renewed civic engagement efforts directed at newcomers. A century ago, when Italians, Poles, and Jews were immigrating in large numbers, an Americanization movement was vast and vibrant. Everyone from state governments to local schools to neighborhood YMCAs took part, promoting love and loyalty for America. The movement fizzled after World War I when new laws dramatically curtailed immigration.[89] Given demographic trends and the potential for

---

[88] Id. Jesse Helms, the former Republican senator from North Carolina, demonstrated a similar interest in developing a better understanding with Mexico before he left office. In 2001, he led four other U.S. senators on a trip to Mexico City, bearing good will and a hand of friendship. In holding three days of joint meetings with Mexican politicians, he recognized that relations between the United States and its neighbors to the south are of unprecedented importance. As Senator Joseph Biden, who was also on the trip, told his counterparts on the Mexican Foreign Relations Committee, "For Senator Helms to initiate and encourage the rest of us to make this trip is a mark not only of the change that's taking place in your country, but also of ours." Keven Begos, *Helms Trip More than Whim; Senators Visited Neighbor to Boost U.S. Relationship*, RICHMOND TIMES DISPATCH, Apr. 22, 2001, at A17.

[89] Jennifer Ludden, *Efforts to Help Immigrants Make Easier Transition into American Culture*, NPR Morning Edition, Mar. 9, 2004.

newcomers to continue to contribute mightily to the nation, socially and economically, it makes sense to reach out to immigrants and refugees as soon as they arrive so that they too might understand the responsibilities of being an American.

Once we recognize that the promotion of civic engagement among new-comers is in our own best interest, we can begin the process in earnest. The examples cited in this chapter represent some good thinking on the subject; however, when we put our creative minds together, the potential for newer, more exciting, and innovative ways of promoting civic integra-tion is enormous. Although state and local governments (including city service agencies and even community policing programs) should lead the way, just think of the amazing things that could be accomplished when other vital institutions become involved: schools, daycare centers, local businesses, chambers of commerce, churches, recreation clubs, neigh-borhood groups, senior groups, and youth groups; they bring such rich possibilities to the enterprise.

We have a choice of Americas – one narrow and one broad. One choice is closed minded, resistant to continuing changes that will continue to breed tension and violence. The other is one that embraces change and encourages integration in the hopes of building a stronger, better com-munity. The choice we make, individually, locally, and nationally, will tell us much about ourselves as a country, as a community, and as human beings. The goal must be to avoid the pitfalls of division, insular living, and unknowing bias. Instead, we should fully embrace newcomers in our midst with open arms, for they are our neighbors and, in a real sense, our own collective relatives.

APPENDIX

Selected state-by-state data show significant changes affected by immi-gration throughout the country.[90]

Alabama: The state's population grew 10.1 percent during the 1990s to 4,447,100 last year. The number of Latinos tripled to 75,830.

Arizona: The nation's second-fastest-growing state surged by 40 percent during the 1990s to 5,130,632 residents. It gained two U.S. House seats in the 2002 elections. Every county grew over the past decade. Experts said

---

[90] *Population Shifts during the 1990s, supra* note 30, at A20.

the boom was driven partly by retirees and agricultural workers moving into western counties and urban expansion around Phoenix. The Latino population jumped 88 percent, meaning Latinos account for one in every four residents. Arizona also had a 26 percent growth in Asian Americans between 2000 and 2004.

Arkansas: The state grew 13.7 percent during the 1990s to 2,673,400 residents. Arkansas's Latino population exploded, growing 337 percent to 86,866. The majority live in northwest Arkansas, where jobs increased more than 50 percent in the past ten years. The number of blacks also grew 12 percent to 418,950.

California: The state's population grew 13.8 percent during the 1990s to 33,871,648, by far the largest population of any state. It added a U.S. House seat in the 2002 elections. Whites for the first time are no longer the majority, with non-Hispanic whites accounting for 47 percent of the total. Latinos make up one-third of California's population. Unlike states where immigration was credited for a rise in population, birth rates were cited for the increase. With a boom in Asian immigration, the Asian American population is now 13 percent of the total.

Colorado: The state added one million residents during the 1990s, growing 31 percent to 4,311,882. It gained a seventh U.S. House seat in the 2002 elections. The boom in the third-fastest-growing state was in farm and ranch land south of Denver and counties that are home to some of the state's ski resorts. The Latino population grew 73 percent and Asians by 68 percent.

District of Columbia: The population fell by 5.7 percent during the 1990s to 572,059. Still, Washington rebounded by more than 53,000 residents since a 1999 estimate, suggesting a comeback for a city that boasted 802,000 residents in 1950. The sixty-one-square-mile district remains overwhelmingly black – 61.3 percent of the population – but the number of blacks dropped more than 12 percent in the 1990s. The city gained racial and ethnic diversity, with the Asian and Latino populations jumping 65.6 and 37.4 percent, respectively.

Florida: The fourth-largest state added three million people over the 1990s, growing 23.5 percent to 15,982,378. Florida added two U.S. House seats in the 2002 elections. The boom was credited largely to Latinos from other states and Central and South America. The number of Latinos grew 70 percent to 2.7 million, or 16.8 percent of the state's population, surpassing blacks as the state's largest minority group.

Miami-Dade County, the state's largest, grew by 16 percent to 2.3 million people and its Latino population jumped 35.5 percent.

Georgia: Suburban growth and an influx of retirees and minorities fueled a 26.4 percent population boom during the 1990s to 8,186,453 last year. It added two U.S. House seats in the 2002 elections. Georgia's Latino population jumped 300 percent, from 109,000 in 1990 to 435,000. The Asian American population grew by 29 percent between 2000 and 2004.

Hawaii: The state's population grew by 9 percent during the 1990s to 1,211,537. In the first census to give Americans the option of marking more than one race, more than one in five – 21.4 percent – of Hawaii's residents said they belonged to at least two races. The national average was 2.4 percent. The Census figures also showed a population shift from Oahu, home to Honolulu and Pearl Harbor, to more rural islands like Maui and Molokai. Hawaii's population is 58 percent Asian American.

Idaho: Urban areas in the fifth-fastest-growing state boomed during the 1990s, helping Idaho post a 28.5 percent population gain to 1,293,953. The Latino population soared, nearly doubling to more than 101,000. Latinos now make up 7.5 percent of Idaho's total population, more than two percentage points higher than in 1990.

Illinois: The state's population grew by 8.6 percent during the 1990s to 12,419,293. Illinois lost one of its U.S. House seats after the 2002 elections. Immigrants, families, and workers added to overall state diversity and helped fuel a Chicago-area boom in which the city gained population for the first time in fifty years. The number of Latinos grew by nearly 70 percent, and the group now accounts for 12.3 percent of the state's population.

Indiana: The state's population grew 9.7 percent during the 1990s to 6,080,485 last. Indiana lost one of its U.S. House seats after the 2002 elections. The state's Latino population increased by 117 percent.

Iowa: The state's population grew 5.4 percent during the 1990s to 2,926,324. Iowa counted 82,473 Hispanics in 2002, a 152.6 percent increase from 1990. By 2005, the Latino population surpassed 100,000. The state remains 94 percent white, though the number of blacks climbed 28.6 percent to 61,853 in 1990.

Kansas: The state's population grew 8.5 percent during the 1990s to 2,688,418. The number of Latino residents doubled to 188,252, growing from 3.6 percent of the overall population in 1990 to 7 percent.

Kentucky: The state's population increased by nearly 10 percent during the 1990s and topped four million for the first time at 4,041,769. Ninety percent described themselves as white and 7 percent as black. Spencer County, a newfound haven for workers in the Louisville area, grew 73 percent since 1990 – the highest rate in the state. While urban areas reported growth, 14 counties that depend on coal and agriculture lost population since 1990. Immigrants have affected these rates. The Asian American growth (75 percent) was centered in urban areas, and Latino growth (173 percent) was distributed, helping agricultural areas from declining even more.

Louisiana: The state's population grew nearly 6 percent during the 1990s to 4,468,976. New Orleans lost more than 12,000 residents, while nearly 47,000 people moved to the neighboring suburbs. Most population gains were across the southern part of the state, home to its most viable water ports. Statewide, the black population grew by 32 percent to nearly 1.5 million people in 2000, and the Asian population also jumped. The final effect of Hurricane Katrina on the state's population is yet to be determined. Latino workers have immigrated into the state to aid in reconstruction efforts, while some Southeast Asian refugee families reportedly have resettled in other states (10,000 Vietnamese resettled in the Houston area alone). In 2003, about 230,000 Latinos lived in the tri-state area (Alabama, Mississippi, Louisiana) affected by Katrina.

Massachusetts: The state's population grew 5.5 percent during the 1990s to 6,349,097. The state's Asian population boomed, increasing by 68 percent, while the number of Latinos grew 49 percent.

Minnesota: The state grew 12 percent during the 1990s to 4,919,479. The Latino population tripled to 143,382, though the state remains 91 percent white or partly white.

Mississippi: The state's population grew 10.5 percent during the 1990s to 2,844,658. Mississippi lost one its U.S. House seats after the 2002 elections. The Latino community more than doubled – up to nearly 40,000 in 2000 from 15,931 in 1990. Whites made up 61.4 percent of the state's population and blacks 36.3 percent.

Missouri: The state's population during the 1990s grew by 9.3 percent to 5,595,211. The Latino population nearly doubled during the 1990s, and Kansas City continued to outpace St. Louis as Missouri's most populous city. St. Louis, mired in a half-century population decline, lost 12.2 percent of its residents as surrounding areas grew dramatically.

Nebraska: The state's population grew 8.4 percent during the 1990s to 1,711,263 – a record. The growth was credited to a growing number of Latinos who accounted for two of every five new residents during the 1990s. Latinos now account for 5.5 percent of Nebraska's population.

New Hampshire: The state's population grew 11.4 percent during the 1990s to 1,235,786. The attraction of high-tech jobs, affordable real estate, and a rural lifestyle backed a population surge in southern and coastal New Hampshire. The Latino population grew by 81 percent, Asians and Pacific Islanders by 74 percent, and blacks by 26 percent. The state remains 96 percent white. The Asian American population grew another 33 percent between 2000 and 2004.

New Jersey: The state's population grew 8.9 percent during the 1990s to 8,414,350. It remains the most densely populated state. The Asian population soared 60 percent, and the number of blacks grew by 10 percent. Latinos accounted for more than half of the state's population growth.

New Mexico: Overall, the state's population grew 20 percent during the 1990s to 1,819,046. The Latino population, one of the largest in the country, increased from 38 percent to 42 percent of the state's population.

New York: The state's population grew 5.5 percent during the 1990s to 18,976,457. New York lost two of its U.S. House seats after the 2002 elections. The number of residents identifying themselves as Latinos increased by 29.5 percent to 2.9 million, the majority living in New York City. Seven percent of the state's population is Asian American.

North Carolina: The state's population grew 21.4 percent during the 1990s to 8,049,313. North Carolina gained a U.S. House seat in the 2002 elections. North Carolina has grown by nearly three million people in the past three decades, with nearly half that growth coming in the 1990s. The Latino community more than quadrupled to 378,963. The Asian Amerian population grew 25 percent from 2000 to 2004. The state is 72 percent white.

Ohio: The state's population grew 4.7 percent during the 1990s to 11,353,140 last year. Ohio lost one of its U.S. House seats after the 2002 elections. The Latino population grew by 55 percent, though the group is still a minority of less than 2 percent statewide.

Oklahoma: The state's population grew 9.6 percent during the 1990s to 3,450,654. Oklahoma lost one of its U.S. House seats after the 2002 elections. The state's Latino population doubled. Most of the gain came in and around Oklahoma's two largest cities, Tulsa and Oklahoma City.

Oregon: The state's population jumped by 20 percent over the past decade to 3,421,399. Whites still account for more than nine out of ten residents, but the number of Latinos more than doubled to 275,000. The number of Asians increased by some 40 percent and the number of blacks 17 percent.

Pennsylvania: The state's population grew 3.4 percent during the 1990s to 12,281,054. It lost two of its U.S. House seats after the 2002 elections. Pennsylvania's two largest cities, Philadelphia and Pittsburgh, both lost population while suburbs ballooned, especially in the east. At the same time, the state's Latino population grew by 70 percent, including many who settled in Pennsylvania Dutch country.

Rhode Island: The state's population grew by 4.5 percent during the 1990s to 1,048,319. Residents who said they were racial minorities grew by nearly 40,000 to 128,877 people – more than 12 percent of the population – and the number of Latinos nearly doubled. The white population declined by 6 percent but still accounts for 85 percent of the population.

South Carolina: The state's population grew 15 percent during the 1990s to 4,012,012. Half of the state's top-ten growth counties were in suburban areas around Columbia, Greenville, and just south of Charlotte, North Carolina. The state's Latino population surged more than 200 percent.

South Dakota: The state's population grew 8.5 percent during the 1990s to 754,844. Rapid City grew by 9.3 percent. Shannon County, home of the Pine Ridge Indian Reservation, saw a 25.9 percent rise, and the state's Asian population soared by as much as 105 percent.

Tennessee: The state's population grew by 17 percent during the 1990s to 5,689,283. The Latino population nearly tripled and now accounts for 2 percent of the state population. The number of Asians almost doubled, though the state remains 80 percent white and 16 percent black.

Texas: The state's population increased 22.8 percent during the 1990s to 20,851,820, making Texas the second most populous state. It added two U.S. House seats in the 2002 elections. The boom was led by Latinos: There were 6.7 million Latino Texans in 2000, compared with 4.4 million in 1990 – a 54 percent rise. The figures also show that 91 percent of the 3.9 million newcomers live in Texas's largest cities and their burgeoning suburbs.

Utah: The fourth-fastest-growing state grew by 30 percent during the 1990s, adding 510,319 residents to 2,233,169. A 138 percent increase in the number of Latinos helped fuel the boom. Asians are the state's second-largest minority group.

Washington: The state's population grew 21 percent during the 1990s to 5,894,121. The Latino population grew by 36 percent.

Wisconsin: The state's population grew 9.6 percent during the 1990s to 5,363,675. It lost one of its U.S. House seats after the 2002 elections. Wisconsin became more Asian, more Latino, and more suburban. In Milwaukee County – the only county to lose residents during the past decade – the Latino population shot up 84 percent.

EPILOGUE

. . . . A Policy of Humanity

My initiation as an immigrant advocate came as a young law student volunteering at a legal aid office in San Francisco's Chinatown/North Beach neighborhood during the summer of 1972. I was actually assigned to the housing law unit at the office, when I struck up a conversation with a tenant client, Mr. Medrano, about a peripheral issue that was bothering him. He was upset because he had visited the local INS office the day before to inquire about the procedures for applying for his wife to immigrate from Mexico. Mr. Medrano was a lawful permanent resident of the United States, so he showed his "green card" (alien registration receipt card) to an INS officer during his visit. The officer challenged the authenticity of the card and proceeded to cut the card in half to take a closer look at its construction. The card was genuine, and the officer returned the two halves to Mr. Medrano and told him to leave. When I heard this story, I offered to return to the federal building with Mr. Medrano to demand a new card. We walked into the building, took the elevator to the tenth floor where Mr. Medrano had been the day before, and we found the same INS officer at his desk. When I confronted the officer, he did not deny what had happened. Without an apology, he simply stated, "Go down to room 100, and they'll take care of it." "Victory!" I mistakenly thought. We trekked down to room 100, only to find a waiting line with about fifty others ahead of us. After a two-hour wait, we received a form for a replacement card, to be filed with a $25 filing fee, and were told that a new card would be issued in six months.

That first glimpse into the callousness and insensitivity that INS officers routinely displayed toward citizens and aliens walking into the building turned out to be a relatively minor example of the mean-spirited side of immigration enforcement that I have since encountered. As a practitioner, I recall the INS denial letter for a foreign student visa holder who needed to change schools to San Francisco to be at sea level because he suffered from Eisenmenger syndrome, a disease where living at higher altitudes exacerbated the symptoms: "If elevation is a problem, the applicant should take a boat back to Ethiopia." I recall two separate occasions during the month of December, when an immigration judge ordered my deportation clients into custody simply because the "pain of being incarcerated during the holidays" would give them second thoughts about returning illegally. I have interviewed clients who were beaten by border patrol officers. I faced INS investigators who took pleasure in spewing racial epithets about Filipino and Mexican detainees. On a more personal level, my friends who work for immigrant rights organizations and I have had the displeasure of receiving rabid hate mail simply for representing individuals facing deportation or for espousing pro-immigrant perspectives in the media.

As a nation, the United States has engaged in unnecessarily harsh measures in the name of protecting our borders. Long before we seriously engaged in protecting our borders against terrorists, we took extreme measures to protect our borders against *bad* immigrants. Some of the most immoral actions taken by our government today in the name of protecting our borders are topics I have discussed more extensively elsewhere: Operation Gatekeeper's enforcement through deterrence strategy that results in needless tragic deaths every day along the U.S.–Mexico border and the procedural barriers implemented for asylum applicants and the failure to give them the benefit of the doubt even though their fear is well-founded.[1] In this text, the issues related to undocumented immigration, the deportation of long-time residents, kinship- versus employment-based immigration, national security, and the integration of newcomers provide the context for further decisions being implemented that involve important moral choices. These choices are made as part of the political process in our name.

An example of such a political moral choice is the criminal prosecution of Shanti Sellz and Daniel Strauss. Both in their early twenties, Sellz and

[1] Bill Ong Hing, DEFINING AMERICA THROUGH IMMIGRATION POLICY 184–208, 233–258 (2004).

Strauss volunteer for the group No More Deaths, a faith-based coalition that sets up camps in the desert borderlands of southern Arizona to provide food and water to migrants risking their lives by crossing the border illegally during the deadliest season: June to September. The group's goal is to save lives, usually by providing food and water. They do not transport anyone, except in dire circumstances under a doctor's orders, and the transport is made with complete transparency in clearly marked vehicles. So when Sellz and Strauss encountered three migrants who were dying in the scorching July desert sun, they transported the three for emergency medical care. They saved three lives, but Sellz and Strauss were arrested, charged with transporting illegal aliens, and face fifteen-year prison terms.[2] There is something seriously wrong with our system when providing humanitarian aid is treated as a crime. The injustice is so serious that Amnesty International announced that Sellz and Strauss would be considered prisoners of conscience if imprisoned. And since the choice is done in our name, as members of a democratic society, we must all share the shame.

Former President Jimmy Carter reminds us that George Washington, inspired to establish a nation that was the antithesis of the cruelty demonstrated by the British military during the Revolutionary War, sought to establish in America a "policy of humanity."[3] With this foundation in mind, the United States has sought to be a champion of human rights throughout the world. But when it comes to immigrants, I believe that we have forsaken this policy of humanity. Instead, we have installed a regime that literally and figuratively criminalizes and punishes aliens, in pursuit of what is more a policy of inhumanity.

Thus, being a boat person becomes a crime. The crime begins with the acute desire on the part of the person to enter the United States, under even the most harrowing circumstances, in order to better herself or himself or the lot of the family. These individuals pay "snakeheads" (the Chinese term for smugglers) to secretly smuggle them in. We punish those trying to enter the United States for this crime. We capture them, imprison them, hold them without bail in many cases; we relocate

---

[2] *More Deaths Shouldn't Be an Option*, TUCSON CITIZEN, Dec. 20, 2005, at 4B; *A Deadly Prosecution; Our Stand: Humanitarians Giving Aid on Border Need Guidance, Not Jail Threat*, ARIZONA REPUBLIC, Dec. 14, 2005, at 8B.

[3] Jimmy Carter, OUR ENDANGERED VALUES: AMERICA'S MORAL CRISIS 132 (2005).

them to places inaccessible to volunteer attorneys, charge them with a misdemeanor, exclude and deport them.

Being a good brother or sister is a crime. This crime begins in the darkness along the border, when you help your younger sibling jump the line to reunite with family members or simply to seek a better life. We capture this good brother or sister, imprison the person, and prosecute him or her for smuggling – an aggravated felony. We deport these good siblings. If they return, we prosecute them again and sentence them up to twenty years.

Indeed, dreaming is a crime. This crime begins with images of a bountiful America swirling in the minds of young workers from abroad. The attraction of America is strong. The picture is one of social and economic payoff for an honest day's work. The portrait is one of opportunity for oneself and one's family. The "crime" occurs once the dream is manifested by crossing the border without documents. We capture these dreamers. We incarcerate them. We charge them with a misdemeanor and deport them. We charge them with a felony if they return.

The justification for criminalizing these behaviors is based on a notion of preserving our borders, our sovereignty, and our resources. The action is based on our fear of being overrun, of job loss, of wage depression, and of unassimilability. The process of criminalizing the immigrant and his or her dreams is multistepped. First the immigrant is labeled a problem through demonization, then he or she is dehumanized, until at last his or her actions or conditions are criminalized. Once immigrants are branded as bad for the economy or as "illegal," they are dehumanized and essentially treated as pariahs no longer human and thus not worthy of our sense of justice or decency.

Identifying immigrants as a problem through demonization involves familiar allegations: they take jobs, they cost a lot, they commit crimes, they don't speak English, they damage the environment, they don't share our values, and they are different. This problematization-demonization process is implemented by the likes of Lou Dobbs, Tom Tancredo, Patrick Buchanan, the Minutemen, and the Federation for American Immigration Reform. They attack with seat-of-the-pants economics. They attack with hysterical statements. They find a ready audience in members of the public (some gullible, others who themselves are malevolent) who look around, see people of color with accents working, and facilely claim that the immigrants must be taking jobs that Americans would otherwise have. This brand of xenophobia is recycled from the worst nativist periods of the nation's history – periods that respectable people look back upon with shame.

After hysteria is heightened, the demonization process continues by asking the public if immigration is a problem. Thus, modern-day polls and surveys claim to reveal that 80 percent of respondents think that current immigration is bad for the country if asked specifically about immigration. But when general polls ask respondents to name serious societal problems, immigration is either ranked low or not even mentioned.

Demonization is an ugly thing. It attacks a person's sense of worth, of self, of identity. It deflates. Long before the demonization reaches the technical exclusion/criminalization stage, the social and emotional exclusion of the targeted individuals commences. Historically, long after the repeal of any exclusionist law, the psychic exclusion endures in the minds of the affected communities.

Even in the face of a robust economy, the modern problematization-demonization process has been wildly successful. Restrictionist strategies have worked, as their proponents have been allowed to define the issues, largely in their own terms of alleged economic and fiscal impact. Until the immigration demonstrations in 2006, pro-immigrant sentiment and immigrant rights groups had been silenced in the media. Given the public's thirst for understanding complicated subjects in the simplest of terms, the media accepts the gut-instinct style of economic claims that blame immigrants for job loss and wage depression. Nuanced findings are not good material for headlines. Driven by the political system's reward to the candidates who offer the most stinging sound bites, politicians point fingers at the disenfranchised, voiceless alien to grab the attention of voters. Like being tough on crime, politicians believe that being tough on illegal immigration will aid in their re-election. The media and politicians serve as convenient and effective conduits for the demonizers. The effectiveness of the demonizers is striking, since even in not-so-robust economic times, economic data and job projections favor more immigration.

As we have seen, aggregate empirical studies support the conclusion that immigrants are a boon to the economy. Certainly variance occurs in labor market analyses of different jobs in different parts of the country. Yet considered in total, the evidence reveals that immigrants create more jobs than they take, and what little wage depression occurs is visited upon earlier Latino immigrant groups. States that have a larger population of immigrants have lower unemployment rates. In fact, the increased presence of undocumented workers also energizes the economy and creates new jobs for native workers. These findings are counterintuitive for those who base their conclusions on sightings of immigrant workers presumed to be holding jobs that U.S. citizens deserve. Moreover, immigrants (undocumented as well as documented) add to the tax coffers more than they take out. A maldistribution of these contributions among local, state, and federal governments might occur. However, blaming immigrants for this maldistribution is out of line; when the numbers are totaled, society comes out ahead financially when it comes to immigrants.

As the level of demonization through anti-immigrant rhetoric has reached new heights, hot talk radio hosts, conservative columnists, and politicians – Democrats and Republicans alike – chime in. Many of these neo-nativists claim that things are different, that times have changed from even just a few years ago. Much of the rhetoric strikes a chord with many well-meaning, but misguided, members of the public who have sensed a lack of control over a variety of issues that affect their lives and search for simple answers. Others – the more racist in our midst – derive a sense of validation from shock jock antics. Of course Asians and Latinos have heard these chants in the past. Once again, "playing the immigration card" has become the fashion. Once again, further subordination of the subordinated feels right. Scapegoating is in.

Once demonized, the immigrant can be dehumanized. Dehumanization commodifies the immigrants. The immigrant-as-commodity is not precious. Rather, the immigrants-as-commodities are likened to "hazardous waste dumps."[4] Although the Supreme Court has ruled that dangerous and hazardous materials are "commerce" subject to scrutiny under the Constitution's Commerce Clause, the immigrant-toxic-waste-dump-commodity has little constitutional protection in this dehumanized state.

---

[4] In *Immigration and Naturalization Service v. Lopez Mendoza*, 468 U.S. 1032 (1984), the Supreme Court refused to extend the exclusionary rule derived from the Fourth Amendment to deportation proceedings. In the process, Justice O'Conner reasoned:

> Presumably no one would argue that the exclusionary rule should be invoked to prevent an agency from ordering corrective action at a leaking hazardous waste dump if the evidence underlying the order had been improperly obtained, or to compel police to return contraband explosives or drugs to their owner if the contraband had been unlawfully seized.

Id. at 1046.

Dehumanization thus silences the immigrants. Dehumanization allows the public to ignore their faces. Dehumanization allows the powers that be to categorize the immigrant at will, allowing them to ignore the idealism, the goals, the aspirations, and the dreams of the immigrant and the images of the Statue of Liberty. In short, it allows what is in the mind of the immigrant to be ignored.

Indeed, the notion of punishing employers for knowingly hiring undocumented workers (with the resulting punishment of prosecuting or at least removing the workers themselves) is representative of the demonization-dehumanization process applied to immigrants. At the end of World War II, initial efforts to completely demonize and dehumanize the immigrant worker by imposing employer sanctions failed. In the mid-1970s, a plan known as the Rodino proposal, to make hiring of undocumented workers illegal, was hotly debated. Finally, the dehumanization effort was accomplished as part of the Immigration Reform and Control Act of 1986.

Refugees also have been subjected to the demonization-dehumanization process. Until 1980, the United States had a proud history (albeit with a few embarrassing footnotes) as a recipient of refugees. As early as 1783, President George Washington proclaimed, "[T]he bosom of America is open to receive not only the opulent and respectable stranger, but the oppressed and persecuted of all nations and religions."[5] For almost two hundred years, significant numbers of refugees were welcomed into the United States. The 1948 Displaced Persons Act[6] enabled 400,000 refugees and displaced persons (mostly from Europe) to enter into the United States. The 1953 Refugee Relief Act[7] admitted another 200,000 refugees. Thousands of refugees entered from mainland China after the 1949 communist takeover, and more than 145,000 Cubans sought refuge after Fidel Castro's 1959 coup. Finally, using special authority, the attorney general permitted more than 400,000 refugees from Southeast Asia to enter by 1980 after the U.S. military withdrawal from Vietnam in April 1975.

Dissatisfaction with ad hoc admissions provided the impetus for reform that ultimately led to the passage of the 1980 Refugee Act.[8] Policymakers

---

[5] Michael C. LeMay, FROM OPEN DOOR TO DUTCH DOOR: AN ANALYSIS OF U.S. IMMIGRATION POLICY SINCE 1820, 7 (1987).

[6] Pub. L. No. 80-774, 62 stat. 1009, *amended by* Act of June 16, 1950, Pub. L. No. 81-555, ch. 262, 64 Stat. 219.

[7] Pub. L. No. 83-203, 67 Stat. 400 (1953), *amended by* Act of Aug. 31, 1954, Pub. L. No. 83-751, 68 Stat. 1044 (1954).

[8] Refugee Act of March 17, 1980, 94 Stat. 102.

were uncomfortable with the attorney general's considerable unstructured power to hastily admit tens of thousands of refugees who were unwanted in many parts of the country. Thus, under the new law, limits were imposed on the annual slots available to refugees irrespective of real humanitarian needs. Under the new law, the human side of refugees could be suppressed.

Since the fall of Saigon (Ho Chi Minh City) in 1975, thousands of Vietnamese refugees have attempted to flee by boat to places such as Hong Kong. Originally, many of them were processed and allowed to enter countries such as the United States. Eventually, however, refugees became less welcomed, and fewer were admitted. As more and more were being kept at holding facilities, it was ultimately decided to send most back to Vietnam. Can we forget the images of refugees who were dragged into airplanes for deportation by Hong Kong/British authorities? Apparently so. A case of boat people dehumanized. The United States has been only somewhat better – its dehumanization of refugees resulted in welfare reform in 1996 that cut off benefits, including food stamps, to refugees in spite of the responsibility our nation had to them.

Once dehumanized and rendered voiceless, the immigrant's actions, status, and dreams may be criminalized. The process is completed: problematize, demonize, dehumanize, and then criminalize. Congress's authority to criminalize and exclude in the immigration area is vast. Indeed, as an enumerated power expressed in Article 1, Section 8, of the Constitution, this power has been labeled "plenary,"[9] just as we have come to label Congress's power over interstate commerce. And just as the Supreme Court has allowed Congress to legislate under the pretext of the Commerce Clause to implement its moral judgments (e.g., wage and hour laws, civil rights protections), Congress has been permitted to legislate and criminalize the behavior of immigrants based on social and moral judgments.

So we decided long ago, as a matter of public policy, to punish those who attempt to cross our borders without proper documents. These individuals – the relatives, the adventurous, the entrepreneurial, the creative, and the industrious – are criminalized. We punish them for being boat people. For seeking freedom. For seeking political freedom. For seeking economic freedom. For seeking political options. For seeking

---

[9] See, for example, *Fiallo v. Bell*, 430 U.S. 787 (1977).

economic options. For wanting a better life for themselves and their children. For being a good sibling. Simply, for dreaming. The decision to criminalize applies to those whose travels across the southern border have been economic and cultural rituals for generations – across a border into territory that for generations was part of Mexico. The decision applies, regardless of the hardships or conditions endured in the journey to the land of opportunity. The decision applies, regardless of the person's venerable aspirations.

Why do we demonize immigrants? Why do we punish them? Why do we criminalize? Former California Governor Wilson explained: "We can no longer allow compassion to overrule reason."[10] So we punish. We have that power. We are a sovereign nation. The Court has upheld that power. We feel compelled to exercise that power. We must protect our borders. We must protect our people. We must protect our economy. We punish dreamers. After all, we cannot take in everyone.

The process of problematizing, demonizing, dehumanizing, and criminalizing makes punishing aliens seem normal to many Americans. We have come to accept the punishment and exclusion of people from other lands. We more readily accept this concept in the post-9/11 era, even though our better instincts tell us to recognize the interdependency of national economies, workforces, and environmental practices. As part of the American mind-set, these misguided policies demonstrate a shameful, mean-spirited side of our character that preys upon decent, hardworking noncitizens. In the name of protecting our borders, our policymakers have adopted these policies, and we as Americans have allowed these policies to be implemented because the demonization is so complete.

Neo-nativists also use fear to urge clamping down on immigrants. Xenophobia teaches us to fear immigrants – to fear being overrun culturally, economically, numerically. Fear is used as a means of persuasion, often bringing out the worst in people and turning us away from reason, understanding, and negotiation. The result is that much of our time and energy is wasted on divisive arguments and debates, distracting us from engaging in productive work, such as incorporating newcomers into our society. Denouncing the newcomer becomes the easy response. Fear restrains us from taking the time to learn about others, to share our views, to collaborate in building a stronger community. Basing decisions on fear rather

---

[10] Letter from Governor Pete Wilson of California to President Bill Clinton (Aug. 9, 1993) (on file with author).

than on sound judgment paralyzes us from following our aspirations to be a great nation committed to justice and equality for all. In the words of Senator Ted Kennedy, ours should be a nation of "hope, not fear."[11]

I chose to believe that most Americans are decent, well-meaning individuals with a solid sense of right and wrong, who often are silenced by a vocal minority of neo-nativists. Americans who have had the opportunity to work or socialize with people of other backgrounds come to realize how much we all have in common. In our hearts, we understand that reaching out rather than lashing out is the right thing to do. Emotionally, we know that having an open heart is the best path. We should strive to be thoughtful and treat people right; to adhere to high standards of truth, justice, humility, compassion, and forgiveness. I believe that the vast majority of Americans, if given the choice, would endorse a welcoming approach toward immigrants – documented and undocumented – but they sense no immediate way to intervene in mean-spirited immigration enforcement methods. Thus, as in many other policy debates, the "fervor and activism of [a] small minority greatly magnify their influence, especially within the U.S. Congress,"[12] when it comes to immigration policy and enforcement.

The quiet majority of Americans who would not condone the callous or insensitive treatment of immigrants and the failure to implement smart integration strategies do have the power to redirect our government's commitments to moral and civil principles of justice and community. In our day-to-day lives, we can show our true preference by making choices and taking actions that are receptive to newcomers. We can listen to, we can learn from, and we can share our ideas with immigrants and refugees. Taking just a little time for such an effort would be noticeable to a newcomer. These small, individual actions can make a difference in our neighborhoods and communities. The little things matter, especially if we couple those efforts with ignoring, if not objecting to, the intolerance espoused by those who are narrow-minded. And they can matter even more if we demand tolerance, humanity, and fairness of our political and civic leaders as well.

---

[11] Senator Edward M. Kennedy's remarks at the 2004 Democratic Convention, July 27, 2004, available at http://www.pbs.org/newshour/vote2004/demconvention/speeches/kennedy.html.

[12] Carter, *supra* note 3, at 11. President Carter pointed out this phenomenon in noting that a persistent majority of Americans believe that assault weapons should be banned, and a majority think that abortions should be legal in all or most cases. Ibid.

The experiment that we call America is a test of our character and our willingness to believe that we can have a strong country that is caring and diverse. Showing compassion and fairness in our immigration policies is not a sign of weakness. Rather, those traits demonstrate a confidence in a rule of law and system of government that metes out punishment when necessary but understands that regulating the lives of those who seek to live within our borders must be done with the utmost compassion, dignity, and understanding. As in previous generations, there is much to admire about individuals who come to our shores seeking freedom and a better life. Whether they are fleeing persecution or entering to seek work in order to better their lives, the newcomers of today are not much different from those of the past. Once here, welcoming newcomers and understanding the challenges that they will be facing are imperative. As they become part of our neighborhoods and communities, some may make mistakes, but we do well to remember that supporting rehabilitation, giving a second chance, and providing ways for individuals to mature are essential elements of a civil society. Although these forgiving traits may immediately benefit the individual, in the end, we all benefit. When an individual finally turns the corner and becomes a contributing member, the entire community benefits – socially, emotionally, and economically.

Thus, when it comes to the treatment of our fellow human beings who have crossed boundaries into our territory, we should consider what has driven or attracted them here before we become too judgmental. There is a reason why Chinese immigrants in the 1800s referred to the United States as "Gold Mountain." These immigrants initially may have been lured by the stories of the discovery of gold, but eventually the attraction of gold was a metaphor – not to be underestimated – for the vast emotional as well as economic opportunities that the new world presented.

The new American empire also should not be underestimated. As U.S. culture, economic influence, political power, and military presence affect the far reaches of the globe,[13] we cannot be too surprised at the attraction that Old Glory holds throughout the world. The ubiquity of America is vast. Although I agree with many commentators that the cost of aggressive

---

[13] Former President Jimmy Carter has warned: "[P]olitical actions have been orchestrated by those who believe that the utilization of our nation's tremendous power and influence should not be constrained by foreigners. Regardless of the costs, some leaders are openly striving to create a dominant American empire throughout the world." Carter, *supra* note 3, at 4.

military actions has created more enemies for the United States, American muscle also is attractive to many foreigners. Coupled with the pervasiveness of American culture throughout the world, American empire appeals to would-be immigrants and refugees who seek the American dream of freedom, prosperity, and consumerism. Migrant workers, refugees, high-tech workers, multinational executives, and relatives (both from the working class and the professions) all respond. Thus, American empire is responsible for luring countless migrants to the United States each year, as the phenomenon reignites the Statue of Liberty's call to those "yearning to breathe free" and the fascination with America. Understood in this light, the debate over the profile of new immigrants is disingenuous. Because the nation has attracted these immigrants, the fitting response is a commitment to integrating the newcomers in order to incorporate them into a system devoted to the political, economic, and social vitality of the nation.

We are in this together. Let us welcome the migrant worker – documented or undocumented – into membership because we have recruited him here and benefited from her labor. Give the convicted alien criminal who has resided here since infancy a second chance to escape the inner-city environment he or she grew up in. Embrace the emotional and economic contributions that kinship immigrants bring with them to the country each day. Recognize that reaching out to and incorporating newcomers advances the national security. And welcome the newcomer into the civic life of our society, so that he or she too can more fully contribute to the community. This is how we continue to build our nation of immigrants. This is how it's done, in a just, humane, intelligent, and moral manner. This is how we fulfill our commitment to a policy of humanity.

Index